Parents On Your Side

A Teacher's Guide to Creating
Positive Relationships
With Parents

Lee Canter
and
Marlene Canter

Contents

Introduction

Since 1991, when the first edition of *Parents on Your Side* was introduced, there has been a growing effort in schools to involve parents in their children's education. Increasingly, teachers and administrators recognize that parent support can be a key factor in a student's success in school. Parents are in a unique position to offer insight, assistance, backup, and encouragement concerning their children.

Yet getting parent support is not always easy. Educators continue to explore the best way to involve parents in their efforts. Noted researcher Joyce Epstein[1] suggests that there must be a multifaceted approach. She has identified six important types of involvement between families, schools, and the community. Her work calls for practices that involve:

- Assisting families with parenting skills
- Recruiting and training parent volunteers in the schools
- Involving families in their children's homework and other academic activities
- Including families on committees and in other school organizations
- Working with community agencies and businesses to provide resources to parents and strengthen school programs
- Communicating with families about school programs and student success

It is this last type of parent involvement—communication—that is the focus of this book.

Through effective communication with parents, teachers can have the greatest impact on their day-to-day success with students. With parents on their side, teachers can more effectively manage most academic and behavioral issues that arise. When the most important adults in a child's life are working together, students benefit enormously.

Today more that ever, teachers are finding themselves in situations that require regular communication with parents. The increasing number of charter schools and community-based schools bring more parents into contact with teachers. The use of email offers a convenient tool for teachers to communicate with parents about homework and their children's progress. Voicemail systems allow parents to call the school at night and hear assignments delivered in the teacher's own voice. Teachers and schools are building websites that describe school events, policies, and class assignments and even allow parents to view student grades on a regular basis. Schools are creating events that bring teachers and parents into more frequent contact. These increased opportunities for parent-teacher interaction, as well as the traditional parent conferences, necessitate that teachers use skill and sensitivity in the way they speak with parents.

The focus of this book is on those communication skills—how to speak with parents, how to listen to them, and how to reach out for their support.

Various changes have been made in this second edition of *Parents on Your Side.* There is greater emphasis on collaboration. We now recognize the need for parents and teachers to combine their knowledge of students' strengths and limitations, then work together to devise an approach that will lead to student success. This revised edition also includes updated references, plus a reorganization of the original material to clarify the strategies you need.

It is our hope that the skills in this book, in combination with your school and community efforts, will lead to greater parent involvement and success for you and your students.

References

[1] Epstein, J. L. (1997, September/October). Six types of school-family-community involvement. *Harvard Education Letter.* [Online]. Available: http://www.edletter.org/past/issues/1997-so/sixtypes.shtml.

Section One

Why Teachers Need Parents and Parents Need Teachers

Teachers need parents because parent involvement has been proven to significantly improve a student's chance for success in school. A parent's influence on both behavior and academic performance can assist you significantly in your educational efforts at school.

Parents need teachers to inspire the way to better involvement in their children's education. Most parents want to get involved, yet some feel that they have no valuable insights to offer or that their involvement is not appropriate or appreciated. Therefore, parents need teachers to reach out to them, elicit their valuable insights, and let them know that their help is greatly appreciated.

The first section of *Parents on Your Side* discusses the need for communication between parents and teachers and examines the ingredients that make such communication effective.

Chapter 1: Why You Need Parents on Your Side

This chapter discusses why communication with parents is valuable for every teacher's repertoire.

Chapter 2: Having an Effective Attitude

This chapter takes a look at attitudes that enable a teacher to effectively communicate with parents.

Chapter 3: Recognizing Roadblocks

This chapter stresses the importance of being aware of teachers' and parents' misconceptions about each other.

Why You Need Parents on Your Side

"Stephanie just doesn't seem to care about school. She rarely does her homework and most of the time she isn't prepared for class. She could be an A student, but she is barely doing C work. I've spoken to her parents. They said they would make sure she starts doing her homework, but they don't follow through."

"Chris was a problem in class all day today—constantly talking back, yelling, and screaming. I tried reaching his mother. She's never at home and she's told me not to call her at work. She doesn't want to be bothered. She said that there's nothing she can do with her son."

"Nothing I've tried has worked with Michael. He just sits there and won't work. Do you know what his mom said when I called her? She said that during the day he was my responsibility. She said that I am the teacher and I should be able to get him to do his work."

Sound familiar? If so, you're not alone. Educators today are expected to teach more and more students with academic and behavior problems, as well as students who are just not motivated to do their best in school. Complicating this situation is the fact that all too often these students have parents who seem unwilling or unable to become involved in their children's education.

Lack of parental support from the parents of Stephanie, Chris, and Michael resulted in their teachers having to handle these situations on their own—with less than positive results. The frustration of these teachers mirrors the frustration of many educators today who attempt to motivate students without the active support of parents.

Teachers speak out for parent involvement.

A 1989 *Instructor* magazine poll asked educators to name the one thing they would like to tell national policymakers about the most effective way to raise student achievement. The answer given most frequently was "more parental involvement." These teachers went on to state that they felt parental involvement was more important than smaller class size, more important than increased control and power for teachers, more important than promoting student responsibility, and more important than decreasing the time students spend watching television.[1]

The *Instructor* poll was supported by the 1996 Phi Delta Kappa/Gallup Poll of teachers, which reported that lack of support from parents is the biggest problem they face in their classrooms.[2]

And a 1993 article in *The New York Times*[3] succinctly sums it up in its title: "What Do Teachers Want Most? Help From Parents."

Clearly, this is in tune with the current nationwide trend to actively recruit parents' support in their children's education. This effort is supported by federal, state, and local programs: *Goals 2000,* for example, sets partnerships between schools, parents, and communities as a voluntary national goal for all schools, and mandates specific practices and programs to grant parental influence as a prerequisite for funding.[4] Such programs are meant to place students at the center of an open and caring three-way communication among parents, school, and community to drive home the same message: School matters for success in life.

Parents are the most important people in a child's life.

Why do teachers and legislators feel parent support is so important? Think about this: Why did you behave in school? Why did you strive to succeed academically? If you were like many others, your parents were an important factor in shaping your attitude toward school.

"In our home we had two rules about school. Rule #1 was: Do what the teacher says, do your best work, and never misbehave. Rule #2 stated that under no circumstances were we ever to break Rule #1. My parents always let us know that they were prepared to do whatever it took to ensure that we succeeded in school. And I knew that they meant it.

"Looking back now, I can see that my parents really empowered my teachers. When my teacher stood in front of the class, my parents were standing symbolically at his side. A request from my teacher was a request from my parents. A demand from my teacher was a demand from my parents. If I got into trouble at school, I got into twice as much trouble at home. My parents never felt that either my teacher or the school was responsible for me. My parents always knew that they themselves were key to my success. They knew that their interest, involvement, and expectations provided the motivation I had to have to achieve my potential.

"Today I'm a teacher, and I know how much more my students could accomplish if I had that kind of support from more of their parents."

You need this kind of commitment from parents today. Parents are the most important people in a child's life. Their love, affection, support, and approval are fundamental needs of all children. And because parents are number one in importance, they are also number one in the ability to influence and motivate their children.

The value of parental involvement and support has been thoroughly studied and evaluated by leading researchers in the educational community.

- A 1986 United States Department of Education study concluded that "the family is critical to success in school." Indeed, the "curriculum of the home" is twice as predictive of academic learning as socioeconomic status . . . [and] parent influence is no less important in the high school years."[5]

- Noted researcher Urie Bronfenbrenner studied a number of educational intervention programs. He concluded that active involvement and support of the family are critical to a child's success in school.[6]

- R. J. Gigliotti and W. B. Brookover studied schools of similar size, geographic locale, and student SES. They found that parent participation was a critical factor in determining the overall effectiveness of the schools, regardless of the economic level of the parents.[7]

- Joyce Epstein of Johns Hopkins University studied teachers who actively sought parent involvement. She found that there were positive changes in student achievement, attitude, and behavior when teachers included parent involvement as part of their regular teaching practices. The students reported that they had a more positive attitude toward school and more regular homework habits.[8]

- Anne T. Henderson summarized nearly 50 studies of parent-involvement programs and concluded the following:

  › Programs designed with strong parental involvement components produced students who performed better than otherwise identical programs that did not strongly involve parents.

  › Schools that relate well to their communities have student bodies that outperform other schools.

  › Children whose parents help them at home and stay in touch with schools score higher than children of similar aptitude and family background whose parents are not involved. Schools in which children are failing improve dramatically when parents are called in to help.[9]

It is said that it takes a village to raise a child. There is no doubt that if the educational village—home, school, and community—is involved and supportive, students benefit.

Parents of the new millennium are anything but a homogeneous group. Their numbers include single mothers, single fathers, stepmothers, stepfathers, double-income households, same-sex partners, parents of various cultural or ethnic origins, newly arrived immigrants, parents of different educational backgrounds, the affluent, the middle class, and an ever-increasing number of poverty-level parents.

These parents—and their situations—may differ in many ways, but in spite of their differences they share something significant in common: Each and every one could be a positive factor in shaping the success of a child. Each and every one could provide the motivation that your students need in order to do their best in school. Thus, it is your responsibility as a teacher to do what is in your power to get their support.

An uninvolved parent, justifiably or not, gives a child the message that the child just isn't important enough to warrant close attention. An involved parent, on the other hand, can provide the boost to a student's self-esteem that will lead to greater success in school and a more fulfilling and accomplished adulthood.

You can learn how to involve parents in their child's education.

Parents on Your Side is a step-by-step program developed to help you, the educator, reach out to parents so that your students may get the support they need to succeed in school and, ultimately, in life. The program is based on two important premises:

1. **You can learn how to communicate effectively with parents.**
   There are teachers today who consistently receive support from all kinds of parents in all kinds of situations. We have studied these educators and found that there are common elements critical to their success. In *Parents on Your Side,* you will learn the techniques that effective teachers use to work successfully with parents.

2. **Parents want to support you.**
   The vast majority of your students' parents really do want to be involved. A 1999 Public Agenda and Public Education Network survey of parents of African-American and white students concluded that, regardless of race or ethnicity, the vast majority of

parents believe that "kids learn best when their families stress the importance of education, [and that] respect for the value of school begins at home."[10]

Parents do care about their children and want to provide needed support. In many cases, however, they just don't know what to do—or if they should do it at all. To put it in perspective, only 25% of parents report receiving systematic requests or directions from teachers on how they can help their children academically. However, when requested to give additional assistance, over 85% of parents immediately responded and were willing to spend at least 15 minutes per day working with their children.[11] In short, when parents are contacted by skilled, trained teachers who communicate effectively, they will respond.

If students are to reach their full potential, they need the support and encouragement of an entire community of concerned, caring adults. That community includes all of us. And it especially includes students' parents. However, not every parent has a positive attitude toward school and education. School can be imposing and intimidating rather than warm and welcoming. It is your job as a teacher to reach out to all parents and to embrace them as partners in their children's education. To do your job effectively, you need to get those parents on your side.

Parents on Your Side will give you the practical skills and confidence you need to get all parents to support your academic, discipline, and homework efforts. You will learn the following:

- How to develop an effective attitude toward parent involvement (chapter 2)

- How to recognize and move past the roadblocks that stand in your way (chapter 3)

- What to do before the school year starts (chapter 4)

- How to plan a productive Back-to-School Night event (chapter 5)

- How to establish a yearlong positive parent communication program (chapter 6)

- How to involve parents in their children's homework (chapter 7)

- How to develop a plan for conducting parent conferences (chapter 8)

- How to communicate effectively (chapter 9)

- What to do when problems arise (chapter 10)

- How to contact a parent about a problem (chapter 11)

- How to conduct a problem-solving conference (chapter 12)
- How to use home-school contracts (chapter 13)
- How to help parents with discipline problems (chapter 14)
- How to deal with difficult parents (chapter 15)
- How to make sure that every parent and student feels successful by the end of the year (conclusion)

In chapter 2, we'll begin by taking a look at the effective attitude shared by teachers who do get parent support.

References

[1] Clapp, B. (1989). The discipline challenge. *Instructor, XCIX*(2), 32–34.

[2] Langdon, Carol A. (1996, November). The third Gallup/Phi Delta Kappa poll of teachers' attitudes toward the public schools. *Phi Delta Kappan, 78*(3), 244–250.

[3] Chira, S. (1993, June 23). What do teachers want most? Help from parents. *The New York Times*, p. 7.

[4] Epstein, J. L. (1995, May). School/family/community partnerships: Caring for the children we share. *Phi Delta Kappan, 76*(9), 701–712.

[5] United States Department of Education. (1986). *What works: Research about teaching and learning*. Washington, DC.

[6] Bronfenbrenner, Urie. (1966). *A report on longitudinal evaluations of pre-school programs*. Washington, DC: Department of Health, Education and Welfare.

[7] Brookover, W. B., & Gigliotti, R. J. (1988). *First teachers: Parental involvement in the public schools*. Alexandria, VA: National School Boards Association.

[8] Epstein, J. L. (1993). *Effects on parents of teacher practices in parental involvement*. Baltimore, MD: Johns Hopkins University Center for Social Organization of Schools.

[9] Henderson, A. (1987). *The evidence continues to grow*. Columbia, MD: National Committee for Citizens in Education.

[10] Farkas, S., & Johnson, J. (1999). Looking at the school: Public agenda asks African-American and white parents about their aspirations and their fears. *Arts Education Policy Review, 100*(4), 24–27.

[11] Gallup, A. (1989). The second Gallup/Phi Delta Kappa survey of public school teacher opinion. *Phi Delta Kappan, 79*(11).

Having an Effective Attitude

The best way to learn how to get parents on your side is from teachers who are already successful at soliciting parental support. In researching this book, we talked to teachers who consistently get the support they need from parents. These teachers may differ greatly in where they teach, how they teach, and whom they teach, but they do not differ at all in their attitude regarding parents.

These teachers share five important qualities, which will be examined in this chapter:

1. Effective teachers know they must have the support of parents.

2. Effective teachers reach out to parents as essential partners in a child's education.

3. Effective teachers demonstrate concern for the child.

4. Effective teachers treat parents the way they would want to be treated.

5. Effective teachers demonstrate professionalism and confidence.

In other words, effective teachers don't just "get" parents on their side; they have an attitude that enables them to work successfully with parents.

Effective teachers know they must have the support of parents.

Effective teachers understand, without a doubt, that when parents are involved, students do better academically and behaviorally. Experience supports this conclusion. Research backs it up. But effective teachers take this knowledge one step further. As professionals responsible for the education of their students, these teachers believe that it is a dereliction of responsibility to allow a student to flounder academically or behaviorally without doing everything possible to help—and "help" means getting parents involved. Any lesser effort would be, in their view, "educational malpractice."

Effective teachers also unequivocally believe that they owe it to themselves to receive support from parents. Teachers are often faced with the responsibility of not only educating students but of helping solve their emotional and behavioral problems, too. It is not in anyone's best interest to struggle endlessly over student problems without the involvement of parents. It's emotionally draining, time consuming, and, ultimately, nonproductive.

For your students and for yourself, you must have parental support. Parents are in a unique position to deliver the help that is needed.

Effective teachers reach out to parents as essential partners in a child's education.

No one—teacher, principal, counselor, or psychologist—can have as profound an impact on student behavior as can parents. Parents are the most important, influential people in a child's life. Parental love and approval are fundamental needs of every child. All children want and need the praise and positive support of their parents.

And yet, parents may not be aware of the influence they have over their children or how to use this influence to their best advantage. When necessary, you must be prepared to guide parents toward positive reinforcement techniques that will motivate their child to greater success in school.

Parents have the most time and opportunity to give their child individual attention. No matter how dedicated a teacher you are, you have a limited amount of time to work one-on-one with students. For example, in a typical elementary classroom, you may spend a maximum of 5 minutes per day working with students individually on their reading or math skills. When you can encourage a parent to spend 15 minutes a night helping a child, you are tripling the amount of individual attention that child can receive. Likewise, the one minute of personal attention a secondary teacher may be able to give a student could be increased as much as 15-fold when the parent helps at home.

Parents can offer disciplinary backing. Realistically, you are limited in what you can do when a student chooses to misbehave. The supportive feedback and corrective actions you exercise in or after class work for some students. There are other students, however, who need to know that parents will also follow through with disciplinary measures at home for misbehavior exhibited at school. When misbehavior at school means a loss of privileges at home, there is a much greater likelihood of a student choosing to behave. By the same token, when improved behavior at school is recognized with supportive feedback at home, there is a much greater chance that the student will continue to choose appropriate behavior.

To illustrate more clearly, look at the parent involvement issue from the perspective of another group of professionals who deal with children: pediatricians. The pediatrician knows that it is her responsibility to diagnose a child's problem, prescribe treatment, and carefully explain to parents what they must do to help their child. The pediatrician then fully expects that parents will support her efforts. If a parent complains with "I work, I can't make sure he takes his medicine," or "I'm too busy to get her to her checkup," the doctor will lay it on the line: "I cannot make sure your child gets better unless you do your part."

The issues that you as a teacher deal with are every bit as immediate and important as those the pediatrician faces. Children who experience school failure have a higher probability of ending up on drugs, in jail, or on welfare. These outcomes can be as serious as most physical problems a child will encounter, and you have as much right to parent support as a doctor does, for teachers and doctors are both professionals responsible for the well-being and growth of a child.

Parents are usually willing to get involved in their child's education, yet for many reasons they are often reluctant to do so. Effective teachers put in the time and effort it takes to get these parents involved. These teachers communicate to parents that they honestly care about their children's success in school and, ultimately, in life.

Effective teachers adapt their schedules to include late evening or weekend conferences in order to be accessible for all parents. Effective teachers contact parents repeatedly and at any time or place necessary to speak with even the hard-to-reach parent. Effective teachers are willing to offer support and guidance to parents who are not sure how to improve their children's academic or behavior skills. Effective teachers show respect and understanding for the parents' concerns and insights at all times, and are willing to adapt their strategies based on a parent's justified criticism. Effective teachers are willing to cooperate with parents, and do their best to listen to and incorporate the parents' insights into a student's problem rather than to impose the teacher's point of view. Effective teachers use proactive strategies to involve parents in their children's life at school before problems even arise, and to establish a positive relationship with the entire family.

Effective teachers do everything in their power to reach out to parents who may feel left out of their children's life at school.

Effective teachers demonstrate concern for the child.

A great concern of parents is that their child's teacher will not put in the time and effort necessary to ensure that their child succeeds in school. Effective teachers know this and take steps to alleviate these parental worries.

Experience has shown them that when a parent believes that a teacher really cares about their child, that parent is not as likely to argue, make excuses, or question the teacher's competency. Instead, the parent will make every effort to support the teacher.

Here are some strategies that effective teachers use to demonstrate concern for their students.

From the beginning of the school year, communicate that you care about the student's success.

It is never too early to show parents you care. Many teachers begin even before the school year starts. A welcoming phone call or note home to parents of incoming students can go a long way toward demonstrating your interest in their children. In chapters 4 and 5, we will be discussing a few strategies that will get your relationship with your students' parents off to a good start.

Establish positive communication with parents.

The key to showing genuine concern is to contact parents when the child is doing something right. When parents hear good news, it's easier for them to believe that you really do care. You will also find that once you've established positive communication with parents, they will be much more receptive when you have to call them with a problem.

Most parents report that they hear from the teacher only when there is a problem. When every communication is negative, it's easy to understand why parents avoid contact with teachers. After all, most parents would like to believe that their child is doing something right at school, at least some of the time. In chapter 6, we will be looking at a variety of ways to communicate with parents in positive ways.

Take every opportunity to show you care.

In every interaction with parents, all eyes are on you. Don't miss any opportunity to let parents know that you care about their child. Failure to show concern may miscommunicate to the parent a lack of caring on your part. From the start, look for occasions that will show your interest and concern. Notes home, phone calls, birthday greetings, and get-well cards not only address the occasion but also consistently demonstrate to parents that your commitment to their child is genuine. Throughout Section 2, you will find useful ideas and tips for how to incorporate proactive relationship-building with your students' parents into your daily life as a teacher.

Effective teachers treat parents the way they would want to be treated.

Teachers who are most successful in getting parent support adhere to the "golden rule" of positive parent relations: Treat parents the way you would want to be treated if you had a child in school. This common-sense approach to positive parent involvement is one of the most valuable qualities you can develop.

By following the golden rule, you will gain two important advantages:

1. Through your words and actions, you will consistently demonstrate to parents that you are a concerned and caring teacher. Your underlying message at all times will be, "I understand your needs, and I will be sensitive to them."

2. You will have a guideline for determining how you will approach and deal with parents in all situations. When you ask yourself, *What would I as a parent want to see happen in this situation?* the answer will usually be surprisingly clear.

For example:

- If I had a child in school, what specific information would I want to hear from the teacher at the beginning of the year?

- How and when would I want to be approached about a problem?

- How would I want to be spoken to?

- How would I want to be listened to?

- Would I want to hear from the teacher when my child is doing well or only when there is a problem?

Putting yourself in the parents' place can take the guesswork out of determining how to handle many situations. Respect for the parents will follow naturally, as will an increased ability to take their input seriously.

You will find the golden rule mentioned throughout *Parents on Your Side* because it is the guiding force behind many of the techniques and suggestions given. Keep it in mind because it applies to all the issues discussed.

Effective teachers demonstrate professionalism and confidence.

You can be the most skilled teacher in the world, but if parents don't recognize your competence, you'll have a difficult time getting their support.

What can you do to demonstrate your professionalism and let parents know you have confidence in your own ability?

Involve parents.

A confident teacher welcomes the support and involvement of parents and is not intimidated by the help a parent can offer. A confident teacher views education as a team effort, and parents as part of that team.

Professionalism in dealing with parents requires that you have a plan for working with parents all year long. Parent involvement is not a twice-a-year event. It is a daily responsibility. It cannot be left to chance encounters and sporadic conversations. You need to know exactly when, how, and why you will contact parents from the first day of school to the last. You need to develop a parent involvement plan.

A parent involvement plan is your plan of action for dealing with parents throughout the year. This plan is not a strict, step-by-step prescription. A successful parent involvement plan is one that you develop to meet your specific needs and the needs of your students and their parents. In the following chapters you will find practical techniques that you can use to get and keep parent support—in all situations, at all grade levels, and with all kinds of parents. These techniques will be your guide for developing a plan of your own.

Demonstrate your confidence.

Show your confidence in every interaction with parents. Each time you meet with a parent, speak with a parent on the phone, or send a note home, you have a new opportunity to shine. Make the most of these opportunities. Stop and think a minute before you speak or write a note. Be professional, confident, and assertive. Then let your words and attitude carry that message forth.

Communicate clearly and assertively.

Assured communication—communication that says, "I know what I'm doing"—is vital to working effectively with parents. Would you hire an attorney who vacillated on how to advise you? Why should a parent be expected to support a teacher who does not appear to have confidence in her own abilities? You have to impress upon parents that you do in fact know what you're doing. You have to learn to project the attitude of self-assurance that earns respect and promotes confidence. That means learning communication skills.

In chapter 3, we will look at some of the roadblocks that keep parents and teachers from communicating effectively.

Recognizing Roadblocks

Despite the nationwide trend to involve parents and communities in the process of formal education, what still defines our role models of administrators, teachers, and parents are attitudes that strictly separate home from school. Administrators tend to call the shots, teachers consider themselves the experts on a student's education, and parents view school with a bias ranging from complacency to combativeness.[1]

These attitudes block the road to an open two-way communication between teacher and parent.

You as a teacher need to recognize, address, and ultimately remove two kinds of roadblocks before you can successfully cooperate with your students' parents. This chapter covers the following:

- Teachers' roadblocks—obstacles that keep teachers from initiating communication

- Parents' roadblocks—obstacles that keep parents from giving support

Be aware of teachers' roadblocks.

A teacher's effective attitude when working with parents is only as effective as the teacher's ability to communicate it.

- If you find yourself doubting whether or not it is your responsibility to handle a problem situation, you may find yourself on unsure ground when you try to solve it.

- If you feel that you've never been trained to work with parents, then you may find yourself stumbling over your own words and actions.

- If you have negative feelings about working with parents in general, they can easily appear as a lack of confidence and competence.

Following are three types of roadblocks that often prevent teachers from asking for the help they need from parents.

Teachers' Roadblock #1: The Myth of the "Good Teacher"

"Our district wants parents happy at all costs. We are basically told to handle problems on our own. If we go to parents for help, they'll think we don't know what we're doing."

"Everyone expects us to handle problems with our students on our own. It's a clear message at this school that if you have to involve parents, the administration thinks you're not up to snuff."

The myth of the "good teacher"—the notion that competent teachers should handle all their students' problems on their own—still permeates many schools and school districts. Many administrators have fostered this myth by discouraging teachers from contacting parents when problems arise. Many parents have fostered this myth by responding in a negative manner when teachers call. The underlying assumption seems to be that teachers should handle it all by themselves, that it is not "professional" to involve parents.

Do you:

- Wait until the last minute before calling a parent about a problem?

- Avoid talking to parents because you are afraid they will judge you?

- Apologize to parents when you do speak with them?

- Negate problems?

- Avoid talking with your administrator about problems you are having with students or parents?

If you answered yes to any of these questions, you probably buy into the myth of the good teacher. This is important for you to recognize. If you feel less than professional when you need to work with parents, you will present yourself to others not as a competent and confident professional but as an unsure, faltering novice.

Here's an example of how the myth of the good teacher can creep into a phone conversation between parent and teacher.

The conversation begins with an apology.

Teacher: *I'm really sorry to bother you at home. I know how busy you are.*

The teacher then proceeds to belittle her own abilities.

Teacher: *I really just don't know what to do with Sara. She had problems again today, and I guess I don't know what else to try with her.*

The teacher minimizes the severity of the problem.

Teacher: *Sara hit another student today. Well, she didn't really hurt her.*

The teacher continues in an ineffectual way to ask for support.

Teacher: *As I said, I'm not too sure what to do at this time. I know you've got six other kids and plenty of problems of your own, but if you have the time, I'd really appreciate it if you'd have a word with Sara.*

The uncertainty communicated with a weak communication style may be why teachers do not get parents on their side. Look more closely at what went on in that conversation.

First, this teacher, like many teachers, began a parent conversation by apologizing. There is no reason to apologize! Apologies are given when you feel that you have done something wrong. You are calling the parent not to bother her but to discuss what can be done to help the child. Making this call is your job and your responsibility.

Second, this teacher belittled her own professional abilities. Teachers often say things to parents such as, "I don't know what to do with him." Such statements do not exude confidence or professionalism. Instead, these statements lead parents to believe that you are incompetent and incapable of handling their child. Obviously, this can be frustrating to parents, especially those with children who have problems.

Let's return to the pediatrician analogy. Assume that your own child is ill. You take your child to the doctor, who runs some tests and calls you back the next day. She says to you,

"I'm really sorry to bother you at home. I know how busy you are. I have the tests back and I'm really not sure what is going on with your child, but I think she has some kind of bacterial infection. As I said, I know you're busy, but if you could find the time, I'd really appreciate it if you'd go to the pharmacy and get your child some penicillin. Okay?"

This is an exaggerated example, but think about it for a moment. How would you feel about this doctor? Would you ever take your child back to see her? Would you have any confidence in this doctor? Would you support this doctor? The answer is the same: no. But this is exactly the situation going on today with many teachers. They do not know what to say. They do not know how to say it. They are so tied up in the myth of the good teacher that they do not feel that they have the right to ask for parent support. This attitude is reflected in everything they say to parents. Keep the pediatrician analogy in mind as you continue to read through this book. You will find that the analogy is pertinent to many of your professional situations.

The myth of the good teacher keeps too many teachers who really are good at everything else they do from working effectively with parents.

Does this roadblock apply to you? If so, you must learn to overcome it if you are going to establish support from parents. In this book, you will learn the techniques and gain the confidence to do so.

Teacher's Roadblock #2: The Myth of the "Bad Parent"

"You can't reach parents, and if you do, all you hear is that they don't know what to do and they want you to handle the problem. Why bother trying to work with them?"

The flip side of the coin bearing the myth of the good teacher is the myth of the "bad parent." Teachers, like everyone else, may be affected by stereotypes. For example, some teachers may believe that parents from a disadvantaged socioeconomic background are less equipped to be good parents. Often parents from disadvantaged backgrounds had very little schooling themselves and thus—so the teachers think—have very little interest in their children's efforts at school. Other teachers may think that parents of different ethnic or cultural backgrounds may not share their educational values. Still others may feel that a single-parent household cannot offer the support necessary to raise an emotionally stable child.

These misconceptions are detrimental to any productive communication with parents. If teachers believe that parents are not doing their job and have no valuable insights to offer, they will most likely not try to reach out to them in order to solicit their help.

Do you:

- Believe that parents don't take the time or make the effort to get involved in their children's education?
- Consider a student's problem proof of a parent's failure?
- Contact parents to complain rather than to get their input?
- Tell parents how to handle their child's problem?
- Disregard a parent's point of view?
- Discard a parent's concern?

If you answered yes to any of these questions, you probably are buying into the myth of the bad parent.

Not only will this attitude keep you, the teacher, from reaching out to parents, it will also keep parents from offering their help, because it is clearly not appreciated.

The truth is that all parents care. They may just not know how to show it, or they may show it in a way that you do not approve of. It is not in your or your students' best interest to underestimate parents. In fact, it is your responsibility to reach out to all parents to get them involved.

Most parents know their children better than you do and care about them greatly. If you cooperate with a parent, you'll be able to see the student in a different context, one that might show you what parents have accomplished rather than where they have failed. Practical tips and strategies for dealing with parents from different backgrounds will enable you to realize if and when your attitude toward a specific student may be informed by negative attitudes about his background. If you reach out to and cooperate with parents, you can and will move beyond your misconceptions to recognize and build upon a family's strength rather than its failures.

The myth of the bad parent may be based on experience.

Nonproductive encounters with parents can lead teachers to develop negative expectations. These negative expectations can easily lead to negative feelings about working with parents at all. When this happens, parent contact quickly breaks down, often resulting in a parent being called only as a last resort, when a problem is totally out of hand or at a crisis state.

Consider this situation: A group of middle school teachers were having academic and behavioral problems with a large number of their students. Upon examination of their grade books, it was apparent that there were students who had not completed an assignment for weeks. Other students had been given 5 to 10 detentions. When asked what contact they had had with parents, it became clear that not one of them had called a parent. When asked why parents had not been contacted, one teacher summed up the attitude of the others: "The parents in this area don't back us up and don't care. They want us not only to educate the children but to raise them, too!" These teachers felt that there was no value in taking the time and effort to work with their students' parents.

A teacher's negative expectations are often a direct result of having been questioned and criticized by parents. Many teachers say that the most stressful part of their job is working with angry, critical parents. When a teacher has had several unproductive conferences with hostile parents, is subjected to parents who threaten to sue or go to the school board, or is threatened with bodily harm, it is easy to understand why the teacher might become defensive or anxious.

The negativity educators sometimes feel toward parents can be a major roadblock to getting parents on your side.

Bear in mind that negative expectations are based on yesterday's experiences. Tomorrow is a new day. Begin the new day armed with a positive attitude toward parent involvement and with the skills and techniques for dealing with parents presented in *Parents on Your Side*.

Teacher's Roadblock #3: Lack of Training in Working With Parents

"I know that I avoid dealing with parents. I'm not comfortable working with parents. I know how to work with kids; I don't know how to work with parents."

"I was trained to do one thing—to teach children. Parents were not even mentioned in my education classes."

Do you find that you avoid dealing with parents because you're just not comfortable working with them? You're not alone. Most teachers will agree that they were trained only to teach students and that parents were never even mentioned in their education classes. A study by the Harvard Family Research Project indicates that only 25% of the teacher education courses reviewed covered communicating with parents.[2] In the vast majority of all teacher education classes, there is, for all intents and purposes, little or no content focusing on this issue. Without training, you may find that you do not have the skills and confidence necessary to get the backing you need from parents.

Just as you need to know how to develop lesson plans for curriculum and create a discipline plan for behavior management, you also need to know how to work with parents. This requires special skills. You must learn to work with all kinds of parents, including those who question or challenge your professional competence.

To accomplish this, you must learn to listen effectively and respond accordingly—because a teacher, just like any business manager, needs to receive training in effective communication skills. *Parents on Your Side* will give you practical tips that will help you to view your students and their parents as your clients, and yourself as a customer-relations officer. We will teach you how to roll out the welcome mat and reach out to even the most reluctant parent.

Be aware of parents' roadblocks.

The roadblocks aren't all yours. Parents have roadblocks of their own that keep them from giving support. Learn to listen. Pinpointing the type of roadblock a parent might be focused on will enable you to use specific techniques to move the parent past the roadblock and get the support you need.

We have identified four parent roadblocks that typically keep parents from backing you. As you consider each one, keep in mind that by recognizing the roadblock, your response can direct the ensuing conversation to a productive conclusion.

Parents' Roadblock #1: Parents Are Overwhelmed

"Ever since my divorce, my life has fallen apart. Sometimes I just don't feel like I can make it on my own raising a family. I know I should discipline my sons to behave at school, but really, I'd just rather the teacher handle it, because I can't cope."

When you hear a parent make comments like these, you need to know that you're dealing with a parent who is overwhelmed, that this parent is coping with a stressful situation in his life. Armed with this information, you can gear your response to moving the parent past this roadblock and avoid getting bogged down in a conversation that accomplishes nothing.

The term *at-risk student* is very popular today. We could coin another term: *at-risk parent*. These are parents who are at risk of being overwhelmed by the stress in their lives. They do not feel that they have the time or energy to support their children's education to the degree necessary to ensure their children's success.

You will find at-risk parents in all kinds of households. While it's true that many at-risk parents are part of the growing population of single parents struggling to raise and support a family on their own, it's also true that at-risk parents can be found in the most affluent two-parent homes. The point is, there can be many reasons why parents are overwhelmed with their lives: poverty, divorce, illness, or job stress. These parents may feel that school is the last thing they have the time or energy to deal with. Overwhelmed parents are a very real roadblock to getting the support you need as you learn to actively listen to what a parent is saying and react appropriately. Listen for words or phrases that will cue you to a parent's state of mind.

Here's an example of a conversation with an overwhelmed parent.

The teacher calls a parent regarding a homework problem. She introduces herself and begins discussing the problem with the parent. Before she gets very far, the parent interjects the following comments:

Parent: *I hear what you're saying, but I come home so tired at night that the last thing in the world I can do is battle with my child over homework. I know he should do it, and I know I'm the one who should be making sure he does it. But I'm just too tired to deal with it. Here are two ways a teacher could respond.*

Teacher A: *Mrs. Jones, Eddie has to turn in all of his homework assignments or he's going to fail this class. That's all there is to it. I don't want that to happen and, I'm sure, neither do you.*

Teacher B: *I hear how difficult it is for you now. I also hear you saying that you really are concerned about how your son does in school. Mrs. Jones, we both want success for him. I'm here to work with you to see that it happens. I'm going to give you some suggestions that will help you check on his homework progress each night easily and quickly.*

The results:

- Teacher A failed to notice the parent's roadblock and consequently will probably end up without the support she needs to solve the problem.

- Teacher B has recognized that she is dealing with an overwhelmed parent. She knows that if she doesn't help move the parent past this roadblock, she won't get the support she needs. This teacher listened and heard. She recognized that the parent was not uncaring or hostile, but overwhelmed. She therefore adjusted her response to lead the conversation in a direction that would not cause the parent anxiety and add to her burden. Chances are good that this teacher will get the support she needs from this parent. And that means the student will get the help he needs.

Parents' Roadblock #2: Parents Want to Help but Don't Know How

"I tell her to study. I tell her to do her homework. She says she will, and then she just doesn't do it. I have no idea how to get through to this kid."

This is a parent who cares but doesn't know what to do. Each year, you will encounter parents who do not have the strength or the skills needed to motivate their children to perform academically or behave appropriately in school or at home. And if parents cannot get their children to behave at home, it's not likely that they will be able to give you the support you need to ensure that their children behave in school. These are parents who need and often will accept your help. They want their children to succeed as much as you do. It is your responsibility to recognize this roadblock and get help to them.

Learn to recognize this roadblock because very often these are the parents who, with guidance and support, will be eager to become actively involved in their child's education.

Here's an example of a conversation with a parent who doesn't know how to help.

A teacher is meeting with a parent about a behavior problem. As the teacher begins to discuss the problem, the parent responds:

Parent: *Believe me, I'd do something if I could. I know the way John behaves at school is wrong; he acts the same at home. I just don't have any idea what to do to help him stop. And what difference would it make anyway? He doesn't listen to a thing I say.*

Here are two possible responses.

Teacher A: *Well, John needs to behave at school. I can't have him disrupting my class.*

Teacher B: *I hear you saying that you really want to help John learn to behave at school. And I know it's not always easy to know how to do it. If you'd like, we can work together to come up with some solutions. I've worked with lots of kids just like John. I can promise you that if we put our heads together, we will come up with some solutions that will get John back on track.*

The results:

- Teacher A has pushed the problem, not the solution, onto the parent. If he had listened more effectively, he would have heard that the parent is really at a loss for what to do.

- Teacher B realized that she was speaking with a parent who was willing to help but just didn't have any idea what to do. Knowing she had to move the parent past this roadblock, she responded by offering further suggestions for what the parent could do to remedy the problem. Through her words, this teacher let the parent know that she was concerned enough about the student to take the time to help solve the problem.

Parents' Roadblock #3: Parents' Negative Feelings About School

"I hated school. I never even graduated. The teachers were always on my case and now they're on my son's case."

Each year, you will encounter parents who themselves had negative school experiences. Often when a parent did not perform well academically, was constantly in trouble, or dropped out of school, the parent harbors negative feelings about school in general and teachers in particular. These parents often do not trust teachers and may feel that teachers do not have their children's best interests at heart. Since these parents had negative experiences in school, they tend to avoid involvement in school activities. It is often difficult to get them to come to Back-to-School Night, parent conferences, school performances, and other events.

Finally, these parents may actually expect their children to have academic or behavioral problems in school just like they did. Their own experiences may lead them to believe that this is just how children behave in school. Thus, these parents tend to feel that there is no reason to get involved in solving their child's problems because there is nothing that really can be done about them.

Because a parent's negative attitude can easily be transferred to the child, it is important to recognize this roadblock and take steps to get these parents positively involved.

Here's an example of a conversation with a parent who has negative feelings about school.

The teacher calls a parent to discuss an academic problem. As soon as the teacher begins to speak, the parent goes on the offensive.

Parent: *You teachers today don't like kids any more than my teachers did. All you ever do is call me and tell me how bad my kids are.*

Here are two possible responses.

Teacher A: *Mr. Smith, I'm calling because your son isn't performing as he should in my class.*

Teacher B: *Mr. Smith, I'm much more interested in calling you to let you know how terrific your son is. He has great potential. That's why it's so important that we both work together to solve this problem. Your son can be doing a lot better in class. I want to see that happen. I care about your son's success, and I know you do, too.*

The results:

- Teacher A ignored the parent's roadblock and continued to address her original agenda. Ignoring the parent's anger won't defuse it. The conversation will probably lead to a dead end. The parent will still be hostile and the teacher will still not have support.

- Teacher B determined that he was speaking with a parent who had strong negative feelings about teachers and school in general. He knew that this parent would never listen to anything until this roadblock was removed. The teacher let this parent know that he in fact was dealing with a teacher who does care.

Parents' Roadblock #4: Parents' Negative View of Teacher Competence

"Schools have gone downhill. I know it. Everyone in the neighborhood knows it. I'm not going to stand by and let my child's teacher ruin his school experience."

From time to time, you will encounter parents who simply do not respect your professional expertise. There are several reasons why this is so. First, hardly a week goes by that there isn't media attention focusing on the "dismal" state of the American educational system, focusing in particular on the poor performance of students. In many instances, the blame is placed on the teachers. Parents cannot help but absorb this constant negativity regarding the educational system.

Second, there are more parents today with a higher level of educational sophistication than ever before. Many of these parents have their own theories of how their child should be educated and will not hesitate to state these opinions, valid or invalid, to the teacher.

Third, there are, unfortunately, still some teachers who are not competent enough to meet the needs of students. The inability of the educational system to remove these teachers has added tremendous fuel to the fire of parental discontent. All it takes is one incompetent teacher in a building to stir the wrath of parents. When these teachers are not removed, the frustration level of parents and colleagues increases and an entire school can be labeled inadequate.

Keep in mind that negative views of a teacher's competence can come across in many forms, from outright hostility to subtle questioning. To defuse this negativity, you need to really listen to what a parent is saying, not just react defensively or in anger.

Here is an example of a conversation with a parent who has negative feelings about school.

The parent calls the teacher about a low grade her daughter has earned.

Parent: *My child is special, and I want a teacher who can meet her special needs. I will not sit by and settle for anything less.*

Here are two possible responses.

Teacher A: *I'm doing the best I can with her.*

Teacher B: *You're right to want the best for your child. That's why I want to work with you to see that she is successful in my class.*

The results:

- Teacher A let the parent get to her. She was probably hurt and became defensive. Her weak response will only make the parent angrier and feel more justified about her assumptions. The teacher's response certainly will not increase the parent's confidence in her.

- Teacher B knows she is listening to a parent who has a negative attitude regarding teacher competence. And she knows that reactionary responses will get her nowhere. She therefore accepts the parent's sense of urgency and demonstrates strength, assurance, and confidence in her own ability.

Be sensitive to obstacles to effective communication.

Recognizing your own roadblocks is the first step toward an attitude that accepts parent involvement as both your right and your duty as a teacher. By listening for parents' roadblocks and responding accordingly, you can open communication and work together to solve problems. Once you recognize the roadblocks that stand in the way of parent involvement, you can start taking steps to remedy it.

It's a matter of sensitivity—of taking the time to think about what you really expect from a parent and what a parent really expects from you. You can't do your best for your students without the support of their parents. And parents can't give that support if they are focused on anger, confusion, or their own negative expectations. Moving every conversation with parents forward to a productive conclusion is the way to get parents on your side. You must always ask for and listen to the parent's point of view in order to demonstrate that you care about the student and his home. Hearing what is said, and adjusting your responses accordingly, is the foundation of effective communication.

References

[1] Cavarretta, J. (1998, May). Parents are a school's best friend. *Educational Leadership, 55*(8), 12–15.

[2] Lynn, L. (1997, September/October). Teaching teachers to work with families. *Harvard Education Letter.* [Online]. Available: http://www.edletter.org/past/issues/1997-so/teaching.shtml.

Section Two

How to Work With Parents to Establish Positive Relationships

Section 2 of *Parents on Your Side* will give you step-by-step suggestions for how to establish a positive relationship with parents from the start. Proactive parent involvement measures are techniques and strategies a teacher employs on a regular basis with all parents *before* a problem arises in order to establish a positive relationship.

Chapter 4: Meeting First-Day Objectives

This chapter offers suggestions to reach out to parents on or before the first day of school. Contacting parents to introduce yourself will get your relationship off to a good start.

Chapter 5: Making the Most of Back-to-School Night

These suggestions will turn Back-to-School Night into a success that will last all year long.

Chapter 6: Establishing Positive Communication With Parents

Positive communication cannot stop at the beginning of the year. This chapter presents a few efficient and effective strategies to keep in touch with the parents of all your students.

Chapter 7: Involving Parents in the Homework Process

This chapter turns homework into a successful activity between parents and students, and makes sure that parents stay involved in their children's daily lives at school.

Chapter 8: Conducting Regularly Scheduled Parent Conferences

This chapter focuses on parent conferences, which are the most effective and efficient way to communicate with parents.

Chapter 9: Demonstrating Sensitivity and Awareness

Awareness and sensitivity, the two most important guidelines offered in this chapter, are the basis and prerequisite for any and all communication techniques discussed throughout this book.

Consistent and continued positive communication with parents throughout the year will help you establish a relationship with parents that you can build upon should problems arise.

Meeting First-Day Objectives

Start working as soon as possible to get the parent support you need. It's up to you to make the first move. From the very beginning, you must clearly communicate that parental involvement and support is necessary and valued. Don't wait until a problem comes up. Don't wait for parents to come to you. Reach out to them right away. Parent contact needs to begin before the first day of school.

The first actions you take will quickly help to establish your reputation with parents as an effective professional who not only cares about the welfare of their children but who has the confidence and skills to take charge. Set immediate objectives for yourself and take the actions that will achieve them. The purpose of meeting these objectives is to break down potential communication barriers, get past existing roadblocks, and set the stage for productive communication and cooperation all year long.

This chapter covers three objectives for you to meet on or before the first day of school:

1. Send a "before school starts" greeting to all parents and incoming students.

2. Open up verbal communication with parents of potential problem students.

3. Communicate your expectations to parents.

Send a "before school starts" greeting to parents and students.

Before the beginning of the school year, you are probably unknown to most of your students' parents, and perhaps to the students themselves. Introduce yourself by saying a friendly hello. Take time during vacation—before school starts—to drop a line to incoming students and their parents. You don't need to say much, just let them know that you're enthusiastic about the upcoming year. Here are two examples.

Sample "Before School Starts" Greetings

Dear Mr. and Mrs. Rosas:

Just a quick note to let you know I'm looking forward to working with Melina this year. It will be a pleasure to get to know both of you. Please feel free to drop by the classroom on the first day of school, September 10. I'd like to say hello!

Sincerely,

Ms. Warner

Dear Melina:

I just received my roster and found out you'll be in my algebra class. I'm looking forward to a terrific year and I hope you are, too. Enjoy the rest of your vacation. I'll see you September 10.

Sincerely,

Mr. Ramos

These brief notes are a preview of the many positive communications parents and students will be receiving from you throughout the year.

Open up verbal communication with parents of potential problem students.

Have you been assigned students who have a history of problems in school? Don't just complain about it in the teachers' room. Do something positive about it. Take some proactive steps to get the parents of these students on your side now, before school and the problems begin, by calling the parents. The goal of your conversation is to establish positive communication and to reassure parents that you care about their child. You also want to exhibit professionalism and confidence in your ability to work with their child.

Remember that parents of difficult students are probably used to hearing from school only when there is a problem. Here's your chance to make a difference and show them that you are a caring and supportive teacher. You are going to turn this situation around and contact them with good news. You'll let them know you are confident that you can all work together to make this a successful year for their child.

Plan what you will say.

Before making the call, write down what you want to cover, and keep your notes in front of you as you speak. This preparation will be well worth it. If you deal effectively with this first phone call, you will probably have far greater support from this parent throughout the year.

Plan to address each of the following points:

1. **Begin with a statement of support.**
   The first words you speak will set the tone for the entire conversation. Be sensitive to the parent's feelings. Keep in mind that the last thing she wants to hear are problems concerning her child, before the school year has even begun. You have to let this parent know immediately that you are calling because you care about her child and because you sincerely want to make the new year a success.

   "Mrs. Hirsch, this is Mrs. Williams. I'm going to be Bobby's fifth-grade teacher. I wanted to speak to you before the school year began because I want to make sure that this year is successful for your child."

2. **Get parental input concerning the problems of last year.**
   Demonstrate your interest in the parent's point of view. Let the parent know that you genuinely care how she feels about what happened the previous year. This is the time to listen for roadblocks. Is the parent overwhelmed? Angry? Unable to deal with the child's problems? Gear your response to what the parent says to you.

   "I would like to know how you see Bobby's experience at school last year."

3. **Find out what the parent feels is necessary to make this year more successful.**
   Listen to the parent's suggestions. She may be able to offer valuable insights that will help you get off to a better start with the student. The information may give you an advantage in dealing with the student from the first day.

   "I'd like to know what you think we need to do to make sure Bobby has a good year this year."

4. **Explain that parent support is critical.**
   Let the parent know how important her support is.

   "I believe that you can help me with Bobby. I will be in touch with you throughout the year because your support is vital. You are the most important person in Bobby's life and he must know that we are working together to help him."

5. **Express your confidence.**

Put yourself in this parent's position. Another school year is starting. If it's anything like the last, it may be a continual round of negative feedback from school. Give the parent something to be optimistic about. The confidence you project will encourage the parent to give the support you need.

"I have complete confidence that by working together we will help Bobby to have a good year. I want to assure you that I've worked with all kinds of students, and I am certain I can make this year a great one for your son."

Sample Phone Conversations

Here's a sample elementary level conversation.

Parent: *Hello.*

Teacher: *Mrs. Gowdy?*

Parent: *Yes.*

Teacher: (Introduce yourself) *This is Mrs. Tomaselli. I'll be Ted's teacher next year.*

Parent: *Oh, hello.*

Teacher: (State reason for call) *The reason I'm calling is that I want to make sure that this year is successful for Ted.*

Parent: *I'm glad to hear that. Last year wasn't very good for Ted at all.*

Teacher: (Get parental input) *Really? Why is that?*

Parent: *Oh, I don't know. The teacher and Ted didn't get along. She was very negative. They had what I guess you would call a personality conflict. I felt that she didn't know how to handle him. She would call me and expect me to do her job. You know, she's the teacher, and she should handle some of those things. I sure didn't know what to do.*

Teacher: *I can see that last year was very frustrating for you.* (Get parental suggestion for solution) *I'd really like to hear any suggestions you might have that could help Ted have a better year this year.*

Parent: *My son needs a lot of attention. He's had a tough couple of years. Ever since my husband and I got divorced, Ted just doesn't seem to care about school. So far no teacher has given him the attention and support he needs.*

Teacher: *I understand what you're saying, and let me assure you that I will do everything I can to make it a positive, supportive year for him. In fact, I've got an idea of something we can do right at the start of* *the year. Every day, I have a special monitor in class, and I think it would be great if for the first few days of school Ted could be my special monitor. That will enable me to give him a lot of personal attention and positive support. I can make sure the first few days this year are really positive for him.*

Parent: *That may help. It's more than the teacher did last year.*

Teacher: (Express need for parental support) *I know that if we work together we can ensure success for Ted.*

Parent: *What do you mean by "working together"? I don't have much time. You know I work full time and have two other children.*

Teacher: *I understand. What I'm suggesting won't take a lot of time. But it'll make a great difference. You know, you are the most important person in Ted's life, and Ted must know we're working together to help him.*

Parent: *I haven't had much success with him in the past.*

Teacher: *I know how frustrating it can be with children, but let me assure you that I've worked with many students like Ted. And I've worked with many of their parents and have had great success. I am going to make it a point to see that Ted has a super year. I want Ted to like school, and I want him to be a success.*

Parent: *You sound like you mean it.*

Teacher: *I do. I mean what I say.*

Parent: *I really appreciate your taking the time to call. No teacher has ever done this before.*

Teacher: *It's my pleasure. I will be in touch with you throughout the year, and I want you to stay in touch with me. (Speak to child) Before I say good-bye, I think it would help if I could speak to Ted for a few minutes to introduce myself to him and share my feelings about this year.*

Here's a sample secondary level conversation.

Parent: *Hello.*

Teacher: *Mrs. Greenfield?*

Parent: *Yes.*

Teacher: *This is Mr. Schwartz. I'll be Gail's social studies teacher next year. (State reason for call) The reason I'm calling is that I noticed that Gail had a lot of trouble with social studies last year. (Get parental input) I'd like to find out why she had these problems and what we can do to make sure they don't occur this year.*

Parent: *Well, I think I can tell you what the problem was. I think she had a poor attitude toward school.*

Teacher: *I hear what you're saying. Can you tell me specifically what happened last year with her schoolwork?*

Parent: *Sometimes she told me she didn't have any homework when, actually, she did. And the few times she did do it, she would race through it just to finish it. She wouldn't care whether she did a good job. She'd do it while she was on the phone with the stereo blasting or the TV on.*

Teacher: *It sounds like you had a few difficulties.* (Get parental suggestion for solution) *Do you have any suggestions about what I can do to help the situation this year?*

Parent: *I really don't know. To be honest, she probably needs a new group of friends. The kids she hangs out with are no good.*

Teacher: *I can't get her new friends, but I think maybe there are some things I can do as her teacher to help.*

Parent: *Well, she says she doesn't believe that teachers really care. Teachers could care less if she comes to class, or if she does or doesn't do her work. It never matters.*

Teacher: *Well, I'm a teacher who does care. I'll make sure she knows that.*

Parent: *I don't know. She hasn't liked teachers, and she hasn't liked school since the seventh grade. She's really been lost. Just lost.*

Teacher: *I think lots of kids get lost today in schools the size of ours. I don't want her to get lost. That's why I'm calling. I want to work with her to make sure she is involved and does her class work and her homework.*

Parent: *She needs a lot of help. She has no idea how to study.*

Teacher: *I can help her there. I can teach her some very simple, basic study skills that will help her to be more successful.* (Express need for parental support) *I will do my part, but I'm going to need your help if we are going to turn things around for Gail.*

Parent: *But she doesn't listen to me. I'm not even usually home when she does her homework. I'm at work, and I don't know what I can do from there.*

Teacher: *I don't want you to worry. I've worked with many students like your daughter. I've also worked with many parents in your position, and let me assure you, we can help her. Throughout the year, I'll give you guidelines and techniques that will help Gail study*

> *more successfully. I'll follow through at school, and you can follow through at home. How does that sound?*

Parent: *I really appreciate your attitude. But I still don't know if it will do any good.*

Teacher: *I know it will. We will work together. We will help your daughter. She is going to succeed in my class. With me doing my part and you doing your part, it will work. You can count on me. I will be behind you 100 percent.*

Communicate your expectations to parents.

If they are to be actively involved, parents need some basic information right at the beginning of the school year. First, they need to know a little bit about you. After all, you are going to be an influential person in your students' lives. It's important that parents have an opportunity to know something more about you than your name and room number.

Second, parents of both elementary and secondary students need to know the teacher's classroom rules and standards. Think a minute about the parent contacts you have had in the past. What precipitated many of these contacts? Chances are it was either a behavior problem or a homework problem. These are, after all, the day-to-day problems that you deal with most often. It is extremely important that you communicate to parents your standards and policies for both areas. You can't ask parents to back up your rules if they don't know them. Before school begins, you should formulate both a classroom discipline plan and a homework policy.

Send home the following on the first day of school:

- A letter of introduction
- A copy of your discipline plan
- A copy of your homework policy

Suggestions follow for generating these items.

Send home a letter of introduction.

Give parents an opportunity to know something about you and your plans for the upcoming year.

- Keep your letter brief; no more than one page.
- The tone of your letter should be upbeat and enthusiastic.
- Take this opportunity to tell parents that you need their support— that the education of their children is a team effort.

- Above all, end the letter with a statement expressing your confidence in the success you expect for all of your students this year.

Sample Letter of Introduction to Parents

Dear Parents,

My name is Mr. Camacho, and I will be your child's fifth-grade teacher this year. I'm looking forward to an exciting, productive year working with you and your child.

Throughout my years of teaching, I have become committed to the importance of parent involvement in a student's education. I firmly believe that your child receives the best education possible when you and I work as a team.

Enclosed with this letter are copies of my classroom discipline plan and my homework policy. Please read both of these carefully. They explain many of my expectations for your child in this class. I need your support of these expectations, and I need you to let your child know also that you support these classroom rules and standards.

I will be keeping in close touch with you all year long. Please do the same with me. I welcome your calls and messages. Any time you have something you'd like to discuss with me, please call the school office at 555-2222. I will return your call as quickly as possible.

I look forward to meeting you at Back-to-School Night on September 24. It's going to be an exciting evening that I know you won't want to miss.

Sincerely,

Mr. Camacho

Formulate your classroom discipline plan.

A classroom discipline plan[1] determines your policies regarding behavior management. It provides a system of guidelines that clarify the behaviors you expect from your students. It also establishes what they can expect from you in return if they follow your guidelines and if they don't. Such a clearly defined policy is the prerequisite for a structured and supportive classroom environment in which all students are treated consistently with fairness. A discipline plan ensures your students' emotional and physical safety and allows you to focus on teaching, and your students on learning.

These guidelines for formulating a discipline plan incorporate the strategies for behavior management developed in our book *Assertive Discipline*. Obviously, there are other behavior management techniques upon which a classroom discipline plan may be based. While *Assertive Discipline* provides effective techniques for classroom management, use the strategies that best suit your teaching style. It is important that you develop some plan that clarifies your policy regarding behavior management. You, your students, and their parents have a need and the right to know which behaviors you expect, and the supportive and corrective measures you will take to encourage and enforce these behaviors.

In defining such a plan, it is important that you don't just copy the suggestions offered here but that you use your own professional judgment to determine which classroom management strategies best fit your situation.

Whichever techniques you choose, a discipline plan is an integral part of any teacher's parent involvement plan. It lets parents know exactly how their children are to behave, what will happen when they do behave, and what will happen when they don't.

A classroom discipline plan should address at least the following three areas:

1. Rules students must follow at all times

2. Corrective actions students will receive for not following the rules

3. Supportive feedback students will receive for following the rules

Having well-defined rules and predetermined corrective actions from the very beginning will assist you in your teaching efforts and give you a basis for effectively communicating with parents. Based on your discipline plan, you will be able to:

- Judge student behavior fairly

- Discuss behavior problems more confidently with parents, because you can accurately describe to a parent

  › The rule(s) that the student has broken

  › The corrective actions following the student's misbehavior

  › The supportive feedback following the student's compliance with your rules

Sample Discipline Plan Letter

Classroom Discipline Plan
Room 5 Mr. Bronson

Dear Parent(s):

These are the rules of my classroom. These rules will be in effect at all times:

- Follow directions.
- Keep hands, feet, and objects to yourself.
- No teasing or name calling is allowed.
- Do not leave the room without permission.

If a student chooses to break a rule, the following corrective actions will be imposed:

First time a student breaks a rule: Reminder
Second time: 5 minutes away from group
Third time: 10 minutes away from group
Fourth time: Teacher calls parents with student
Fifth time: Send to principal

Severe misbehavior, such as fighting or verbal abuse, will result in the immediate imposition of the **Severe Clause:** Send to principal.

Students who behave appropriately will be supported with verbal reinforcement, positive notes sent home, small rewards, class parties, and other special privileges.

I have already discussed this plan with your child, but I would appreciate it if you would review it together, then sign and return the form below.

Thank you for your support.

Sincerely,

Mr. Bronson --

I have read the discipline plan and have discussed it with my child.

Parent's signature _____

Student's signature _____

Date _____

Send your discipline plan home.

Once you've defined your classroom discipline plan, it is important that you allow parents to take a look at it so that they may know how their children will be dealt with at school in case of discipline problems. Include a sign-off portion that is to be returned to you, indicating that the parent has read the discipline plan. (See page 42.)

Determine your homework policy.

Because homework provides a day-to-day connection between home and school, it is one of the best opportunities you have for positive interaction with parents. Homework has the potential to be a powerful part of your parent involvement program. Too often, however, homework becomes a bone of contention between parents, students, and teachers. Any positive interaction that might result from it is lost in a sea of misinformation and unfulfilled expectations.

If you want parents to give the support you need regarding homework, it is important that your homework standards are clearly spelled out. As much as you need to develop a discipline plan to communicate your disciplinary standards, you need to develop a homework policy to clearly communicate your homework standards. A homework policy clearly states your expectations for everyone involved in the homework process: student, teacher, and parents.

Elements of a Homework Policy

A homework policy should:

1. Explain why homework is assigned.

2. Explain the types of homework you will assign.

3. Inform parents of the amount and frequency of homework.

4. Provide guidelines for when and how students are to complete homework.

5. State that you will keep a record of assignments completed and not completed.

6. Explain how homework will affect students' grades.

7. Inform parents and students of test schedules.

8. Let parents know how you will positively reinforce students who complete homework.

9. Explain what you will do when students do not complete homework (effect on grades, for example).

10. Clarify what is expected of the parent.

Look more closely at each of these elements of a homework policy.

1. **Explain why homework is assigned.**

   You can't assume that parents understand why homework is given or how important it is. Therefore, you must explain the benefits of homework. For instance, your rationale could include that homework is important because:

   • It reinforces skills and material learned in class.

   • It prepares students for upcoming class topics.

   • It teaches students to work independently.

   • It aids in evaluating student progress.

   • It teaches students to assume responsibility for their own work.

   • It teaches students organizational and time-management skills.

2. **Explain the types of homework you will assign.**

   It is important that both parents and students know that you are doing your part to ensure that students have the ability to do the homework you assign. Your policy should state that the homework you assign requires only those skills students have already learned in class.

3. **Inform parents of the amount and frequency of homework.**

   If parents are to back up your homework program, they must know when to expect assignments. Research has shown that regular homework assignments are more effective than homework assigned inconsistently. It is important, therefore, for you to include in your homework policy:

   • The days of the week on which you will assign homework.

   • The amount of time it should take students to complete homework

   The amount of homework you assign will depend on your community, your district, your principal, your class, and even the individual student.

4. **Provide guidelines for when and how students are to complete homework.**

   For students to meet your expectations about completing homework, you must clearly explain how you expect them to do their assignments. Typical expectations include:

   • All assignments will be completed.

- Students will do homework on their own and to the best of their ability.

- Students will turn in work that is neatly done.

- Students will turn in homework on time.

- Students are responsible for making up homework assignments missed due to absence.

5. **State that you will keep a record of assignments completed and not completed.**
   Your policy should state that you will keep a daily record of all homework assignments completed and not completed. The fact that you will check all homework is enough to motivate many students to do their homework. Also, this type of record keeping says something to both students and parents about the value you place on each and every assignment.

6. **Explain how homework will affect students' grades.**
   Students and parents alike need to know if homework will be graded separately or as a percentage of another grade. Many schools list homework as a separate item on report cards. Others consider homework as part of a subject grade. The system you use should be stated in your homework policy.

7. **Inform parents and students of test schedules.**
   It is important that parents and students (especially in upper grades) know when tests will be scheduled and how they will be evaluated. The following is an example of a homework policy statement regarding tests for a math class.

   "Tests will be given periodically, usually on a Wednesday or a Friday. Adequate notice will be given for all tests. To prepare for tests, go over notes and corrected homework assignments. Any test that receives a D or an F must be returned within two days signed by a parent."

8. **Let parents know how you will positively reinforce students who complete homework.**
   Research has shown that positive reinforcement is useful in motivating students to do homework. Your policy, therefore, should include:

   - Supportive feedback for individual students—praise, awards, and notes home to the parents

   - Rewards that can be earned by the entire class

9. **Explain what you will do when students do not complete homework.**
It is important that students and parents clearly understand the corrective actions that will be imposed for not doing homework. Examples of actions that can be taken include the following:

- Have parents sign completed homework every night.
- Have elementary students miss recess to complete homework.
- Have secondary students eat lunch while completing homework.
- Have students complete homework after school.
- Lower students' grades.

Whatever corrective actions you choose must be clearly spelled out in your homework policy.

Let parents know that homework missed for legitimate reasons must be explained in a signed note from them.

10. **Clarify what is expected of the parent.**
Since you do not follow the homework and the students home, it is up to parents to see that homework is completed. Your homework policy needs to cover the specific type of support you expect from parents. You should expect parents to

- Establish homework as a top priority for their children.
- Make sure that their children do homework in a quiet environment.
- Establish a daily homework time.
- Provide supportive feedback when homework is completed.
- Not allow children a way out of doing homework.
- Contact you if children have problems with homework.

Send your homework policy home.

Parents need to receive your homework policy before the first homework assignments are given. Take a look at the sample homework policy letters to parents on pages 47 to 50. Notice that each of the elements previously listed is included in the letters.

It's worth the effort.

Take a moment to look back at the first-day goals in terms of moving parents past their roadblocks. How do you think parents will react to receiving these notes, letters, and phone calls?

- An overwhelmed parent will be relieved and pleased that his child has a teacher who is taking charge and who obviously cares about the student. This parent will appreciate the confidence the teacher has shown in taking a proactive stance.

- A parent who wants to help but doesn't know how to do so will feel that the ice has been broken. With the introduction that has been made, she will feel much more comfortable approaching you for help.

- Finally, a parent who has negative feelings toward school in general or teachers in particular will most likely have been nudged just a little bit closer to a more positive attitude toward both.

You are setting the stage for a full year of positive parent involvement. By meeting each of the objectives above, you demonstrate to parents that you are committed to your parent involvement program. This in turn will communicate that you are committed to their children's success. Certainly, this will be greatly appreciated.

Putting in time and energy early will save you even greater effort in the future. These are preventive actions that will put your parent involvement program on the right track from the start.

Reference

[1] Canter, L., & Canter, M. (2001). *Assertive discipline: Positive behavior management for today's classroom.* Bloomington, IN: Solution Tree Press.

Sample Homework Policy for a Fourth-Grade Class

Room 6 Homework Policy

To the family of _____

Why I assign homework:

I believe homework is important because it is a valuable aid in helping students make the most of their experience in school. I give homework because it is useful in reinforcing what has been learned in class, prepares students for upcoming lessons, teaches responsibility, and helps students develop positive study habits.

When homework will be assigned:

Homework will be assigned Monday through Thursday nights. Assignments should take students no more than 1 hour to complete each night, not including studying for tests and working on projects. Spelling tests will be given each Friday. I will give students at least 1 week's notice to study for all tests, and one written report will be assigned each grading period.

Student's homework responsibilities:

I expect students to do their best job on their homework. I expect homework to be neat, not sloppy. I expect students to do the work on their own and ask for help only after they have given it their best effort. I expect that all assignments will be turned in on time.

Teacher's homework responsibilities:

I will check all homework. Because I strongly believe in the value supportive feedback plays in motivating children to develop good study habits, I will recognize students when they do their homework and offer incentives.

Parent's homework responsibilities:

Parents are the key to making homework a positive experience for their children. Therefore, I ask that parents make homework a top priority, provide necessary supplies and a quiet homework environment, set a daily homework time, provide praise and support, not let children avoid doing homework, and contact me if they notice a problem.

If students do not complete homework:

If students choose not to do their homework, I will ask that parents begin checking and signing completed homework each night. If students choose to make up homework the next day, their homework will be accepted but they will receive a one-grade reduction on that assignment. If they choose not to make up missed assignments, students will receive a grade of F for the assignment missed.

If there is a legitimate reason why a student is not able to finish homework, please send a note to me on the day the homework is due stating the reason it was not completed. The note must be signed by the parent.

Please read and discuss this homework policy with your child. Then sign the bottom portion of this letter and return it to school.

Mrs. Kerns -

I have read this homework policy and have discussed it with my child.

Parent's signature _____

Student's signature _____

Date _____

Sample Homework Policy for a Ninth-Grade Social Studies Class

Homework Policy
Mr. Jaworski   9th Grade Social Studies

To the family of _____

Why I assign homework:

I believe that homework is a valuable aid in helping students make the most of their experience in school. I give homework because it reinforces what has been taught in class, prepares students for upcoming lessons, and helps students develop self-discipline, responsibility, and organizational skills.

When homework will be assigned:

Homework will be assigned Monday, Tuesday, and Thursday nights, and should take students no more than 1 hour to complete (not including long-range projects and studying for tests).

Tests:

Tests will be given periodically, usually on a Wednesday or a Friday. Adequate notice will be given for all tests. Any test that receives a D or an F must be returned within 2 days, signed by a parent. Students will have at least 2 weeks' notice to study for tests, and one written report will be assigned each grading period.

Student's homework responsibilities:

- All assignments will be completed and turned in on time.
- Students are responsible for making up homework missed due to absence.
- Students will turn in work that is neatly done.

If students choose not to do their homework, the following corrective actions may occur:

- Parents will be asked to sign completed homework each night.
- Students may be required to complete homework during lunch or after school.

If there is a legitimate reason why a student is unable to finish homework, please send a note on the day the homework is due stating the reason it was not completed. The note must be signed by the parent.

Parent's homework responsibilities:

Parents are the key to making homework a positive experience for their children. Therefore, I ask that you make homework a top priority, provide necessary supplies and a quiet homework environment, provide praise and support, and contact me if you notice a problem.

Teacher's homework responsibilities:

I will check all homework and keep a record of assignments completed and not completed. Because I strongly believe in the value supportive feedback plays in motivating students to develop good study habits, I will recognize students with a variety of incentives when they do their homework.

I am looking forward to enjoying an exciting, productive year at school. Please do not hesitate to call me if you have any questions regarding this homework policy or any other matter.

Please read and discuss this homework policy with your child. Then sign the bottom portion of this letter and return it to school.

Sincerely,

Mr. Jaworski --

I have read this homework policy and have discussed it with my child.

Parent's signature _____

Student's signature _____

Date _____

Meeting First-Day Objectives

Reminders

DO

- Initiate parent contact before the first day of school.
- Formulate a classroom discipline plan before school starts.
- Write your homework policy before school starts.
- Send parents a letter stating that you need their support and that the education of their children is a team effort.
- Contact parents of potential problem students to let them know you are committed to their children's success in school this year.
- Send your discipline plan and homework policy home as soon as school begins. Ask parents to read and sign both documents.
- Carefully explain your discipline plan and homework policy to students on the first day of school.
- Feel confident in your ability to have a successful year!

DON'T

- Don't avoid contacting, by phone or by letter, non–English speaking parents. Find a translator to help you and reach out to these parents. Please refer to chapter 9 for further discussion of communicating with parents from different cultural or linguistic backgrounds.
- Don't wait for parents to come to you. Reach out to them first—before school starts.

Meeting First-Day Objectives
Checklist

Refer to this checklist when you start your first-day objectives.

HAVE YOU:

☐ Sent welcome notes to parents and students before school begins?

☐ Sent home a letter of introduction?

☐ Contacted parents of problem students before school begins?

☐ Sent home a copy of your classroom discipline plan?

☐ Sent home a copy of your homework policy?

Making the Most of Back-to-School Night

Chapter 5

B ack-to-School Night can be one of the most important events of the school year for both elementary and secondary teachers. It's your opportunity to meet parents, explain your policies and programs in detail, answer any questions about your class, and, most important, assure parents of your commitment to their children. The professionalism and confidence you project at Back-to-School Night can be instrumental toward getting parents on your side. Back-to-School Night can be a solitary event, unrelated to the rest of the year, or it can be the beginning of a dynamic year in which you and parents team up to become partners in their children's education. It all depends upon how you plan and deliver.

Unfortunately, we know that more than half of all parents don't attend Back-to-School Night. You may find that the very parents you want and need most to attend are the ones who don't show up. Don't just accept this; take action. Make a commitment to do all you can to encourage full parent participation. Use a variety of techniques to motivate parents to attend.

This chapter will outline the following ideas to help you plan and implement a great event:

- Remove logistical problems that may keep parents from attending.

- Send Back-to-School Night invitations.

- Involve students in planning.

- Use parent motivators to boost attendance.

- Reach out to parents who cannot come.

- Plan the classroom environment.

- Know exactly what you will say to parents.

- Present special Back-to-School Night activities.

- Keep the spirit alive.

Remove logistical problems that may keep parents from attending.

Some parents may not attend Back-to-School Night because they have other commitments. Try to accommodate parents' work schedules (if you are aware of them), and make sure that Back-to-School Night is set for a day and time that most parents are likely to be available.

Many parents cannot get away at night because they do not have a babysitter. Work with your administrators to set up a schoolwide babysitting service for Back-to-School Night, and you will see better attendance. Make sure that all parents are informed of the service.

If transportation to and from school has been a problem that kept parents from attending Back-to-School Night, set up a schoolwide carpool service. Make sure all parents are aware of this service.

Send Back-to-School Night invitations.

Make sure parents receive personalized invitations from you. Let them know that you are really counting on their attendance and that Back-to-School Night is an important responsibility for both of you. Use the invitation to publicize some of the events planned and, most important, list compelling reasons why parents should attend. Include a tear-off RSVP portion that will encourage parents to commit to attending. Be sure to send this invitation well in advance, so that parents can make plans. Send a follow-up reminder a few days before. Invitations can be sent via email as well.

Involve students in planning.

Students at any grade level can help you create an inviting classroom atmosphere by designing "Welcome Parents" signs and other classroom posters or displays for Back-to-School Night. In addition, try to involve students in preparing some of your Back-to-School Night activities or presentations. (See pages 63 to 65 for suggestions.) By doing so, you will generate enthusiasm they will pass on to parents.

Use parent motivators to boost attendance.

Your first Back-to-School Night objective is to get parents there. To boost parent attendance, you may have to offer a few incentives. Try some of these ideas.

Sample Back-to-School Night Invitation

To: _____

You're invited to **Back-to-School Night!**

Place _____

Date _____

Time _____

- See what we're doing in class.
- Learn what you can do at home to help your child be successful in school!
- Participate in the Back-to-School Night raffle! Prizes!
- Enjoy a video/slide presentation starring your child!
- Take home a **FREE** Parent Handbook filled with great ideas for you and your child.

Please join us.

Working Together We Can Make a Difference!

Babysitting will be available in Room 10.

- -

For carpool information, please call 555-5555.

☐ I will be attending Back-to-School Night.

☐ I won't be able to attend Back-to-School Night.

Name _____

Parent of _____

Hold a Back-to-School Night raffle.

Attending parents get to place signed raffle tickets in a jar. During a subsequent school day, the teacher pulls out several raffle tickets and gives prizes to the winning students. School supplies (markers, pocket dictionary, compass) make excellent prizes. Inform parents of the raffle ahead of time. And be sure to tell students, too, so they can help motivate their parents to participate.

Play Back-to-School Night lotto.

Each parent who attends Back-to-School Night writes his or her name in a space on a special Back-to-School Night lotto board. Later, in school, the teacher pulls the winning numbers and awards prizes to students whose parents' names were drawn.

Give Back-to-School Night bonus tickets.

Any student whose parent(s) attends Back-to-School Night receives a ticket entitling the student to a special privilege or award, such as free reading time, a pencil, or a notepad.

Reach out to parents who cannot come.

Some parents simply cannot come to Back-to-School Night. Others just choose not to come. Regardless of the reason, you owe it to yourself and your students to make another effort to contact them with your Back-to-School Night message.

The next day, send home any materials you distributed at Back-to-School Night. To avoid penalizing a student whose parents didn't attend, make sure you don't forget to give these parents a chance to participate in the raffle or lotto or any other incentive activity you used. Remember that you don't want to disenfranchise any parent. You want them all solidly behind you. Your willingness to go the extra mile will further demonstrate your commitment to all your students.

Plan the classroom environment.

First impressions really count at Back-to-School Night, so make a point of creating an environment that is inviting and friendly. You want parents to feel involved and welcomed. Let the room speak for you. Set the mood by hanging a bright "Welcome Parents" poster in the front of the room.

Here are other items that should be displayed:

- Class schedule (on board)
- Displays of students' work completed and curriculum in progress
- Centers or areas labeled clearly

Sample Letter to Parents Who Did Not Attend

Dear Parent(s)

We missed you at Back-to-School Night.

I am sending you the Parent Handbook that I distributed at Back-to-School Night. It's filled with lots of information that will be useful as the year goes on. Please call me if you have any questions at all about anything in the handbook.

At Back-to-School Night, all the parents filled out raffle tickets for a classroom drawing. We will be having this drawing in a couple of days and students will win prizes such as pencils, rulers, and other school supplies. To make sure your child participates in the raffle, please fill out the coupon on the bottom of this letter and send it back to school as soon as possible.

- -

Back-to-School Night Raffle.

Working together we can make a difference!

Parent's name _____

Student's name _____

Nametags help everybody get to know each other.

Introducing yourself to parents and parents to each other will be easier if everyone is wearing nametags. Put a supply of adhesive-backed tags near the classroom door and, as they enter, ask parents to write their names on the tags. You may wish to prepare nametags that leave a space for the student's name also. This will help you identify parents who may have a different last name than the student has. Nametags will help parents get acquainted with each other, too.

Know exactly what you will say to parents.

Be prepared. Know what you are going to say, when you are going to say it, and how you expect parents to participate. Back-to-School Night should be carefully orchestrated so that all your goals will be met. Make sure you prepare an outline of the topics you want to talk about with parents. This is no time to get nervous and leave out important information. It's perfectly okay (and a smart idea) to refer to note cards as you speak.

Your Back-to-School Night goal should be to convince parents of two things:

- Parents are the most important people in a child's life and, as such, are in a unique position to help children achieve their highest potential.

- You as their teacher sincerely care about the children and are committed to seeing them succeed.

Everything you say or do should be geared to achieving these goals. Always remember that communication is more than words. Make sure that your body language conveys your love for teaching, your interest in your students, and your confidence in your ability to make the upcoming year a success for everyone, academically and personally. (See chapter 9 for more information on using body language in your communication with parents.) Smile, share stories about your students, create a good laugh, and show your enthusiasm.

Following are the major points that should be included in your Back-to-School Night presentation. If any of your student's parents are non–English speaking, make sure you have a translator available. Remember to look directly at parents as you speak, even when using a translator. Smile, make eye contact, and project the confidence you want the parents to feel.

Emphasize to parents that they are the most important people in their child's life.

Make sure you emphasize that research has proved over and over again that the best schools, the best teachers, and the best principals are not as important to a child's achievement in school as a parent is. Let them know that it is for this very reason that you want to work with them to educate their children. Make sure they know that you find their input, support, and backing extremely important and valuable.

Explain when and how you will communicate with parents.

Tell parents that you intend to communicate with them regularly. Explain that you will let them know when their children are successful. Say that you will also contact them if their children are not doing as well as they could. Explain that regular parent contact is central to your teaching plan because you firmly believe that when parent and teacher and student are working together, every student can be successful.

Invite parents to contact you.

Show parents that you are accessible. Emphasize that for you, communication is a two-way street. Communication is cooperation. Invite parents to contact you with concerns, problems, and suggestions. Mention your office hours, but emphasize that parents should feel free to contact you at any time. Give out your email address, unless you are uncomfortable doing so.

Describe your classroom discipline plan.

Discuss your discipline plan to ensure parents that you will deal with student misbehavior fairly and consistently. Make sure parents know that supportive feedback is as central to your discipline plan as are corrective actions. Refer to the copy of the plan you already sent home. Allow parents to ask questions regarding your plan and, if necessary, explain your rationale. Make sure they know that the behavior management techniques you use are meant to keep your classroom safe and conducive to learning. Emphasize that the goal of your discipline plan is to help your students self-monitor their behavior in order to be more successful.

Describe your homework policy.

Refer to the copy of your homework policy you sent home for parents to read. Emphasize that homework is a meaningful way to increase the learning effect of any curriculum. Make sure parents know that you will enlist their help if problems arise. Show your confidence that homework can and will be a positive experience for students and parents.

Tell parents what you need from them.

Make sure parents know that you need and expect the following from them.

- Support for your academic efforts: Ask parents to let their children know that education is important to them.

- Support for your disciplinary efforts: Ask parents to communicate to their children that they expect them to follow the established classroom rules. Ask parents to follow up with appropriate disciplinary measures at home.

- Support for your homework policy: Ask parents to make sure that their children take homework seriously. Parents should see that their children have a quiet place to do homework, set a time when homework has to be done every day, and enforce and encourage doing homework with disciplinary techniques such as providing support and rewards and corrective actions.

Make sure parents understand that their support is in their children's best interest. Emphasize that they are the most important people in their children's lives.

Convey your confidence.

Express your firm belief that the cooperation between parents and teacher will make the coming year positive for students, parents, and teachers. If everyone does his share, the students will succeed.

Listen, take notes, and be ready with further suggestions.

As you speak, be sure to pause occasionally and ask parents if they have any questions or suggestions. Take notes on what is asked, on what parents suggest, or on any other issues that may arise. You should respond to all these concerns in a Back-to-School Night follow-up letter (see page 65). It's important to let parents know you are listening to them and that you take their concerns and suggestions seriously.

Here are some other points you may want to include in your presentation.

Give parents suggestions for how they can help at home.

Remember that parents often don't help their children with schoolwork because they just don't know what to do. Be prepared to give parents some specific ideas for helping their children at home. If, for example, students are beginning to print, send home a manuscript letter practice sheet. If students are learning multiplication facts, send home copies of flash cards that can be cut out. If students will soon be tackling a term paper, give the parents guidelines for helping with that project. Be sure to explain to parents how these materials are to be used. Follow up throughout the year with "helping at home" updates as the curriculum changes.

Introduce parents to power reading.

Reading comprehension skills are the basis for success in all subject areas. Parents can help their children develop these skills at home with the power reading technique. Here's how to introduce it.

"First, read aloud to your child for 5 minutes. Be sure that the book from which you are reading is at your child's reading level. Model good reading

for them by pronouncing words carefully and clearly, and by making appropriate pauses for periods and commas.

Next, listen to your child read aloud from the same book for another 5 minutes. Your child should begin at the point where you stopped reading. Remind your child to take it slowly and read so that the words make sense. This is why your oral reading is so important. It's setting an example for your child. Don't stop and correct your child while he is reading.

Finally, ask questions about what was read. Check how well your child was listening and reading by asking general questions about the material you read aloud and the material your child read aloud. Talk about the story together.

Power reading is an excellent way to improve reading skills and demonstrate the importance you place on reading. Start a book that is of particular interest to your child, and continue using the same book for power reading sessions until it is completed."

Send parents home with a power reading tip sheet in which you outline the guidelines.

Invite parents to help at school.

Volunteers can be a great help to you in your classroom. Do some recruiting at Back-to-School Night. Think about the kind of help you would like to receive from parents, then put together a volunteer request letter. Make sure you offer some creative alternatives for working parents who can't be in the classroom during the school day (they like to help, too). Ideas might include creating posters for the classroom or helping out on a Saturday classroom improvement project. Don't hesitate to ask parents what they'd like to do; you just might have a talented storyteller, musician, puppeteer, scientist, or chef among them.

Present special Back-to-School Night activities.

You've encouraged parents to attend, created an inviting atmosphere, and spoken to them with assurance and clarity. Don't let it end there. There are other activities that you can incorporate into Back-to-School Night that will round out the evening and help make a lasting impression. Below are some effective suggestions that can make the event an even greater success.

Take parents on a tour of the classroom.

Parents are interested in what their children are learning at school, so take this opportunity to show off your classroom. Don't assume that parents understand the reasons behind your classroom organization and materials. Explain everything. Let them know why you have a listening center filled with a jumble of headsets (for individualized instruction). Explain the reason for the hamster cage (to teach responsibility). Point out your classroom library with pride, and tell the parents how it will be used. Explain to parents that the classroom and its contents will be the students' learning laboratory for a year. Get the parents excited about it. Your educational plans will come alive for parents if they are given the opportunity to feel a part of them. Encourage parents to ask questions about anything they see.

Give parents a "private screening."

All parents love to see their children (whatever their age) in a starring role. Present a slide or video presentation showing students in their daily classroom routines—entering the classroom, working in small groups, doing independent seat work, moving to centers, and so on. Don't forget a group shot of the entire class. Make sure every student appears in the slide show. This will communicate to parents that you really do care about all your students.

Make recordings.

Play a recording of students discussing classroom activities. Have elementary students record a song to be played for parents.

Have students write notes to parents.

Have each student write a note to the parents to be left in the student's desk. (In upper grades, the notes could be kept in a class folder and distributed to parents.) At Back-to-School Night, the parents read the notes and write a return message to their child. In elementary grades, the parents' notes can be left for students on their own desks.

Create and distribute a Parent Handbook.

Hand out a packet of information that parents can take home with them. This Parent Handbook is a convenient way to give parents a lot of information in one package. Here is a list of items you might want to include:

- Class roster (It's especially helpful for parents of primary children to know the names of their child's classmates.)

- School staff list, address, phone number, hours, email address(es), website address

- Map of the school

- Schoolwide rules
- Discipline plan (if not sent in a separate letter)
- Daily classroom schedule
- Grade-level curriculum
- Manuscript or cursive writing guide
- School/calendar year showing all school holidays and other school closures
- Blank teacher/parent communication forms
- Policies about absences, medical appointments, making up class work
- Tips on how to help a child study at home
- Suggested reading lists
- Power reading tip sheet
- Health concerns (nutrition, exercise, or sleep)

Write the name of each student on a Parent Handbook. After Back-to-School Night, send home to parents the handbooks that were not picked up at school.

Keep the spirit alive.

Don't let the enthusiasm generated by Back-to-School Night just fade away. Use it to your advantage. Let parents know how much you appreciated their participation. A few days afterward, send a brief note home thanking parents for attending. Update them on any items that might have come under discussion at Back-to-School Night. And because it's sometimes difficult for parents to speak up and air their concerns in front of a whole group, you might also include a "return message" section where parents can write back to you with any questions they may have. This follow-up note is also an excellent way to make contact with parents who did not attend Back-to-School Night.

The sense of teamwork, camaraderie, and excitement you cultivate at Back-to-School Night is a great way to help parents overcome the roadblocks that keep them from giving you support. By doing so, you will also increase your own confidence in just how successful you can be in getting parents on your side.

Making the Most of Back-to-School Night

Reminders

DO

- Plan your Back-to-School Night schedule as thoroughly as you would a day in class.

- Have translators available if necessary.

- Speak to every parent. Call them by name, and refer to their child by name (nametags can help make this easier).

- Plan what you will say. Keep your notes with you as you speak.

- Provide a program that allows each student to be highlighted in some way (photographs, tape recordings, a video, class-work, artwork).

- Focus on the responsibility of parent and teacher to work as partners in children's education.

- Encourage parents to offer their special talents and interests to the classroom as the year goes on.

- Listen to parents. Take notes about any questions or concerns that are brought up. Follow up on these concerns.

- Provide relevant, informative material for parents to take home.

- Reach out to parents who didn't attend. Send all Back-to-School Night materials home the next day.

- Send out a Back-to-School Night follow-up letter.

Making the Most of Back-to-School Night

Reminders (Cont'd)

DON'T

- Don't expect parents to come just because the school sent home a notice. Reach out to them. It's up to you to get the parents of your students there.

- Don't talk only about curriculum. Remember that your first goal should be to convince parents of the important role they play in their children's education.

- Don't talk down to parents or be intimidated by them. Approach them as equals, but keep in mind that you are the professional educator.

- Don't make the mistake of thinking that exciting Back-to-School Nights are for elementary classes only. Parents of older students also appreciate a motivating presentation.

Making the Most of Back-to-School Night
Checklist

Refer to this checklist as you plan your Back-to-School Night.

HAVE YOU:

☐ Sent home invitations to parents that explain why Back-to-School Night is so important?

☐ Planned to use a "parent motivator" to help get parents to attend?

☐ Written down what you want to say to parents?

☐ Created a welcoming environment in your classroom?

☐ Created a Parent Handbook to give to parents at Back-to-School Night?

☐ Decided on the activities you will present?

☐ Arranged for a translator if necessary?

☐ Decided to send a Back-to-School Night follow-up letter to parents?

Establishing Positive Communication With Parents

S	*how you care.* For effective teachers, these are really words to live
	by. Every day, all year long, positive communication is imperative
	to show that you care and to get past the roadblocks that keep
parents from supporting their children at school. Parents see educators who
consistently communicate positive news to them as educators who truly care
about their children. And the more parents feel you care, the more they will
listen and support you. Unless you are prepared to pursue consistent positive
communication with parents, you will have a difficult time getting all the
parents on your side.

In this chapter, you will learn some proven techniques teachers use for positive communication with parents. You will learn how to do the following:

- Place positive phone calls.

- Send notes, cards, and letters.

- Make home visits.

- Plan parent communication activities.

- Keep a record of positive contacts.

If you are a middle school or secondary school teacher, don't let the
large number of students you teach deter you from making positive contact
with parents. In upper grades, the best way to reach every parent is through
a schoolwide plan in which all teachers work together so that all parents
receive regular, planned positive contact. Design a simple schedule according
to which every teacher is assigned a group of students whose parents should
be contacted as soon as there is something positive to report. Such a schedule
should rotate students among teachers at least twice a year.

Of course, establishing such a schedule may prove too cumbersome at
your school. Even if you're on your own, you can still reach out to parents
regularly. Careful planning is the answer. You'd be surprised at the number of
students you can reach if you just schedule time for positives. A quick positive
phone call, for example, is easy to make and takes only a couple of minutes.

Make two brief calls each afternoon, and you've reached 10 parents a week. Multiply that by 36 weeks, and you've reached 360 parents. As you read about the positive communication techniques in this chapter, give thought to how you could schedule them into your week. Then set a goal of reaching a specific number of parents each week.

Above all, keep this in mind: It won't happen if you don't schedule it.

Place positive phone calls.

One of the most effective parent communication techniques at your disposal is a quick phone call home to let parents know how well their child is doing. It doesn't have to be a long conversation—just a brief update and a few friendly words. Get into the habit of phoning parents with good news, and it won't be so difficult to call them when there is a problem to be solved. You will have already established a comfortable relationship, and parents will be much more likely to listen to what you have to say.

Try to make these calls at a time when you are most likely to reach the parents. For example, call working parents in the evenings or on Saturday mornings. If you only reach voicemail, don't just hang up—leave a message. Parents will be delighted to come home to a positive message.

Plan exactly what you will say.

Here are the points you'll want to cover in a positive phone call.

1. **Describe the student's positive behavior.**
   Begin the call by telling the parent the specific behavior the student exhibited in your classroom.

   "Brandon is off to a great start this semester. He's completed all his class assignments and homework this week."

2. **Describe how you feel about the student's positive behavior.**
   Let the parent know how pleased you are with the student's good behavior or academic performance. Remember that this may be the first time the parent has heard anything positive about her child in a long time.

   "I'm very pleased that Doug is showing such improvement in math this year. His hard work is getting results."

3. **Ask the parent to share the content of the conversation with the student.** Your conversation with the parent will have an even greater impact if the parent tells the child about the call. It is important for the student to know that both you and the parent are proud of her accomplishments.

"When Tonya gets home, please share our conversation with her. I think it will be great for her to know that I called and how pleased we both are with her performance in school."

Sample Phone Conversation

Here's a sample positive phone conversation.

Teacher: *Mrs. Suarez, this is Mrs. Endicott, José's math teacher. I just wanted to let you know how well José is doing in school. He is a really hard worker. He gets right to work on all of his assignments, follows directions beautifully, and always seems to do the best job he can.*

Parent: *Well, he does seem to be enjoying school more this year.*

Teacher: *I'm glad to hear that. I really enjoy having him in my classroom.*

Parent: *I appreciate your telling me this. It's really made my day!*

Teacher: *Well, I believe it's just as important to tell parents when their child is doing well in school as it is when the child is having problems.*

Parent: *That makes sense to me.*

Teacher: *It makes sense to me, too. There's one last thing. Please let José know that I called and how happy I am about how well he's doing in class. I want to be sure he knows that his good work is noticed by all of us.*

Parent: *I sure will! Thank you!*

Send notes, cards, and letters.

The school year will be filled with occasions that call for positive parent communication. Take advantage of as many of these "good news" opportunities as possible. In many cases, you may want to use email to send a quick note or a birthday or get-well greeting.

Write positive notes to parents.

An effective way to give parents supportive feedback on their child's performance in school is to send home positive notes. A positive note consists of a few lines mentioning some good news about their child. Once you get into the habit of sending home a predetermined number of notes each week, it will become a natural part of your routine. And this habit will pay dividends: It will be much easier to contact parents about a problem if they've already heard from you in a positive context.

- Keep a file of ready-to-use positive notes and preaddressed envelopes in your desk. Save ready-to-use notes in your computer, too.

- Plan to send home a specific number of notes each week.

- When writing notes, address the parents by name and mention the student's name, too. Keep the notes brief and to the point.

Sample Positive Note

October 14

Dear Mr. and Mrs. Brown,

   Just wanted to let you know what a terrific job Kiana did today in giving her oral report to the class. Her presentation was both informative and entertaining. You should be proud of the good work she is doing!

Sincerely,

Mr. Smith

Send home good behavior messages and academic awards.

In addition to personalized notes, send home behavior messages or academic awards to parents. Many of these awards are commercially available with a preprinted message ("Thought you'd like to know that _____'s behavior in class today was terrific!"). All you have to do is add the child's name and send the award home with the student.

The Spotlight is on YOU for good behavior!

Send birthday greetings.

Add your good wishes to birthday celebrations by sending home greetings to students on their special day.

For students: What better way to let parents know that you care about their child than by sending home a birthday card. When it arrives in the mail, everyone in the family sees that you do care. If you have access to a computer and printer, you can easily run off cards that are personalized both with words and graphics. Keep a class birthday list in your plan book so that you can be prepared.

For parents: Have students create a birthday card for each parent as an art project at the beginning of the year. File them away by date, and send home when appropriate.

Send get-well cards and make phone calls.

When students are sick, parents are worried, work schedules are upset, and life becomes more complicated for families. This is a good opportunity to show your concern for your student and his parents. When a student is sick for more than a few days, send home a get-well card. Pick up the phone or send a quick email to see how the child is doing. You can also use this opportunity to update the parent on the child's classwork.

Here's an example of a get-well phone call.

"Mrs. Lee? Hi. This is Sandra Hyatt, David's teacher. We've missed David this week, and I just wanted to give you a call and see how he's doing. The whole class sends their best wishes. We're looking forward to having him back.

"I know he may be concerned about the work he's missing, but tell him to concentrate on getting well! I'll work with him on catching up when he's feeling better."

Write thank-you notes.

Throughout the year, parents will help you in many ways: donating supplies to the classroom, volunteering time, chaperoning field trips or dances, or helping their child with a project. Don't let these good deeds go unrecognized. Parents will be more motivated to help out again if they feel that their contribution was appreciated. Keep a supply of thank-you notes on hand, and use them often. Students too will notice and feel proud when these acknowledgments go home.

Each Friday spend a few minutes reviewing the week. Jot down the names of parents who made that special effort you appreciate, and send home a note to each.

Make home visits.

Nothing is quite as personal, or demonstrates your concern and caring, as a visit to a student's home. This is especially true when the purpose of a home visit is simply to say hello, meet the family, and talk to the parent about the positive things the student is doing in school. A home visit can be a wonderful experience for student, parent, and teacher. For the parent, it's an opportunity to meet the teacher in comfortable, familiar, and relaxed surroundings. For the student, it's a chance to clearly see that home and school are a team that's working together. For you, a home visit can give you a better perspective on a student's life away from school.

You will find that once you have met personally with parents under such positive circumstances, it will be all the easier to contact them about any problems that arise as the year proceeds.

- Try to make as many home visits as you can at the start of the year.

- Be sure to call the parent ahead of time to schedule a date and time for the visit. Don't just drop in!

Plan parent communication activities.

When parents are connected with what's going on in your classroom, it will be easier for you to stay connected with them. Keep parents informed about schoolwork and other classroom activities.

Create a daily "school-to-home" journal.

When parents ask their child, "What happened in school today?" the answer is often, "Nothing." You can encourage better public relations than this. A daily journal that goes back and forth between home and school can keep parents and students communicating. At the end of each day, have students write a few sentences telling what went on in school that day. Each night, have students take the journals home to be read by their parents. Have parents sign the day's entry, and have the student return the journal to school.

Send home a weekly envelope containing student work.

The more a parent knows about a child's work at school, the higher the probability you will get the support you need. Plan to send home a folder or large envelope each Friday containing student work from the previous week. Label the folder "Special Delivery to Parents." The folder should include space for the parents to sign, indicating that they looked at the child's work. You may also wish to include space for parents to make comments. Students should be instructed to return the folder to school on Monday. (Positive notes and awards can be sent home in the folders, too.)

Compose a weekly classroom newsletter.

Send home a newsletter each week informing parents about classroom activities and upcoming events. Newsletters can also be posted on the school's website. Make sure that your students do some, if not most, of the work on the newsletter. This method of communication will be most effective if students help create it.

Here are two newsletter ideas.

Weekly Family Letter (for primary grades)

Every Friday, each student writes three or more sentences telling what he did during that week. The sentences are turned in, and the teacher compiles them into one big letter (typed), making sure that at least one sentence from each child is included. The letter is addressed to "Dear Family." On Monday, the teacher gives each student a copy of the letter. Students mark what they wrote on their copy and take it home to show to proud parents.

Suggestions for use: Send home a note to parents with the first Weekly Family Letter. Make sure they understand that this letter will be a weekly group effort and that their child's writing will be included each week. Suggest that they ask their child to read the whole letter to them each week and to spend some time talking about the events recorded in the letter.

Keep all the weekly letters in a three-ring binder. As the weeks go by, students will enjoy looking back at their classroom experiences. You may wish to occasionally include photographs to add further interest to this very lively history.

Family Newsletter (for upper grades)

Older students will enjoy having a hand in planning and producing a weekly (or biweekly) newsletter. As a class project, decide on regular columns that will be included in the newsletter. Assign committees to be responsible for gathering the information for and writing each column. Rotate assignments throughout the year.

Suggestions for columns:

- A Message from the Teacher
- We're Proud of These Students!
- Upcoming Projects and Assignments
- Special Events
- Opinion Poll

- What We Need (what parents can do specifically to help the class or school)

Keep a record of positive contacts.

Because you want to be sure that all students and parents are receiving equal, positive attention, it's important to keep track of the calls you make and the notes and awards you send home. Set up a column in your roll book or plan book to record this information. List each student's name. When a note or award goes home, or a phone call is made, jot down the date on the line next to the name. Get into the habit of reviewing this list regularly.

While you should not ignore the achievements of high-performing students, bear in mind that it is extremely important to send home positive notes to parents of students with potential academic or behavior problems, or to parents of students who have had problems in the past. The more the parents of these children hear good news, the greater the probability of getting their support when you need it. Also, recognizing a difficult student for a positive achievement may even help this student to stay on track and keep up the good work.

Establishing Positive Communication With Parents

Reminders

DO

- Make special effort to communicate positively with parents of students who have had problems in the past.

- Set goals for sending home a specific number of positive notes each week.

- Make positive home visits at the start of the year, and all year long.

- Keep track of all parent communications.

- Phone parents with positive updates on academic and behavior successes.

- Keep the positive momentum going all year long.

DON'T

- Don't underestimate how important positive notes and phone calls to parents are. They really do want to hear good news from you.

- Don't forget to give positive reinforcement to the students who always behave and do their work. They shouldn't be ignored.

- Don't forget to say thank-you to parents any time they help you out.

- Don't make negative communication the first contact you have with parents.

Establishing Positive Communication
With Parents
Checklist

Refer to this checklist as you plan positive communication with parents.

HAVE YOU:

☐ Set goals for sending home positive notes to parents? How many notes will you plan to send home each week?

☐ Started making positive phone calls to parents? Once you try it, you'll like it. It's easy, effective, and always welcomed.

☐ Made a birthday list of students and set aside birthday cards so you'll always be prepared?

☐ Put together a collection of get-well cards and thankyou notes for use throughout the year?

☐ Set up a record-keeping system to keep track of your positive communications?

☐ Planned to send home a classroom newsletter to keep parents informed about what's going on in your classroom?

Involving Parents in the Homework Process

Homework has the potential to be the most consistent day-to-day contact you can have with parents, particularly in the upper elementary grades and in secondary school. Yet parents complain that homework is often the greatest cause of conflict between them and their children. Likewise, teachers complain that students don't complete assignments and parents won't follow up to see that they do. The result is that in most classrooms an important parent involvement resource goes to waste. Changing homework from an irritant into a positive is what you will find in this chapter.

Too often, homework remains a mystery to parents. They don't understand why homework is given, when it will be given, how it is expected to be done, or what they can do to help. In short, parents' responsibilities in the homework process are usually never really addressed. All they know for sure about homework is that it's often a problem. This is unfortunate for both parent and student because the homework process also has the potential to increase a student's self-esteem. When parent and child work together, the child knows that he is important enough for the parent to stop what she's doing, pay attention, and get involved. And that's a good feeling for a child to have.

Teachers who are committed to involving parents in the homework process start by developing a homework policy. The policy establishes a firm foundation for homework by stating the expectations of everyone involved—students, parents, and teacher. Your homework policy is just the beginning, though. You need to follow through all year long by keeping parents well-informed about class work, upcoming tests and projects, and ways in which they can help their children study more successfully.

This chapter covers four ways you can turn homework into an asset of your parent involvement plan:

1. Help parents help their children do a better job on homework.

2. Keep the lines of communication open.

3. Assign family learning activities on weekends.

4. Help parents solve their children's most common homework problems.

Help parents help their children do a better job on homework.

Most parents want to help their children do well with homework, but they don't know how or where to begin. Start off the year by providing parents with useful homework and study skills tips so they can begin immediately to improve their child's homework performance.

Plan to send homework and study skills tip sheets home at the beginning of the school year. (Guidelines for creating the tip sheets follow. Some sample sheets are also included.) When preparing the tip sheets and distributing them to your students' parents, use these guidelines:

- Each study skills and homework tip should be self-contained on its own page. Include as much specific information as possible.

- Rather than send all study skills and homework tips home at once, you may choose instead to send specific tips home in correlation with assigned work.

Homework and study skills tips should also accommodate a particular child's personal learning style. Often a child exhibits a learning style different from that of his parents. This may cause problems between parents and students that significantly hamper the success of your homework policy. If this is the case, make sure you assist the parents in understanding and accommodating their child's personal needs. Help the parents understand that not everybody learns best in the same way: Some children may study better lying on the floor rather than sitting at a desk; some may concentrate best while listening to soft music.

Accepting and supporting a child's own learning style may help the child to learn about his strengths and weaknesses, which help or hinder his achievements in class. Accepting and supporting a child's own learning style may help the child accept his own personality as unique, which in turn may increase his self-esteem.

Accommodating a child's learning style should not be taken as an excuse for accepting distractions. Phone calls, television, and noisy interruptions by siblings or friends are not part of a calming work environment.

Give parents homework tips.

Good homework habits must be developed if a student is to do homework successfully. These five homework tips will guide parents in helping their children organize and complete homework each night.

Homework Tip #1: Set up a study area.

To do homework successfully, a student must have a place at home in which to work. The study area must be well-lit, quiet, and have all necessary supplies close at hand. The study area should accommodate the student's particular learning style. For example, if the student needs absolute quiet to concentrate, nobody else should be allowed in the area while the student is doing his homework.

Homework Tip #2: Create a homework survival kit.

Students can waste a lot of time in last-minute frenzied searches for homework supplies. Parents can put together a homework survival kit for their children that contains all the usual materials the children might need to complete their homework assignments. These materials can include pens, pencils, pencil sharpener, paper, ruler, scissors, and glue.

Homework Tip #3: Schedule daily homework time.

Probably the touchiest homework issue students deal with is finding the time to do homework. Every parent knows that kids will find time for sports, TV, and talking on the telephone, but somehow time runs out when homework needs to be done. Parents can help their children schedule daily homework time and get them to stick to it. It is best if the student is encouraged to do her homework as soon as possible after school and at a time when parents are available to help if necessary.

Homework Tip #4: Encourage children to work independently.

Homework teaches students responsibility. Through homework, students learn skills they must develop if they are to grow to be independent, successful adults. Parents should encourage their children to work on their own. In other words, parents should only offer help once all resources for independent work have been used. Parents should encourage their children to use reference books and dictionaries to collect information. Parents should encourage their children to call a friend with questions before they ask parents for help. Attempting to use resources other than a parent to complete homework will help the student to develop creative problem-solving skills.

Homework Tip #5: Motivate children with praise.

Because children need encouragement and support from the people whose opinions they value the most, praise is the best motivational tool parents can use. Consistent praise can increase a child's self-confidence, develop a sense of pride in personal achievements, and motivate him to do the best work possible.

Give parents study skills tips.

Knowing how to study is an important part of successful learning. But good study habits don't just happen. They must be taught in school and reinforced at home.

Give parents guidelines for helping their child in three key study areas: long-range planning, writing reports, and studying for tests. Send these study skills tips home only if appropriate to the ages and needs of your students. (Samples of tip sheets you might prepare for parents are provided.)

Study Skills Tip #1: Provide help with long-range planning.

Assignments such as book reports, written reports, and science projects are often overwhelming for students (and parents) because they require advance planning and time management. Because students usually don't know how to structure their time, the bulk of the work is often left until the last minute. Give parents a long-range planner, and guidelines for helping their child use it.

A long-range planner can help students break down a big assignment into smaller tasks. Ask parents to take time to help their children determine the steps that have to be followed to complete the project, then to establish the date each step will be completed. If each goal is met, there will be no last-minute panic before the report is due.

Study Skills Tip #2: Provide help with written reports.

Written reports are often difficult for students to handle in an organized manner. Here are three suggestions for parents that can make the job easier:

1. Use a long-range planner (instructions provided in Study Skills Tip #1).

2. Use a written report checklist (see page 85). A written report checklist should address the length of the report, the format and style you expect the report to follow, as well as whether you expect illustrations or other additional materials.

3. Use a proofreading checklist (see page 86). Proofreading should be a part of every written assignment. The checklist should address such issues as grammar, spelling, organization of content, style, and effort.

Sample Study Skills Tip: Long-Range Planner

Long-Range Planner

Directions:

1. Break down your big assignments into smaller steps.
2. Write down your due dates for each step.
3. Fill in the final due date for the project on your last step.

Assignment _____   Due Date _____

_____

1. _____   Due Date _____

_____

2. _____   Due Date _____

_____

3. _____   Due Date _____

_____

4. _____   Due Date _____

_____

5. _____   Due Date _____

_____

6. _____   Due Date _____

_____

7. _____   Due Date _____

_____

Study Skills Tip #3: Help your child study for a test.

Students can study more effectively if they learn how to manage their time and how to use study techniques specifically tailored for test-taking. Provide parents with general tips on how to help their child prepare for studying, and specific tips for studying a textbook (see pages 87 and 88).

Keep the lines of communication open.

The guidelines in *Parents on Your Side* have emphasized the importance of consistent communication with parents. This is especially true with homework. Here are some ideas that can keep the home-school connection working effectively.

Institute a parent-teacher homework memo procedure.

When you need a reply to a homework question or problem, use a parent-teacher homework memo. Write your message on the top portion of the memo; ask parents to respond on the lower part and return the memo to you. You may wish to send parents a supply of memos at the beginning of the school year, along with a letter encouraging them to write whenever they have a homework-related question they would like to discuss with you.

Send home positive homework notes to parents.

Just as you send positive notes to parents about students' good behavior or academic success, you can also send home notes relating specifically to homework. These notes are especially effective if they relate to assignments parents have been involved with, or if they address homework problems that have been solved.

For example:

"Just a note to let you know what a great job Austin did on his report on mammals. I know how much hard work he put into it. Thanks so much for helping him get the library books he needed!"

"Susan has turned in all of her math assignments during the past 2 weeks, and she earned an A on her test today. Now she understands that doing homework makes a difference in how well she does on tests!"

As with other positive notes you send, follow these guidelines:

- Plan to send home a specific number of positive homework notes each week.

- Be specific. Tell the parent exactly what the student did to earn the note.

- Keep a record of notes sent home.

Sample Study Skills Tip: Written Report Checklist

Written Report Checklist

Directions:

When a report is assigned, write or check off the requirements below.

Subject of Report: _____

Date Report Is Due: _____

1. How long should the report be? How many paragraphs ____ or pages ____ do I need to write?

2. Should the report be typewritten or handwritten?
   Typewritten ☐   Pen ☐   Pencil ☐

3. Should I write on every line or every other line?
   Every line ☐   Every other line ☐

4. Should I write on one side of the page or both?
   One side ☐   Both sides ☐

5. Where should I put the page numbers?
   Top ☐   Bottom ☐

6. Should I put the report in a folder?
   Yes ☐   No ☐

7. Should I add photos or illustrations?
   Photos ☐   Illustrations ☐

Other: _____

_____

_____

_____

Additional Notes: _____

_____

_____

_____

_____

Sample Study Skills Tip: Proofreading Checklist

Proofreading Checklist

Directions:

Use this checklist each time you complete a draft of your report.

Subject of Report: _____

Date Report Is Due: _____

- ☐ The title of the paper is suited to the subject.
- ☐ The paper is well-organized, and the introduction is clear.
- ☐ I have put in all capital letters, commas, periods, and apostrophes.
- ☐ Every sentence is a complete sentence.
- ☐ Each paragraph has a topic sentence that tells what the paragraph will be about.
- ☐ I have used descriptive words to make my paper more interesting.
- ☐ The paper contains specific information about the subject.
- ☐ I have read my paper aloud, and it says what I want it to say.
- ☐ The last sentence lets the reader know the paper is finished.
- ☐ I have completed at least one rough draft of the paper.
- ☐ I have checked the paper for spelling errors.
- ☐ This is my best work.

Give positive homework notes to students.

Students put lots of effort into homework. Let them know you both notice and appreciate the work they do. Pay particular attention to students who have improved their homework habits. Your praise will increase the likelihood that these new habits will continue.

"Terrific job on your outline. I can tell that you really used your resource materials."

"Thank you for writing so neatly. Now your stories are even more fun to read!"

Sample Study Skills Tip: How to Help Your Child Study for a Test

How to Help Your Child Study for a Test

Whenever an upcoming test is announced, follow these steps to help get your child off to a good start.

1. **Determine what the test will cover and organize all study materials.**

   Help your child find out exactly what material a test will cover: chapters in a textbook, class notes, homework assignments, and so on. Make sure they are available for study.

2. **Schedule time for studying ahead of time.**

   Don't allow your child to wait until the last minute to study. Break down study tasks throughout the week. It is better to study a little bit each day than to cram the night before a test.

3. **Use effective study techniques.**

   - As your child studies, he should write important information on index cards. Later, these cards can be used to review for the test.

   - Review homework and class notes. It is helpful to underline or highlight important points.

   - Review study questions and past quizzes and tests. Also, make sure your child reviews study questions in the textbook, which provide an excellent review of material covered.

Send home test update slips.

Students often forget to study for tests until the last minute, and parents sometimes hear about tests when it's too late to help their children study. Test update slips can help both student and parent to prepare for tests. Send home these notices well in advance of important tests. Have both the student and parent sign the slips and return them to class. This form of home-school communication can be a very positive force in promoting good study habits.

Sample Study Skills Tip: How to Help Your Child Study a Textbook

How to Help Your Child Study a Textbook

Often, the material covered on a test will be from assigned reading in the class textbook. Here is what you can do to help your child master the material in any textbook:

1. **Survey the chapter.**

   The first step in studying a textbook is to survey the chapter. Have your child follow these steps:

   - Read all headings and subheadings.

   - Look over all pictures, maps, charts, tables, and graphs.

   - Read the summary at the end of the chapter.

   - Read through the study questions listed at the end of the chapter.

   - Finally, go back and make up a question from each main heading.

2. **Read the chapter and take notes.**

   After a survey of the chapter, your child should go back and read it all the way through. Notes should be taken on a separate sheet of paper. These notes should include answers to the questions made from the chapter headings, and a chronological listing of events that occur in the chapter.

   In addition, your child should take notes on index cards. Important facts (names of persons, terms to know, or significant concepts) are listed on the front of the card. The back should be used for listing important points that may be asked on the test.

3. **Review the chapter.**

   After reading the chapter, your child should look over the notes and make sure all the main points are understood. Then she should answer the study questions given at the end of the chapter, as well as the questions formulated from the main headings. Your child should review all the notes and all the key points of the chapter.

Encourage the use of homework assignment books.

Assignment books ensure that students write down all homework and that parents have an opportunity to see what those assignments are. Students keep the assignment book in their notebook, take it home each day, and bring it back the next day. If appropriate, you may ask parents to sign the assignment book each night, indicating that homework assignments have been completed.

Using an assignment book prevents students from saying that they don't know what their assignments are and ensures that the parents know exactly what is expected of their children each night.

For younger students, consider sending home a weekly homework calendar that lists all assignments for the week. It's easy for young children to forget their homework assignments. A homework calendar allows parents to check what's been assigned and what their child has completed.

Ask parents to sign completed homework.

Sometimes just asking a parent to sign completed homework assignments is enough to motivate students to finish them. Use this technique whenever you want to make sure a parent is checking a student's work.

Assign family learning activities on weekends.

Parent-child homework assignments can be worthwhile experiences for everyone. Yet few things are as frustrating to a parent as arriving home from work at night, exhausted, and finding out a child has an assignment that requires parental input and is due the next day. It's not fair to the parent, and it's not fair to the student. What should be a pleasant activity instead turns into a stressful duty.

Teachers often avoid assigning homework on the weekends, but maybe it's time to reassess. After all, many parents have more time to spend on a child's work during the weekend than they do during the week. Try this idea: Tell parents that students will be bringing home a weekend assignment once a month that will involve parents in some way. Explain your reasons for these assignments.

Try these ideas for family learning activities.

Smart Shopper

Go to the grocery store together. Pretend you have $25 to spend. Your job is to plan a lunch and dinner for four people. Make sure each meal is

Sample Family Learning Activities Letter

Dear Parent(s):

Although it's important that students learn to do their homework on their own, I believe there are times when they can benefit from working with parents on a project. For this reason, I am planning to send home a variety of family learning activities throughout the year. These activities are designed to involve you and your child in a creative and interesting activity. I know you are busy, so I will let you know ahead of time when each assignment is coming. I will plan these assignments for weekends, when you and your child will have more time to do and enjoy them. It is my hope that these activities will be fun for everyone.

Sincerely,

Mrs. Wilkinson

well balanced. Write down the menu and the cost of each item you will have to buy.

Walk 'n' Talk

Go on a walk in your neighborhood with a parent. Together, write down 10 things you see, 10 things you smell, 10 things you hear, and 10 things you touch.

Finders Keepers

Using items found at home, work with your parent to create:

- Something funny to look at
- Something that can move forward
- The tallest structure you can make that still balances
- A structure that is 4 inches high and 3 inches wide

Speak Out!

Interview your parent to find out about _____.
For example:

- Your family tree
- Her opinion of the United Nations
- His favorite book

- What she would do in case of an emergency (such as an earthquake, tornado, or flood)

- His opinion about the best place in the world to live

Turn It On!

Watch a video or a TV show about Earth's environment on Saturday night.

Parent: List 10 things you will do to help the environment.

Student: List 10 things you will do to help the environment.

Read your lists to each other. Are any items the same? Decide on four things each of you will begin doing right away.

> NOTE: In consideration of different family situations, you may wish to offer a choice of three activities.

Help parents solve their children's most common homework problems.

When problems with homework persist and you can't solve them yourself, you need more involvement on the part of parents. Prepare parent resource sheets to use throughout the year to help parents deal with specific homework problems. The resource sheets offer a plan of action for parents to follow when:

- Children do not do their best work.
- Children refuse to do their homework.
- Children fail to bring home assignments.
- Children take all night to finish homework.
- Children will not do homework on their own.
- Children wait until the last minute to finish assignments.
- Children will not do homework if parents are not home.

Sample resource sheets are provided for all these topics. When you prepare your own, however, keep in mind that the sheets need to explain that parents should:

- Clearly and firmly state their homework expectations to the child.
- Institute daily homework time (as explained on the resource sheets) and determine loss of privileges if the child still chooses not to do homework.

- Give praise and supportive feedback for work well done.
- Provide backup incentives for continued good work.
- Back up their words with action.
- Contact the teacher if all else fails.

How to use the parent resource sheets

- When there is a homework-related problem you need help with, contact the parent by phone or make arrangements to get together in a face-to-face meeting.

- Together, determine the specific problem the child is having. For example: takes all night to get it done, forgets to bring assignments home. (Review the guidelines on pages 148–153 for conducting a problem-solving conference.)

- Select the appropriate resource sheet and together go over each of the steps to make sure the parent understands what is to be done. Give the parent a copy of the sheet to take home. Don't give the resource sheet to a parent if you feel that he will be intimidated by it. Instead, make sure the parent is given clear verbal guidelines to follow.

- Set a time (in a week or two) to follow up with the parent to determine whether the strategy has been effective or if further action is necessary.

Sample Parent Resource Sheet:
What to Do When Your Child Does Not Do Her Best Work

Solving Homework Problems

What to Do When Your Child Does Not Do Her Best Work

If your child rushes through homework to talk on the phone, use the computer, watch TV, or get together with friends, state that it is not okay to do incomplete or sloppy work. Use these tips to help your child take responsibility for doing homework well.

1. **Schedule daily homework time.**
   Allot a time each day when all other activities stop and your child must go to her study area and do homework.

2. **Tell your child what you expect.**
   Say, "I know you can do a better job. I want you to take your time and do the best work you can. Sloppy work is not acceptable."

3. **Praise your child for work well done.**
   Say, "Great job getting your homework done," or "I like how neat your paper looks. Keep up the good work." Praise is the best way to encourage continued best efforts.

4. **Institute mandatory homework time.**
   This means that your child must use the entire scheduled daily homework time for homework or other academic activities whether or not homework is completed. For example, if 2 hours are allotted each night, the entire time must be spent on homework or, if homework is finished, on reading, reviewing textbooks, or practicing math. Your child will learn that nothing can be gained by rushing through homework and will be encouraged to slow down and do a better job.

5. **Provide additional incentives.**
   To encourage your child to continue good work, give a reward or a point toward a prize each time homework is completed. For example, when five points are earned, reward your child with an extra privilege.

6. **Contact the teacher.**
   If after trying these steps your child is still not doing her best work, you must work together with the teacher to improve your child's performance.

**Sample Parent Resource Sheet:
What to Do When Your Child Refuses to Do Homework**

Solving Homework Problems

What to Do When Your Child Refuses to Do Homework

When your child would rather battle with you than do homework, it's time to set firm limits. Your child may openly refuse to do homework or lie to you or the teacher about why it hasn't been done. You must make it clear that choosing not to do homework is choosing not to enjoy certain privileges.

1. **State clearly how you expect homework to be completed.**
   Say, "I expect you to do all of your homework every night. Under no circumstances will I tolerate your refusing to do your assignments."

2. **Back up your words with action.**
   Say, "You can choose either to do your homework or to lose these privileges: You will not leave this house. You will not watch TV, listen to music, or use the telephone. You will sit here until all of your homework is done. The choice is yours." Stick to your demands. It may take your child several days to realize that you mean business.

3. **Praise your child when homework is completed.**
   Say, "You've been getting all of your homework done. You should feel proud of yourself."

4. **Use a homework contract.**
   This motivator is a written, signed agreement between you and your child that states a reward or a point toward a prize will be earned for each day that homework is brought home and completed. (The younger the child, the more quickly the prize is earned.)

5. **Contact the teacher.**
   If problems continue, request that additional discipline be provided at school for incomplete assignments. Your child will learn that the school is supporting your efforts.

**Sample Parent Resource Sheet: What to Do
When Your Child Fails to Bring Home Assignments**

Solving Homework Problems

What to Do When Your Child
Fails to Bring Home Assignments

When your child continually fails to bring home assigned homework, take action.

1. **State that you expect all homework assignments to be brought home.**
   Say, "I expect you to bring home all assigned work and all the books you need to complete it. If you finish your homework at school, I expect you to bring it home so that I can see it."

2. **Work with the teacher to make sure you know what homework has been assigned.**
   Students can use a weekly assignment sheet to record assignments. Ask the teacher to check and sign the sheet. When your child completes the assignments, you sign the sheet and have your child return it to the teacher.

3. **Provide praise and support when assignments are brought home.**
   Say, "It's great to see that you remembered to bring home all of your homework. I knew you could do it."

4. **Institute mandatory homework time.**
   If your child still fails to bring home assignments, institute mandatory homework time, which requires spending a specific amount of time on academic activities (reading, reviewing textbooks or class notes) whether homework is brought home or not. When students learn that they are expected to study in any case, they will be encouraged to bring home their assignments.

5. **Use a homework contract.**
   This motivator is a written, signed agreement between you and your child that states a reward or a point toward a prize will be earned for each day that homework is brought home and completed. (The younger the child, the more quickly the prize is earned.)

6. **Contact the teacher.**
   If the forgetfulness continues, discuss with the teacher the possibility of imposing loss of privileges at school. Your child will know that you and the school are working together to ensure responsible behavior.

Sample Parent Resource Sheet: What to Do When Your Child Takes All Night to Finish Homework

Solving Homework Problems

What to Do When Your Child Takes All Night to Finish Homework

Some children spend hours on homework when it's not necessary. They may stop and start and be easily distracted. In cases like this, here's what to do.

1. **Schedule daily homework time.**

    Allot a time each day when all other activities stop and your child must go to his study area and do homework. Say, "I expect you to get all of your homework done during this time. Your taking all evening to do it must stop."

2. **Make sure homework is done in a quiet area.**

    If your child has been working in a distracting environment, make sure there is no TV, stereo, or interruptions by siblings. If necessary, you may need to change the location of the study area.

3. **Give praise and support when homework is done on time.**

    Say, "I am really pleased to see that you got your homework done on time. I'm so proud of you."

4. **Give additional incentives when appropriate.**

    To help develop the habit of completing homework on time, play Beat the Clock. First determine how long homework should take. Then, at the start of homework time, set a timer. If homework is finished by the bell, a special privilege is earned.

5. **Back up your words with action.**

    Say, "You can either do your homework during daily homework time or lose these privileges during that time: You will not leave this house. You will not watch TV, listen to music, or use the telephone. You will sit here until all of your homework is done. The choice is yours." Stick to your demands. It may take your child several days to realize that you mean business.

Sample Parent Resource Sheet: What to Do When Your Child Will Not Do Homework on His Own

Solving Homework Problems

What to Do When Your Child Will Not Do Homework on His Own

If your child will not do homework without your assistance, first make sure that he is making a genuine effort to try to work alone. Follow these steps.

1. **State that you expect your child to work alone.**
   Say, "I expect you to do homework without my help. I will not sit with you or do your work for you, but I will be available for questions every so often."

2. **Schedule daily homework time.**
   Allot a time each day when all other activities stop and your child must go to his study area and do homework. Say, "I expect you to get all of your homework done during this time."

3. **Give praise and support when your child works independently.**
   When you see your child working alone, say, "I am really proud of the way you are doing all of this work on your own. I knew you could do it."

4. **Help your child build confidence.**
   If you think your child feels that homework is too much to handle on his own, "chunk" the assignments by breaking them down into smaller chunks that can be handled successfully.

5. **Offer help only after your child has genuinely tried to solve the problem independently.**
   There will be times when something is really too hard for your child to understand, but make sure that you don't step in until he has made a sincere effort to solve the problem at least twice.

6. **Back up your words with action.**
   If the problem persists, tell your child that at the end of homework time he must sit in his study area until the work is finished. Don't let tears, anger, or indifference manipulate you. Relying on you for help will only lead to greater dependence instead of the confidence you are trying to build.

Sample Parent Resource Sheet: What to Do When Your Child Waits Until the Last Minute to Finish Assignments

Solving Homework Problems

What to Do When Your Child Waits Until the Last Minute to Finish Assignments

If your child puts off starting long-range assignments and goes into a frenzy at the last minute, use the following suggestions.

1. **State that you expect long-range projects to be planned and completed responsibly.**
   Say, "I will not tolerate your putting off projects until just before they are due. This waiting until the last minute must stop."

2. **Ask the teacher for a long-range planner.**
   This planning sheet will help your child learn how to break down a large project into small, easily completed tasks over the period of time given for the project. Help your child fill in the steps on the planner.

3. **Give praise and support for your child as each step is completed.**
   Say, "You finished reading the book by the date you scheduled. Keep up the good work."

4. **Give additional motivators when appropriate.**
   If your child needs additional motivation to complete a project on time, institute a system that allows her to earn a point toward a reward or privilege each time a step is completed according to the schedule.

5. **Back up your words with action.**
   If the problem persists, impose restrictions. If your child fails to complete a step on the planner on time, take away a privilege (watching TV, using the phone) until the step is completed. Unless you set limits, your child is not going to believe that you mean business.

Sample Parent Resource Sheet: What to Do When Your Child Will Not Do Homework If You Aren't Home

Solving Homework Problems

What to Do When Your Child Will Not Do Homework If You Aren't Home

If your child will not do homework unless a parent is home, take these steps.

1. **State that you expect homework to be done whether you are home or not.**

2. **Schedule daily homework time.**
   Allot a time each day when all other activities stop and your child must go to his study area and do homework.

3. **Tell the person responsible for child care about daily homework time.**
   The caregiver should know when and where your child is expected to do homework.

4. **Monitor your child when you're not home to make sure homework is done.**
   Telephone your child, if possible, at the beginning and at the end of daily homework time to make sure the homework is getting done.

5. **Give praise and positive support.**
   Praise your child for work done in your absence. "You're doing a great job on homework when I am not here. Keep it up!"

6. **Use additional incentives, if necessary.**
   A homework contract can help your child develop the habit of doing homework without your supervision. It should state: that homework will be done whether you are home or not; the amount of time for completing homework; the number of points earned for completing homework; the reward earned when a certain number of points is attained.

7. **Back up your words with action.**
   Say, "You can do homework during daily homework time or you can choose not to have privileges. You will sit there until homework is finished." Make sure you follow through.

8. **Contact the teacher.**
   If the problem persists, discuss the possibility of imposing loss of privileges at school so that your child knows you and the teacher are working together to help your child behave responsibly.

Involving Parents in the Homework Process

Reminders

DO

- Let parents and students know exactly how you will deal with homework. Send home your homework policy before you give the first homework assignment.

- Give parents tips for helping their children do homework.

- Send home positive homework notes to parents.

- Assign a homework study buddy for each student.

- Let parents know about upcoming tests.

- Plan your homework when you plan your classroom lessons.

- Require students to write down all homework assignments in an assignment book or on an assignment sheet.

- Make sure that all your homework assignments are appropriate to the age and skill level of the student.

- Make sure that students understand how to do each homework assignment. Explain the assignment before students go home.

- Collect and comment on all homework. Students must know that you are paying attention to the work they do.

- Comment in a positive way on how each student did on an assignment, whenever possible.

DON'T

- Don't give last-minute, thrown-together homework assignments.

- Don't give homework assignments that have no objective.

- Don't give assignments that bear no connection to lessons.

- Don't expect students to know how to study unless they've been taught study skills.

- Don't overload students with homework. Be sensitive to the realities of their lives.

- Don't give only drill and practice homework.

Involving Parents in the Homework Process

Checklist

Refer to this checklist as you plan your homework program.

HAVE YOU:

☐ Sent home a homework policy to all parents?

☐ Sent home homework and study skills tips to all parents?

☐ Planned to teach homework skills to your students?

☐ Set goals for yourself for sending home positive homework notes to parents?

☐ Set goals for yourself for sending home positive homework notes to students?

☐ Planned to assign family learning activities throughout the year?

Chapter

8

Conducting Regularly Scheduled Parent Conferences

Successful parent conferences are an essential part of getting and keeping parent support. A regularly scheduled conference can be a pleasant, informative, and productive meeting for both parent and teacher—an opportunity to get to know one another and interact on behalf of the student.

A regularly scheduled conference isn't the time to surprise parents with negative information about their child's behavior or performance in school. These problems should never be saved for routine conferences. They need to be dealt with as soon as they occur.

This chapter covers two important areas to help you ensure that parent conferences are constructive and worthwhile for parent, student, and teacher:

1. Prepare for the conference by planning exactly what you will do.

2. Conduct the conference professionally and enthusiastically.

Prepare for the conference by planning exactly what you will do.

As with all parent contacts, planning makes the difference between a mediocre, lackluster meeting and a motivating, successful conference. The confidence you need to project at a conference is the result of careful planning. Follow each of the following steps, and ensure a more productive conference for everyone.

Step 1: Send home a conference invitation.

Your invitation should be warm and friendly, but it must be informative as well. You will be supplying the parent with information *and* asking for some in return. This way, both of you will approach the conference better prepared and better informed.

Include the information that follows in your invitation.

Explain the purpose of having a parent conference.

Parents may not even know why they are being asked to come to a school conference. They may think that it's to hear bad news about their child, or that the conference is really a waste of their time. You need to let them know why you hold parent conferences and what you hope to accomplish. Stress the importance of the parent being there. Inform parents that you are holding conferences for the parents of all students.

Sample Parent Conference Note to Parents

On November 11, 12, and 13, I will be holding conferences for the parents of all my students. This conference is a very important part of the school year. It is our opportunity to get to know each other better and to plan how we will work together for your child's benefit.

Offer parents flexible time choices.

A majority of parents work outside the home and can't always come to school in the middle of the day. It is extremely important that you recognize this fact and act accordingly. Few situations are as unsettling to a parent as feeling prevented from participating in their child's education.

Whenever possible, set up conference times early in the morning, late in the afternoon, in the evening, or even on weekends. If you feel that a parent may be more willing or able to attend a conference when it is held outside of school, suggest a public meeting place such as a coffee shop or a restaurant. It may not be as convenient for you, but parents will appreciate your willingness to recognize the realities of their lives. No matter when and where you hold the conference, make sure it is conducted in a professional manner.

Give parents as much choice as possible in choosing the day of the week and the time for the conference. Your invitation might include a portion that is returned to you indicating when the parent can attend. (Suggestion: Some teachers circulate a parent-conference-time schedule at Back-to-School Night. The schedule lists all dates and times available for conferences. Parents sign their names next to the dates and times desired. As conference time approaches, reminders are sent home to parents.)

Ask parents to let you know what they would like to discuss.

Include a section on the invitation for the parent to list any issues he would like to discuss at the conference. This gives a parent the opportunity to think in advance about what he would like to talk about. And having this information ahead of time will better prepare you to address the parent's concerns.

Write a personal comment on the invitation.

Whenever you personalize a reproduced letter that goes home, you are showing parents that you've put in just a bit more effort and care. Take a minute or two to jot down a friendly line, such as "I'm looking forward to talking with you," on the parent conference invitation. And be sure to sign your name. Parents will notice these personal touches.

Step 2: Plan the physical environment.

It's difficult to feel professional (or to be perceived as such) when you are sitting face-to-face with a parent who is stuffed behind a primary desk or perched precariously on an undersized chair. Make sure parents are comfortable during the conference. Arrange to have adult-sized chairs in your room.

If possible, set up a coffee maker and offer coffee and/or tea. Make a positive impression before the conference begins by giving some thought to the comfort of parents as they wait their turn. Place two chairs outside the door, along with a stack of student textbooks and workbooks for parents to look at.

Step 3: Put together samples of each student's classwork.

Have examples of the student's classwork available for the conference. This will demonstrate that you took considerable time and thought to prepare for the meeting about this specific student. It communicates not only that you take your job seriously, but also that you genuinely care about this particular student. Throughout the conference, use the work to help you illustrate statements you are making to the parents regarding the student's performance in the classroom.

Step 4: Fill out a Parent Conference Planning and Note Sheet for each student before meeting the parent(s).

A parent conference must be tightly structured. You have only a limited amount of time, and much to discuss. Prepare yourself by noting all the issues you wish to discuss. Knowing in advance what you are going to talk about can save you from inadvertently leaving out important points. If you are prepared, you'll be more relaxed. And when you are relaxed, your confidence will show and the parent will, in turn, feel more confidence in you.

Use the Parent Conference Planning and Note Sheet on page 108 to structure your conferences. Each of the points listed should be addressed when you meet with parents. Notice that three of the points are to be filled in with parent comments during the conference.

Sample Parent Conference Invitation

Dear Parent(s)

During the week of November 14 to 18, I will be holding conferences with the parents of all my students. I am looking forward to this
opportunity for us to talk about your child's educational experiences
this year. At the conference we will discuss your child's progress in
school, my goals for the remainder of the year, and any other issues
that affect you or your child. I am certain that this meeting will be
productive for all of us! Working together, we can make this the best
year ever for your child.

Sincerely,

Mr. Chung

Please take a few moments to fill out the lower portion of this
letter. When completed, send it back to school.

- -

Parent's name _____

Student's name _____

Please check off your first and second choices of the dates and
times most convenient for you. I will do my best to set our meeting
for your first-choice time.

These are the dates I prefer:

☐ Monday, November 14   ☐ Thursday, November 17
☐ Tuesday, November 15   ☐ Friday, November 18
☐ Wednesday, November 16

These are the times I prefer:

☐ Morning   ☐ Afternoon   ☐ Evening

If you have concerns or questions you'd like to discuss with me at
the conference, please write them down below. I would like to take
that opportunity to talk about the issues that are important to you.

_____

_____

_____

Here is a detailed look at each point listed on the planning sheet and how it would be approached in the conference.

1. **Begin by sharing an example of the unique qualities of the child.**
Parents come to conferences to learn about their child's progress. They also want to be satisfied that the teacher knows about, understands, and appreciates the unique qualities of their child. It is important for you to show parents that you've taken the time and shown the interest to get to know their child. For example:

   "Kara has a real passion for art. It is a pleasure to watch her when she is involved in painting."

   "Maureen is a leader among her classmates. Let me tell you how she handled a tough situation between several students."

2. **Give an update on any past problems the student had.**
If you have dealt with the parent about a problem in the past, make sure you spend some time updating the current status of the situation. It's important to attend to this as soon as possible because the parent will most likely be anxious about it, and that anxiety may keep him from listening to anything else.

   "I'm happy to tell you that Erin is turning in all of her homework assignments now."

   "Felipe is doing much better controlling his temper. I can see the effort he's making."

   "Math continues to be a problem for Taylor, but during this conference we're going to discuss what can be done to help him at home."

3. **Discuss the academic strengths of the student.**
Focus on the positive academic strengths of the student. Show examples of class work at this time. If appropriate, you may wish to use the student's report card as a guide for this discussion.

   "Here's where Jaime was at the start of the year in reading. Now look at this. He's moved ahead three levels. You can see from these tests that his comprehension skills are excellent."

   "Troy did a great job organizing and writing this term paper. His research was thorough, his note cards well written, and the final paper was carefully thought out and interesting to read."

Sample Parent Conference Planning and Note Sheet

Parent Conference Planning and Note Sheet

Student's Name _____ Time _____

Parent's Name _____ Date _____

1. Example of student's unique quality:

   _____

2. Past problems of the student to be updated at the conference:

   _____

3. Academic strengths of the student:

   _____

4. Academic weaknesses of the student that should be discussed:

   _____

5. Parent input on student's academic performance:

   _____

6. Academic goals for the student for the rest of the year:

   _____

7. Social strengths of the student:

   _____

8. Any weaknesses in the area of social development the student has:

   _____

9. Social development goals for the student for the rest of the year:

   _____

10. Parent input regarding student's social behavior:

    _____

11. Additional issues parent wishes to discuss:

    _____

4. **If appropriate, discuss the academic weaknesses of the student.**
   If the child is having academic problems, let the parent know you are taking steps to improve the situation.

   "I'm aware, of course, that Kenneth is struggling to keep up in Spanish. I have some lessons on tape that I think will help him. I'd like to send them home with you. Here's how to use them . . ."

   "Algebra I is very difficult for Brittany. I've arranged to have her work with a senior tutor 2 days a week during class time."

5. **Get parental input on the student's academic performance.**
   Ask parents how they feel their child is doing in school. It is important that parents have the opportunity to give feedback. If they feel that there's a problem you are overlooking, you need to address the issue and clear up any misunderstanding. Ask questions such as:

   "Are you satisfied with your child's academic performance?"

   "Do you have any concerns about how your child is doing in school?"

   Take notes on what the parents say, and make sure parents know that you find their input important and valuable. Let them know that, if appropriate, you are prepared to adjust your dealings with their child accordingly.

6. **Discuss academic goals for the student for the remainder of the year.**
   Talk to the parent about what you'd like to see the child accomplish the rest of the year. Get the parent's input, too. Knowing that both of you have the same goals will help establish a rapport that may be needed if difficulties arise later.

   "I would like to see Jonelle reading at grade level by June. Considering how well she's doing now, I think we will meet this goal. What goals would you like to see Jonelle achieve?"

   "Rebecca's research skills should improve considerably over the next few months. We will be doing some assignments geared toward this goal. How do you see Rebecca's progress? Do you have any suggestions?"

7. **Present the social strengths of the student.**
   Discuss the student's social behavior in your class by focusing on his strengths in relating to peers. Be prepared to give specific examples.

   "Larry is always there to help out a friend. His loyalty is really valued by the other students. They know they can count on him."

   "Raffi's exuberance and spirit make him someone that students and teachers enjoy being with."

8. **If appropriate, discuss the student's weaknesses in social interactions.**
Be sensitive. Link any suggestions or observations you have to a positive statement or observation.

"I'd like to see Ben feel more confident about himself when he's in a group. He's a smart boy, but I'm not so sure he thinks so."

"As you are aware, Paula too often lets anger control her. I think, however, that the behavior contract you are using at home and I'm using at school is making a difference."

9. **Discuss your goals for the student, in the area of social development, for the remainder of the school year.**
"I would like to see Kathryn become a bit more assertive in class. I know she has opinions she'd like to offer, but she holds back. I'm going to have the students do some cooperative learning activities. The small-group setting should help Kathryn overcome some of her hesitance."

10. **Get parental input regarding the student's social behavior.**
Ask the parent how she perceives the child is doing socially. Make sure you open the door to a discussion of the parent's suggestions for improving the situation.

"Do you feel that your child is happy in school?"

"What are your concerns regarding your child's relationships with other students?"

"How do you think we could help Yuki feel more confident about herself?"

11. **Finally, talk about any other issues parents may wish to discuss.**
Ask if there's anything else the parent would like to talk about with you. At this time, you should also address any issues that the parent wrote about on the conference notification.

Conduct the conference professionally and enthusiastically.

Set a professional, caring tone.

The attitude you project at the conference is what will ultimately win a parent's confidence, trust, and support. Keep the "golden rule" of parent communication in mind at all times: Treat parents the way you would want to be treated. At a conference, the parent is your guest in the classroom. You are the host, and it's your responsibility to see that it is a pleasurable, productive, and informative experience.

Greet the parent warmly.

First impressions do count. Whether it's 6:30 in the morning or 7:30 at night, wake up, put on a smile, and make the parent feel welcome. Greet the parent at the door, and give a firm handshake before sitting down. Offer coffee or tea and spend a moment or two putting the parent at ease.

Refer to your planning sheet as you proceed through the conference.

Your planning sheet helped you focus on your goals as you planned for the meeting. Be sure you use this valuable resource during the conference, too. Keep it in front of you as you speak, and jot down points of interest as they come up.

Use effective listening and communication skills.

The way you speak and listen to a parent can have great impact in enhancing that parent's trust and confidence in what you are saying. Your body language carries part of your message.

Make sure that your words and your actions communicate that you are an open and caring teacher, here to help your students succeed. Be sensitive to the parent, treating him the way you would want to be treated if your own child were the object of the conversation. With this in mind, be on the lookout for any roadblocks that may appear, and use your communication skills to move the parent past the roadblock.

This conference is a good opportunity for you to interact with parents in a positive, supportive atmosphere. Make the most of it. Don't ignore a parent's feelings of stress, hostility, or confusion. Take these feelings seriously, and address them openly. Your confident, professional attitude and appropriate responses can turn an uninvolved parent into a supportive one.

In chapter 9, we will discuss effective communication skills that will help you succeed in your interactions with parents.

Close the conference on a positive, optimistic note.

At the close of the conference, rise, shake the parent's hand, and walk together to the door. Make sure your parting comments are sincere. Leave the parent with a positive, confident feeling that you are an educator who really cares, and who will be there for the child all year long.

"I'm so glad we've had this conference, Mrs. Peterson. I think the goals we both have for your son are clear. And now that we know each other better,

I'm sure we can work together to make this year a real success for Rob. I look forward to speaking to you again soon."

Conducting Regularly Scheduled Parent Conferences

Reminders

DO

- Arrive at the conference site before the parent.
- Greet the parent warmly.
- Usher the parent to the seat you've selected.
- Look the parent in the eyes when speaking.
- Address the parent often by name.
- Say something complimentary about the student early in the conference.
- Hand the parent the child's work to look over. Point out examples of work that should be noted.
- Have study or academic tips available to give to parents.
- Ask the parent for his input regarding the student.
- End the conference on time, and schedule another one if needed.
- Make detailed notes of what was discussed.

DON'T

- Don't surprise parents with new problems. Parents should be notified the moment a problem arises.
- Don't make small talk. Use every moment of the parent's time to discuss the student's progress.
- Don't discuss other students, even if the parent tries to.
- Don't do all the talking. You want to maintain control of the conference, but you should allow the parent time to discuss his concerns and ideas. You may learn something important that can help you in dealing with the child.

Conducting Regularly Scheduled
Parent Conferences
Checklist

Refer to this checklist when you plan your parent-teacher conferences.

HAVE YOU:

☐ Sent an invitation that explains why parents should attend the conference?

☐ Made flexible time choices available to parents?

☐ Asked parents to let you know what they would like to discuss?

☐ Organized samples of each student's class work?

☐ Planned where parents will sit for the conference?

☐ Arranged for coffee or tea?

☐ Filled out a Parent Conference Form for each student?

☐ Collected appropriate study or academic tips to give parents so that they can help their child at home?

Demonstrating Sensitivity and Awareness

The key to parent involvement is communication. The key to successful communication is sensitivity and awareness. This chapter addresses two important ways to boost your skills:

1. Practice sensitivity in your interactions with parents.

2. Show that you are aware of a family's special situation.

Practice sensitivity in your interactions with parents.

Successful communication depends on more than what you are prepared to say. It also depends on how you listen and react to what a parent says. You can't anticipate a parent's words, but the following techniques will help you show parents that you are sensitive to their feelings and are prepared to adjust your own behavior accordingly.

Be aware of your body language and tone of voice.

Body language and tone of voice carry an important part of your message. Therefore, it is very important that you are aware of and adjust these communication tools to convey caring, accessibility, openness, and warmth.

- When meeting with a parent face-to-face, lean forward slightly while he is speaking. This shows that you are interested in what is being said.

- Maintain eye contact. Do not cross your arms. Instead, show openness and a willingness to listen.

- Make sure there are no physical barriers between you and the parent. It's best to sit next to each other at a table. Don't sit at your desk with the parent on the other side. The seating arrangement has to reflect that you accept the parent as an equal partner in her child's education.

- In all conversations with parents, your tone of voice should show your confidence and calmness. Make sure that irritation, frustration, or annoyance doesn't creep into your manner of speech. Don't raise your voice, and remain calm and polite at all times. Speak to every parent the way you'd like to be spoken to.

- In all conversations with parents, you must be willing to listen to what the parent has to say. Don't take over the conversation. Don't interrupt. Feel free to add some verbal assurances ("I understand") to show that you are listening.

Use the reflective listening technique.

It is important, especially if a parent is upset, that you convey your empathy with what he is saying. A technique called reflective listening is very effective to show that you are sensitive to a parent's situation. When you use this technique, you simply reflect back in words that you heard what the parent said and understand how he feels. You are not making a judgment about what is being said. You are not agreeing or disagreeing. You are simply letting the parent know that you hear and you understand. This is a powerful technique that will demonstrate to a parent that you respect the feelings he is expressing.

Preface your reflective response with comments such as "I hear how upset you are," or "I understand how upset you are about all of this."

Here are some sample comments from parents, with the teacher's reflective response.

Parent:　*I don't know what to do with that boy. He just won't listen to me.*

Teacher:　(Reflective response) *I hear how upset you are about your son.*

Parent:　*I honestly believe his problems are caused by other children.*

Teacher:　(Reflective response) *I hear what you are saying.*

Parent:　*You need to understand that I'm a single mom. I work. I don't have any time to deal with this.*

Teacher:　(Reflective response) *I understand how overwhelmed you must feel.*

Parent:　*I fight every night with him to try to get him to do his homework.*

Teacher:　(Reflective response) *I hear how frustrated you are.*

Parent:　*I really don't know if she should be held back.*

Teacher:　(Reflective response) *I understand what a difficult choice that must be.*

Reflective listening is a valuable skill. Combined with an awareness of your body language, it can greatly increase your ability to communicate with parents.

Use a translator when necessary.

When dealing with parents from a different cultural or linguistic background, you may need to use the services of a translator. Here are a few important guidelines to keep in mind:

- Sit facing the parent, with the translator seated next to you.

- As you speak, always look directly at the parent, never at the translator. When the translator speaks, continue to look at the parent.

- Keep your eyes on the parent when he speaks, not on the translator. Continue to do so when the translator speaks.

In other words, make sure that the conference is between you and the parent, not between you, the parent, and the translator. Pay attention to your body language. Lean forward as you speak. Maintain eye contact, and through your gestures and attitude, exude warmth and caring that will transcend spoken words in any culture.

Show that you are aware of a family's special situation.

Today, a teacher can't assume that one method or style of communication will fit the needs of all. Teachers work with many kinds of families, including stepfamilies, single-parent and two-parent families, same-sex parents, families torn by poverty or wrestling with divorce, two-income families, transient families, non–English speaking families, and families of various ethnic or cultural backgrounds. An effective teacher must at all times be aware of the varying realities of the families of his students.

Throughout *Parents on Your Side,* you are given a wide variety of suggestions to guide you in your communications with parents. Before you put any of these ideas to use, take time to think about the person with whom you will be communicating. Make every effort to satisfy yourself that you are, to the best of your ability, communicating in an appropriate manner.

Take special care to be aware of the cultural diversity of your students and to gain an understanding of their varying cultural expectations and values. Let that knowledge guide your words and actions throughout the year. Acceptable behaviors or manners in one culture may not be the same in another.

Your professional judgment must lead you as you communicate with every parent. Yet it is always appropriate to practice sensitivity and show awareness toward a parent's specific situation, particularly if it is different from your own. Your behavior is guided by your own values, beliefs, and expectations, as is the behavior of your students' parents. Let your attitude and behavior show that you accept the parents' background and are willing to work with them to help their children succeed in school.

Demonstrating Sensitivity and Awareness

Reminders

DO

- Be aware of your body language and tone of voice in all of your communications with parents.

- Communicate confidence and calmness at all times, and demonstrate openness and genuine interest in what a parent has to say.

- Practice reflective listening to show you empathize with a parent's situation.

- Educate yourself about appropriate ways to communicate with parents from different social and cultural backgrounds.

DON'T

- Don't treat every parent alike. Make every effort to adjust your behavior and attitude to suit the individual with whom you are dealing.

- Don't allow your preconceptions about a parent's background to come between you and an open dialogue with the parent.

- Don't dominate a conversation.

- Don't interrupt.

- Don't let irritation, frustration, or anger affect your tone of voice, body language, or attitude toward a parent.

Demonstrating Sensitivity and Awareness

Checklist

Refer to this checklist as you plan your communication with parents.

HAVE YOU:

☐ Educated yourself about the expectations, behaviors, and values guiding the particular parent with whom you are meeting?

☐ Honestly evaluated your own preconceptions about the parent's specific background?

☐ Reviewed the tips on body language and reflective listening?

☐ Prepared the meeting room to communicate that you consider the parent a partner in the child's education?

Section Three

How to Work with Parents to Solve Problems

Successful communication with parents often includes involving parents in solving a student's behavior or academic problem. This section of *Parents on Your Side* will offer practical advice on how to enlist parent support in problematic situations.

Chapter 10: Documenting Problems

In order to be able to communicate with parents effectively about a problem with their child, it is essential that you have sufficient information about problems as they appear. This chapter will give some suggestions on how to keep a record of student behavior and performance.

Chapter 11: Contacting Parents at the First Sign of a Problem

In this chapter, you will learn how to contact parents when problems arise. Contact them as soon as possible in order to avoid the problem getting worse.

Chapter 12: Conducting a Problem-Solving Conference

If a student's behavior or performance does not improve, it may be necessary to conduct a problem-solving conference with the parent. This chapter will offer advice on how to prepare for and conduct such a conference so that it is most effective.

Chapter 13: Using a Home-School Contract

This chapter will show you how to prepare and manage a contract between you, the parent, and the student to improve the student's behavior. The contract stipulates the desired student behavior, the teacher's disciplinary measures administered in case of problems, and the parent's follow-through at home.

Chapter 14: Providing Support for Parents' Disciplinary Efforts

This chapter offers suggestions for you to pass on to parents who need your help in dealing with their children's behavior or academic problems. These suggestions comprise disciplinary techniques and ideas to help parents reach out to their children.

Chapter 15: Dealing with Difficult Situations

In your career, you will encounter difficult parents. This chapter will offer general strategies for dealing with a parent's angry criticism and for reaching even the most reluctant parent.

Chapter 10

Documenting Problems

When it comes to their child's poor performance, parents often resist believing what they are told. Nobody likes to hear bad news. It's especially hard for parents to hear anything negative about their child. They may feel it reflects on their parenting abilities or feel that it's something they have no control over. They may take the bad news personally and may resist your efforts to improve the situation.

Therefore, it will benefit both you and the parents to keep accurate documentation of all academic or behavioral problems as they occur. Documentation will strengthen your position as a professional, help you communicate clearly to parents, and provide strong evidence to parents who may question your word.

Early in the school year, your experience and intuition will guide you in recognizing those students who may have problems. It is vital that you begin documenting their actions immediately. Having anecdotal records will be necessary when you seek the support of administrators and parents.

This chapter addresses the following ways to use documentation in your efforts to change a problem into a solution:

1. Document situations in a nonjudgmental manner.

2. Choose a record-keeping system.

3. Use your documentation.

Document situations in a nonjudgmental manner.

Detailed record-keeping of the situation is not meant as an excuse to try and find fault with a particular student. Rather than labeling a student as incorrigible, make sure to document an unbiased account of what the student did and what you did to help the student correct the behavior.

A nonjudgmental record of the situation will enable you to remain fair and impartial when meeting with parents and administrators.

Be specific in your description of the problem.

When you write your documentation, keep away from vague opinions.

"Sean misbehaved all day long."

"Kerry didn't do anything she was supposed to do today."

Base your statements on factual, observable data.

"Yesterday, Sean threw his lunch tray on the ground and shoved other children in three separate instances."

"Today during reading, Louise repeatedly jumped up and bothered her neighbor."

Consistent, specific documentation will enable you to give a nonjudgmental account of a student's performance. Documentation enables you to tell parents exactly what's going on—behaviorally, academically, or with homework.

Choose a record-keeping system.

Use any of the following methods for documenting student performance:

- A small notebook or computer file with one page designated for each student. Insert a page for the student only when the first infraction occurs. Secondary teachers usually designate a documentation section for each class period.

- $3\frac{1}{2} \times 5\frac{1}{2}$ inch index cards, alphabetically arranged in a file box, one for each student.

- A loose-leaf notebook with one or more pages per student. (This is especially useful for a class with many difficult students.)

An anecdotal record should include the following information:

- Student's name and class

- Date, time, and place of incident

- Description of problem

- Action taken

Sample Documentation on 3½ × 5½ Inch Index Card

Johnson, Kim   Period 4

10/8	Kim cut math class. Phoned Mr. Johnson. Said he won't let her go out with friends if it happens again.
10/20	Kim cut class. Sent note to Mr. Johnson.
10/24	Kim cut class. Sent note to Mr. Johnson to arrange a conference. No response as of 10/26.
10/30	Called Mr. Johnson. Left message to return call. No response.
11/20	Principal sent note to arrange conference.

Sample Documentation in Small Notebook or Computer File

Lois Simon   Grade 4

Date/Time	Place	Rule Broken	Action Taken
9/15 10:45	Classroom	Refused to return to seat	Reminder
9/15 1:20	Classroom	Running in class	Lose 10 minutes recess
9/15 1:40	Classroom	Called out without raising hand	Lose 20 minutes recess
9/18 2:00	Hallway	Ran out of line for drink of water	Reminder
9/18 2:40	Gym	Continued playing after whistle blew	No gym next week

Organize and file your documentation.

Create a separate folder for each student with behavioral or academic problems. Include the following information in each folder:

- Student's name and class
- Home phone number
- Work phone number(s)
- Emergency phone number

Keep your anecdotal record in the file.

In addition, keep copies of all correspondence you have had with parents regarding the student's problem(s). Make notes during phone calls, and write down any agreements reached between you and the parent. Make copies of any letters or notes that you have sent to parents as well as copies of all notes and letters received from them. Don't leave anything to memory.

Maintain your records so that you will have a complete chronological history of the student's problem(s). Later, when you need to refer to them or show them to an administrator or parent, a complete and accurate timeline of events will enable you to present the problem clearly and professionally. Confidence comes from knowing you've done everything possible to solve a student's problem and from having the records to prove it.

You may need to record your class.

If you are dealing with a particularly difficult situation—if you feel that a parent may not trust you, or if a parent believes you are the cause of the problem—it may be useful to record your class so the parents can hear exactly how their child behaves.

There are two ways to do this with two distinctly different outcomes.

- Do not tell the student you will be recording the class. This method allows parents to actually witness their child's problem behavior.

- Tell the student ahead of time that you will be recording the class. Often mentioning that you will be recording the class may be enough to improve the student's behavior. This in itself may be a solution to the problem, and you may never have to play the recording for the parents.

Use your documentation.

Have documentation records with you when you meet with parents. This will make sure that:

- Parents can read the specific behaviors their child engaged in.

- No one can question how you handled the situation.

- Your word cannot be pitted against that of a student.

- You and the student's parents can address specific problems directly and find solutions.

In severe cases, the anecdotal record will show that the student has been given due process and will justify the following:

- Intervention of the principal
- Removal of the child from your class to be placed in another class
- Referral to a counselor or therapist
- Suspension
- Removal from school
- Special education placement

REMEMBER: Having specific records of a student's problems will enable you to hold a more effective problem-solving conference. You will feel confident knowing you did everything you could to deal with the problem yourself. You will not be flustered and will not have to rely on your memory.

Documenting Problems

Reminders

DO

- Begin documenting problems as soon as they appear.

- Make sure your documentation relates factual, observable data.

- Use your documentation when you seek support from an administrator or parents.

- Use the documentation to help you pinpoint specific problems a student is having.

- Include the time, place, and details of the incident, and the names of those involved.

- Organize your files chronologically so that you can present a clear, accurate picture of the history of the problem.

DON'T

- Don't use documenting a student's problem behavior to find fault with him.

- Don't include your own opinions in your documentation.

- Don't let your documentation lapse. To be effective, you must keep consistent, up-to-date records.

Documenting Problems

Checklist

Refer to this checklist as you begin to document student problems.

HAVE YOU:

☐ Begun documenting problems as soon as they appear?

☐ Based your documentation on factual, observable data?

☐ Avoided writing down vague opinions?

☐ Created a documentation file for each student as the need arises?

☐ Included all pertinent communication and notes in the file?

☐ Organized your documentation chronologically?

Contacting Parents at the First Sign of a Problem

A common complaint among parents is that teachers wait too long before contacting them about a problem. It doesn't matter whether it's the first week of school or even the first day. As soon as you become aware of an academic or behavioral problem that parents should know about, contact them. This issue is at the core of any parental involvement plan. Parents can't be expected to get involved if they don't know what's going on.

In this chapter, the following topics will help you make the decision to call parents and follow through successfully:

- When should you contact a parent?
- The best way to contact parents is by phone.
- Make sure you contact hard-to-reach parents.
- Follow up on the initial contact.
- File your notes and records.

When should you contact a parent?

How do you know when you should contact a parent about a problem? Many situations are very clear: severe fighting, extreme emotional distress, a student who refuses to work or turn in homework, or a student who cannot do the work. You don't think twice about involving parents when these situations occur. But what about the day-to-day instances that may not be so obvious? In most cases, your own good judgment will be your best guide.

If you are uncertain about contacting a parent, again use the "your own child" test. This test will put you in the position of the parent and help clarify whether or not parental help is called for.

Follow these steps:

1. Assume that you have a child of your own who is the same age as the student in question.

2. If your child had the same problem in school as that student, would you want to be called?

3. If the answer is yes, call the parent. If the answer is no, do not call the parent.

For example, if your own child forgot to bring her book to class one day, would you want to be called? Most likely the answer is no. If, on the other hand, your own child forgot her book 3 days in a row, you most likely would want to know. The "your own child" test will help to focus your attention on problems that need parental involvement, and it will guide you to treat parents the way you would want to be treated.

You will find that by using this test you will increase your contact with parents. And increasing contact with parents will increase the probability of parent support.

The best way to contact parents is by phone.

Once you've decided that you are going to contact a parent, how are you going to get in touch? A phone call is unquestionably the best way to contact parents when there is an issue that needs prompt attention. It's personal, it's immediate, and it gives you the opportunity to clearly explain the situation and answer right away any questions the parent may have.

Calling parents should not make you nervous or hesitant. You know that you are making the call in the best interests of your student. You have every right and obligation to involve the parent if you think the situation calls for it. Relax. You can conduct a productive call. Planning is the key. You'll find that you can handle any call if you know in advance what you are going to say.

Write down what you will say.

Remember that before you pick up the phone, you need to outline what you are going to say to the parent. These notes will be your script for conducting the call, and the writing process will help you think through and clarify the points you want to make. Having the notes in front of you while you're speaking will keep you from getting nervous and forgetting important details.

Plan to address each of the points listed on the sample planning sheet below. Fill out a sheet like this each time you prepare for a problem-solving phone call.

Sample Parent Phone Call Worksheet

Parent Phone Call Worksheet
Initial Phone Call About a Problem

Teacher _____ Grade _____

Student's Name _____

Name of Parent(s) or Guardian _____

Phone number(s) _____

Date of call _____

Brief description of problem: _____

_____

Write down important points you will cover with parents.

1. Begin with a statement of concern.

2. Describe the specific behavior that necessitated the call.

3. Describe the steps you have taken to solve the problem.

4. Get parental input.

5. Present your solutions to the problem (what you will do; what you want the parent to do).

6. Express confidence in your ability to solve the problem.

7. Inform parents that you will follow up with them.

Notes: _____

_____

_____

_____

_____

By addressing these points, you will find that your phone conversation will be both informative and effective. Let's take a closer look.

1. **Begin with a statement of concern.**

   Your introductory statement will set the tone for the entire conversation. Remember that even though you're calling about a problem, you can still project a positive, supportive, and sensitive attitude. Keep in mind that you're not calling to place blame or complain. You're calling because you care about the student.

Through your words, let the parent know that the welfare of his child is your utmost concern. When a parent hears concern rather than an accusation, he will be much more receptive to you.

The following examples illustrate this point.

"Mrs. Grozny, I'm calling because

- *I'm concerned about how little work Theo is doing."*

- *I'm concerned that Linda does not get along with the other students."*

Notice that the statements express concern for the student and outline the problem in a more positive way that invites further dialogue.

2. **Describe the specific behavior that necessitated the call.**
   Tell the parent in specific, observable terms what the child did or did not do. An observable behavior is behavior you can watch going on, such as talking out, not turning in assignments, refusing to follow directions, or hitting a classmate. Always mention the specific behavior and the number of times the problem has occurred.

   "The reason I'm concerned is

   - *Seth shouted out in class four times today."*

   - *Lorenzo has refused to do any of his work in class for 2 days now."*

   - *Nicole had two fights today with other students."*

   These specific statements about observable behavior tell the parents exactly what happened. Avoid making vague statements that do not clearly communicate the problem.

   "He's having problems again."

   "She's just not behaving."

   Comments such as these don't give parents any real information at all. In fact, they may give the parent the impression that you don't like and are picking on the child. Uninformative, negative comments will only serve to make parents defensive.

   In addition, avoid making negative, judgmental comments such as:

   "The reason I'm calling is

   - *your child has a bad attitude."*

   - *your child is mean to other students."*

   - *your child is lazy."*

   Again, statements such as these give no valid information and will immediately alienate a parent.

3. **Describe the steps you have taken to solve the problem.**
   It's important that parents recognize that you have already taken appropriate action to deal with the situation—that you're not calling them in lieu of attempting to solve the problem yourself. Be specific. Tell them exactly what you have done.

   "I discussed your child's behavior with him and reviewed the rules of our classroom discipline plan. He understands the corrective actions for not following them, and, accordingly, twice he has been last to go to recess. I have also made a point of giving him extra positive attention when he is behaving."

   "When Lynne refused to do her work in class, I had her stay in my room during lunch to complete the assignment. In addition, I have spoken with her on three occasions regarding how she needs to complete her assignments. To further encourage her, I've been giving her a point whenever she does her work. When she earns five points, she can have extra free time."

   "I had a conference with your son about his fighting. He was sent to the principal's office when he continued to fight, and the principal and I had a conference regarding how to help him."

4. **Get parental input.**
   Ask the parent if there's anything she can add that might help solve the problem. The parent may have unique insights into the student's personality, and may know why the student continues to have a problem and how to help him move beyond it. Listen carefully to what the parent has to say, and be prepared to take suggestions into account.

   "Is there anything you can tell me that might help us solve this problem?"

5. **Present your solutions to the problem.**
   Be prepared to tell the parent exactly what you are going to do, and what you would like the parent to do. Don't dispense parenting advice. It is not your place to change a parent's child-rearing methods. It is your place, however, to ask a parent for her support in your efforts to educate the child. In an initial phone call about a problem, the most important thing you can ask the parent to do is let the child know that you called and that you and the parent both are concerned about the problem.

   "Here's what I will do at school: I'll continue to give Gary plenty of positive support when he does turn in homework on time. When he doesn't, he will have to complete it during detention. Would you tell Gary I called, and that I am concerned that he isn't turning in his

homework? Tell him that you are concerned also. I want Gary to know that both of us are working together to help him do better in school."

6. **Express confidence in your ability to solve the problem.**
   Whenever there is a problem, parents may become anxious. They need to know that they are dealing with a skilled teacher who has the confidence and the ability to work with their child to eliminate the problem. Keep the pediatrician analogy in mind. When a child is ill, a parent wants to hear the doctor say, "Don't worry. I know how to solve the problem. It will be taken care of." The last thing a parent wants to hear is, "I don't know how to handle this, but I'll do my best." Let parents know that you know what to do. Emphasize that with the parents' support you know you will get results. Your tone and attitude during this conversation should help express your confidence.

   Make statements such as:

   "Mr. Hill, I've worked with many children like Tom. Don't worry. Together we will help him."

   "Mrs. Jacobs, I've had a lot of experience with young people who have the same problem as Tamar. I know that by working together we will get results!"

   "Mrs. Rivera, it's going to be just fine. Don't worry. I know how to motivate children like Carlos, and I know that together we will get results."

7. **Inform parents that you will follow up with them.**
   When you tell parents that you will follow up on this conversation, you are promising that something is going to happen, that the problem is not going to be swept under the rug. Follow-up contact is vital if parents are going to believe in your commitment. It is also vital for positioning yourself to enlist their support in the future. Before ending the conversation, tell parents when they can expect to hear from you again.

   "I will contact you in 2 days and let you know how things are going with Tamar."

   "I'll call you tomorrow and tell you about David's success!"

Be sensitive and alert.

Your phone call should not be a one-sided conversation. You are building a foundation for future cooperative efforts with the parent. Be sure to ask for parental input at comfortable, appropriate intervals. Don't push parents, but open the door for them to add any insights they may have. If and when they do, make sure you take the time to really listen to any concerns they may express.

Parents know and care about their children, and even though they may not have been able to get a handle on the particular problem you are contacting them about, they may offer insights that are extremely valuable to your efforts.

Take parents seriously: Don't discount their comments, and always show your willingness to listen and learn. Put yourself in the parent's position and approach him in the manner you would like to be approached. Listen for any roadblocks that might appear and help the parent move past them.

Sample Initial Phone Call About a Problem

Below is a conversation that incorporates all of the points discussed. Notice that while asking the parent for cooperation, the teacher not only gives the parent specific information but also shows plenty of professional confidence.

The teacher begins with a statement of concern and then describes the specific behavior that necessitated the call.

"Mr. Jonas, this is Judy Spelling, Sandra's teacher. I'm calling because I'm concerned that Sandra has not been turning in her homework assignments. Last week, she didn't turn in three math assignments and two social studies exercises. Today, I did not receive another math assignment."

Now the teacher describes the steps she has already taken to solve the problem.

"I have discussed this situation with Sandra and reviewed the homework rules with her. She knows that her report card grade will drop if she keeps missing homework. Can you think of anything that might help us solve this problem?"

The teacher asks for parental input. She listens carefully to the response and shows her willingness to possibly adapt her own strategies to the parent's suggestions.

The teacher then presents her solutions to the problem.

"Mr. Jonas, I'd like us to work together to help Sandra develop better homework habits. Here's what I'd like to do: I am going to attach a slip to each assignment that goes home. Please ask to see all of her assignments each night. When she has finished the work, sign the slip. Chances are, your checking the work will be enough to motivate Sandra, but I'll also add a little extra incentive here at school. Each time I receive a completed assignment on time, Sandra will receive a point. When she earns 10 points, I will reward her with extra time in the library, which she does enjoy."

The teacher expresses confidence that the problem can be solved.

"Mr. Jonas, I'm certain that by working together we can help Sandra do a better job at school. She's a bright girl with a lot of potential. Please tell Sandra I called you and that I am concerned about this problem. Let her know that you are concerned about it, too."

Follow-up contact is arranged and the conversation concludes on an enthusiastic, upbeat note.

"I am going to call you next Monday and let you know how everything is working out. I'm sure I'll be calling with good news! In the meantime, be sure to give Sandra plenty of praise when she does her homework. Believe me, it makes a difference.

"I'm glad we've had this opportunity to talk. I look forward to our next conversation."

Make sure you contact hard-to-reach parents.

Don't give up trying to contact a parent just because you've dialed home twice and not received an answer. You have to make every effort to reach a parent. You wouldn't accept defeat if the child were physically ill and needed her parents. Somehow you'd find a way to get through. Keep in mind that a problem ignored will probably get worse, and then parents will wonder why they weren't informed earlier. Remember that it is your responsibility to make all possible effort to contact a parent.

Here are some additional strategies you can use.

Send a letter.

If you cannot reach a parent by phone, a letter home is your next option. This letter should be mailed, not sent home with the student. Be sure to include the same details you would have addressed in a phone call.

- Show your concern for the student.

- State the specific problem the student is having.

- List the steps you have taken to help the student with the problem.

- Explain what you would like the parent to do.

- Let the parent know that you are confident that working together, the problem will be solved.

- Ask the parent to contact you by phone or note to discuss any comments she would like to make.

Sample Letter to a Parent Who Is Hard to Reach

Dear Mr. and Mrs. McCafferty:

I'm writing because I'm concerned about how little work Danny has been doing at school. For the last 2 days, he has refused to do some of his assignments during class. As a result, I have had him stay in during recess to complete them. To help motivate him to do his work appropriately, I have told him he will receive a point each time he does his work in class. He knows that when he earns five points he will receive extra free time.

I would like your help in backing me up on this issue. Danny needs to know that his parents—as well as his teacher—insist that he does his work in school. Each day, I will send home a note to you, letting you know how well Danny is doing. Please sign the note and send it back with Danny the next day. I hope this will be enough to get Danny back on track.

Please call me if you have any questions. Danny is an intelligent, inquisitive boy. I'm sure that by working together we can help him do a better job in school. I will contact you next Monday to talk about how he is progressing.

Sincerely,

Mr. Elwood

Contact either the father or the mother.

Teachers generally call the mother when there is a problem. Even if the father answers the phone, the teacher will often ask to speak to the mother. This reluctance to speak to the father has no place in a professional teacher's repertoire. Make as much effort to reach the father (at home or at work) as you do the mother.

When necessary, call the parent at work.

When you can't reach a parent at home by phone or through a note, your next step is to call the parent at work. Don't fall into the trap of feeling that you shouldn't "bother" a parent at work. Think back to the pediatrician analogy. Would a doctor hesitate to call a parent at work about a child's medical problem? Would you hesitate to call a parent at work if the child was physically ill? Your behavioral and academic concerns about your student are every bit as important. Don't avoid action because you're afraid a parent might be angry. Make that phone call with the knowledge that it is your professional duty to do so. The assurance and competence you project when you speak with the parent will help defuse any resentment a parent may feel.

Call the student's emergency number.

The school has on record an emergency phone number for each child. Most often it is the number of a friend or relative who lives nearby. In those cases where a parent doesn't seem to react to your efforts at contacting her, calling this number is an effective method. When a neighbor rings the parent's doorbell to say the school is having a problem with her child, the parent will usually respond immediately.

Send a registered letter.

A registered letter can have an enormous impact on a parent who seems to be avoiding you. It emphasizes the importance of your message and also prevents a parent from saying he never received your communication.

Follow up on the initial contact.

If your child's teacher called you about a problem, wouldn't you want her to call again with a progress report? Wouldn't you want to know what was happening? Follow-up contact with parents is always necessary whether the problem has improved or not. Remember that you are building a relationship you want to grow and improve throughout the year. The parent needs to know that you will not go away—that you care too much about the student to give up.

Contact the parent when the problem behavior has improved.

It is very important for you to let the parent know that there is no longer a problem and then thank the parent for the support and help given. Let the parent know it was your teamwork that helped resolve the issue so quickly and satisfactorily. Most parents never receive supportive feedback from teachers. It's a real boost when they hear that their child has improved and that they played a part in that improvement.

Follow up with a phone call.

When making a call to parents about a student's improvement, be sure to include these points in your conversation:

- Describe the progress the student has made.
- Point out how the parent's cooperation helped the child.

- Tell the parent that you will continue to stay in touch.

Teacher: *Mr. Nelson, this is Ms. Jensen. I just wanted to let you know that since we last spoke, Brian has really improved. He is doing all his work. There is no arguing and no fighting. He seems much happier in class.*

Parent: *That's great news. He seems happier at home, too.*

Teacher: *I want to thank you for all the support you gave. By working with your son at home, and following through, you have helped him make some important changes. You should be pleased with the results.*

Parent: *Thank you. It was worth the effort, and Brian is proud of himself for improving.*

Teacher: *I'll continue to stay in touch. And if you ever have any questions or concerns, please feel free to call me. Again, thanks so much for your support.*

Follow up with a letter.

Although a phone call is the best way to follow up with parents, you may in some circumstances prefer to send home a note. Include the same information that you would in a call.

Sample Follow-Up Letter

Dear Mr. Duffy,

Elliot has had perfect attendance all month. Thank you for cooperating with the school and for supervising him more closely. I know he will have an excellent year. Please call me if you have any concerns at all about his progress at school. I'll stay in touch with you, too.

Sincerely,

Miss Crowe

Contact the parent if the problem has not improved.

If the problem has not improved, you must contact the parent regarding further action. The goal of this phone call will be to agree upon the next steps both you and the parent will take. Once again, write down what you want to say before you make the call.

Begin with a statement of concern.

Teacher: *Mrs. Carroll, this is Mr. Tanaka. I'm calling because I'm worried that Terry is still continuing to fight at school.*

Describe the problem behavior.

Teacher: *He lost his temper again at recess when he did not get his way in a game and he hit a child.*

Describe what you have done.

Teacher: *I've continued to speak with him and work with him on improving his behavior. We've also taken away recess when he does fight.*

Get the parent's input.

Teacher: *What do you do at home when you receive notes from me about his fighting?*

Parent: *I try to ground him. It really doesn't work because he gets so upset. I can't even keep him in his room. He gets so worked up, I can't deal with him.*

Show your understanding and concern.

Teacher: *I understand how difficult that must be.*

Tell the parent what you will do and what kind of support you need.

Teacher: *I feel that we need to work further to help Terry. I think the best thing we can do to help him now is for you to come in and talk with me and Mr. Lowes, our principal. Mr. Lowes is very skilled at helping teachers and parents deal with children who have trouble not fighting. I feel very confident that if you and I work together with him, we can all come up with a solution to help Terry stop his fighting.*

Parent: *Well, I hope you're right. But I don't know if anything will work. That's just the way Terry is.*

Express your confidence.

Teacher: *I understand how frustrated you are. That's why we have to work together to help him. As I said, Mr. Lowes and I have handled many students just like Terry, and I'm confident that we can help him have a better year. I'd like to meet as soon as possible. Could you come in tomorrow at 3:30?*

File your notes and records.

Communication isn't complete until you've filed all notes and records pertaining to your parental contact. This includes your planning sheets, notes taken during the conversation, and any follow-up data you may have. See the guidelines on pages 124 to 127 for maintaining documentation records.

Contacting Parents at the First Sign of a Problem

Reminders

DO

- Use the "your own child" test when you are unsure about contacting a parent about a problem.

- Make a phone call your first-choice means of reaching a parent.

- Make every effort to contact a parent. Don't give up after one or two tries. You can reach a parent if you really want to.

- Always write down what you want to say before you phone a parent.

- Be prepared to describe the specific behavior that is causing problems.

- Let the parent know what steps you've already taken to correct the problem.

- Make sure you ask for the parent's suggestions for how to deal with the problem. Be prepared to adapt your efforts accordingly.

- Be prepared to tell the parent what you are planning to do about the problem.

- Let the parent know that you're confident the problem can be solved.

- Tell the parent there will be follow-up contact from you.

- Follow through with your promise!

DON'T

- Don't apologize for "bothering" the parent. Remember that you are acting in the child's best interests.

- Don't hesitate to call a parent at work if you can't reach her at home.

- Don't try to reach the student's mother only. Contact with fathers is also important.

- Don't make vague statements about the student's behavior.

Contacting Parents
at the First Sign of a Problem
Checklist

Refer to this checklist each time you prepare to make initial contact with a parent about a problem.

HAVE YOU:

☐ Used the "your own child" test to help you decide whether or not to contact a parent?

☐ Written down all the points you want to cover with a parent?

☐ Aggressively tried to contact hard-to-reach parents?

☐ Included the student's father, as well as the mother, in problem-solving discussions?

☐ Made follow-up contact whether or not the problem has improved?

☐ Kept written records of all parent communication that has taken place?

☐ Kept copies of all notes you sent home and received from parents?

Conducting a Problem-Solving Conference

When a phone call or note to a parent doesn't solve a problem, or if a specific problem seems to warrant it, you need to schedule a face-to-face problem-solving conference. This chapter will help you plan and conduct the conference so that it will be more successful.

A problem-solving conference is your opportunity to meet with a parent and discuss a student's specific problem at school. The conference gives you a chance to gather information on the problem and present it to the parent in an organized, professional manner. It also provides an opportunity for you to listen to a parent's input and use that information to help the student. The goal of the conference is for parent and teacher to agree upon a plan of action for solving the student's specific problem.

Plan and conduct the conference.

Step 1: Decide who will be involved in the conference.

The first thing you need to consider is whether or not to include the student in a problem-solving conference. Some teachers try to include the student, others prefer not to. Use your own criteria to determine when the student's presence will be appropriate.

Here are some reasons teachers have for *not* including a student in a parent-teacher conference.

- Teachers may be concerned that the parent will not be able to openly discuss sensitive matters. Parents are often understandably concerned about hurting the child by discussing shortcomings or problems in front of him.

- There may be occasions when a teacher believes that the student's presence would be highly disruptive. This is particularly true in situations involving younger students who cannot sit still, or with older adolescents who may be hostile and verbally abusive throughout the meeting.

There are times, however, when it can be a very good idea to include a student in the conference, as follows. Keep in mind that a student's age and maturity must always be considered.

- **Student input on the problem is needed.** Sometimes you and the parent may need to hear the student's opinion about why he is having trouble in class or with homework. In addition, you may find that when teacher and parent are at a loss for solutions to a student's problem, the student himself may be able to provide an answer. The student may, for example, point out that a seating change could help, or that he needs to be given some specific study skills.

- **Student commitment to change is needed.** Having a student sit in on a parent-teacher conference can help make the student aware of the seriousness of the problem. When the student sees both the parent and teacher taking the time to discuss the problem, she may be convinced that change really is needed. Many teachers find that if they are using a home-school contract (see chapter 13), it is important to have the student be a part of the process.

- **You want to demonstrate that parent and teacher will work together to help the student.** Many students, especially those involved in power struggles, try to play home and school against one another. If this is the case, it is vital that the student be present to hear both parent and teacher say that they will not tolerate the student's poor academic efforts or behavior problems. The student needs to see firsthand that the teacher and parent are a team and that there will be continued, consistent communication between home and school. The student needs to clearly understand that there will be corrective actions imposed at both home and school if he continues to behave inappropriately.

> NOTE: If you do decide that a student's presence at a conference is warranted, you may want to meet with the parent first, then at a suitable point invite the student to come in and continue the conference.

Plan a team conference if it is warranted.

A team conference is one that involves more than one teacher. To help solve a student's problem, middle school and secondary school teachers, as well as some elementary teachers, often need to meet as a team with a parent. The goal of such a conference is not to gang up on a parent or overwhelm her with complaints, but to let the parent know that all of you are in this together, and that working as a team you can solve the student's problem.

In a team conference, one teacher must be designated to serve as facilitator. It will be the responsibility of this teacher to do the following:

Contact the parent to arrange a time for the conference.
Offer flexible time choices.

Conduct a preconference planning session.
Meeting with a group of teachers may be intimidating to a parent. It is vital that every teacher involved is in agreement ahead of time about the goals of the conference and the means of achieving these goals. The preconference planning session is the time to iron out these issues.

Follow these steps:

- **Isolate one or two problems to be discussed.**
  It is not productive to overwhelm a parent with everyone's complaints about the student. You don't want to turn the meeting into a dumping session. Even if there is more than one problem to deal with, narrow down the field to one or two to be discussed at this particular conference.

- **Coordinate documentation that will be presented.**
  The parent needs to see specific documentation of the student's problem behavior from each teacher involved.

- **Write down all the points the team wishes to discuss.**
  It is important that when the team of teachers meets with the parent, you've already worked out an agenda of points to cover. Use a Problem-Solving Conference Planning Sheet (see sample on page 149) to plan what will be said. It is the responsibility of the facilitator to keep the conference focused by sticking to the points on the agenda.

Lead the team conference.
Follow the guidelines for conducting a problem-solving conference. Plan to have all members of the team contribute by addressing different points.

The facilitator must see that the conference stays on track—that the teachers stick to addressing the issues that were planned. The facilitator should also pay attention to the parent's feelings.

In a team-conference situation, it is particularly important that teachers be sensitive to the parent. After all, there's only one of them and several of you. The facilitator must take special care to see that everyone listens to what the parent has to say. Above all, an atmosphere must be generated that instills confidence and optimism. Remember that your goal is to solve the problem and take steps toward getting parent support in the future.

> Whatever the variation of your problem-solving conference, the final two steps remain the same.

Step 2: Plan and write down what you will say to the parent.

Before your meeting, write down the important points you want to cover with the parent. Doing so will help you develop the skill and confidence that will allow you to conduct a more productive conference. Plan to take your notes with you for referral. Doctors look at notes during a consultation. Lawyers do, too. It's perfectly acceptable, and professional, to do so. It most likely will give parents even more confidence in you. The sample Problem-Solving Conference Planning Sheet on page 149 lists the points you should cover in the conference. Use a planning sheet like this to prepare for each problem-solving conference you hold.

As you prepare, keep in mind how a parent may feel at the conference. You are meeting because of a problem, so chances are the parent may be anxious, upset, or worried. Be sensitive to the parent's feelings. A friendly, positive atmosphere will produce more results than an intimidating setting. Once again, make a mental note to put yourself in the position of the parent. Ask yourself, *How would I feel if I were the parent in this situation? How would I want the teacher to treat me?* Then let that awareness guide your words and actions.

Step 3: Gather documentation.

An important part of a problem-solving conference is describing the specific problem and then presenting documentation. Parents often need to see proof that a problem does exist. Make sure you have all your documentation with you at the conference. Have it ordered chronologically so that you can present a clear picture to the parent of what has transpired.

Sample Problem-Solving Conference

Here are step-by-step guidelines for conducting a problem-solving conference:

1. **Begin with a statement of concern, updating the situation.**
    Because a problem-solving conference can be stressful and upsetting to parents, it is important that you begin the conversation by showing your concern for the student rather than just by bluntly stating the problem.

    "Mr. Stein, I'm still worried about John's misbehavior at recess."

Sample Problem-Solving Conference Planning Sheet

Problem-Solving Conference Planning Sheet

Teacher _____ Grade _____

Student's Name _____

Parent(s) or Guardian _____

Date of conference _____

1. Begin with a statement of concern, updating the situation.
2. Describe the specific problem and present pertinent documentation.
3. Describe what you have already done to solve the problem.
4. Get parental input on the problem.
5. Get parental input on how to solve the problem.
6. Tell the parent what you will do to help solve the problem.
7. Explain what you need the parent to do to solve the problem.
8. Let the parent know you're confident that the problem can be worked out.
9. Tell the parent that there will be follow-up contact from you.
10. Recap the conference.

Notes: _____

_____

_____

_____

_____

"Mrs. Davis, I'm still concerned about Jenny's inability to turn in her homework assignments."

2. **Describe the specific problem and present pertinent documentation.** Explain in specific, observable terms what the child did or did not do. Remember that an observable behavior is one that you can watch going on, such as failing to turn in assignments or fighting. Show the parent your records that document the child's behavior. Make sure the documentation is not judgmental and is impartial.

"This week John was involved in four fights. You can see here that he was sent to the office twice on Tuesday and again on Wednesday and Thursday."

"You can see from these records that Jenny did not turn in any math assignments this week."

3. **Describe what you have already done to solve the problem.**
   As you show your documentation, explain how you have dealt with the problem. If appropriate, refer to your classroom discipline plan and point out that you have been acting in accordance with that plan.

   "As you know, I have given John detention each time he's been involved in a fight."

   "I have reminded Jenny that her final report card grade will drop if homework is not turned in. I have also sent her to detention to finish her work."

4. **Get parental input on the problem.**
   Listen carefully to what the parent has to say. As you listen, take special care to show the parent that you respect his opinion. Too often, parents and teachers don't show respect to one another. As a professional, it's up to you to take the lead by showing parents you value what they say. If appropriate, be prepared to adapt your disciplinary strategies to incorporate the parent's comments and suggestions.

   Here are some questions you may want to ask.

   "Has your child had similar problems in the past?" (It may be useful to examine school records to determine if the child did have problems previously and if the parent was aware of them.)

   "Does your child have similar problems at home?"

   "Why do you feel that your child is having this problem?"

   "Have there been any changes (divorce, separation, siblings, a move) at home that could be affecting your child's behavior?"

5. **Get parental input on how to solve the problem.**
   Most parents know their child better than anyone and might have good ideas about how to solve specific problems. Chances are, you'll hear something like "Well, I guess I'll have to do something to make sure he behaves in school." That's your opportunity to move in and enlist their help. Seize the moment.

   Ask the parent:

   "Are you dealing with this problem at home as well? How have you handled it so far?"

   "How do you feel we can work together to help your child solve this problem?"

If a suggestion seems to make sense, show your willingness to use it in your own disciplinary strategies.

"This seems like a good way of dealing with this. Maybe I can do something similar at school. Let me think about this, and I'll get back to you."

6. **Tell the parent what you will do to help solve the problem.**
   You've already explained what you have previously done and what effect it has had. Now explain your new plan of action to resolve this issue. Let the parent know exactly what you are going to do. Then check for understanding to make sure everything is clearly understood.

   "Mr. Stein, since this problem has continued, I am going to change the disciplinary corrective actions for John. From now on, each time he fights he will be sent immediately to the principal and you will be called. He won't receive any reminders first, and he won't be sent to detention."

   "Mrs. Davis, since the problem wasn't solved, I am going to develop a behavior contract for Jenny. Every time she fails to turn in homework, she will go to detention. Every time she does turn in her homework, she will receive a point. Ten points and she's earned a bonus grade."

   NOTE: If there is to be a home-school contract, introduce it now. (See chapter 13 for complete guidelines.)

7. **Explain what you need the parent to do to solve the problem.**
   Now you must explain, just as carefully, what you would like the parent to do to help solve the problem. Be careful not to dispense general parenting advice. Be very specific in your requests for support. Make sure the parent knows that you are asking for help with a specific problem rather than for a change of his parenting style.

   "Mr. Stein, we need to work together to help John improve his behavior. His fights are completely unacceptable. Any time you are called about a fight, I'd appreciate it if you would follow through at home with your own disciplinary measures. Taking away privileges often works to convince children that you mean business. Whatever you choose to do, remember that you must do it consistently and not back down."

   "Mrs. Davis, it is extremely important that we work together to help Jenny get into the habit of turning in all her homework assignments. To do this, I would like you to check each night to see that all assignments are completed. Your signature on her homework will show me that you've looked it over. Please understand, I don't expect you to correct the work, just to make sure that it's complete."

Pay close attention to any parental roadblocks that might appear. (Does the parent sound overwhelmed? Negative? Confused?) Use your communication skills to move the parent past the roadblock.

8. **Let the parent know you're confident that the problem can be worked out.**
   Well-chosen words will punctuate your message with assurance.

   - Use the word *confident* when you speak to the parent.

   - Use both the parent's name and the student's name.

   - Reassure the parent that you are experienced in dealing with this type of problem.

   "Mr. Stein, I am confident that together we can make this a better year for John. I've dealt with many children who have had this problem, and I can assure you that we will be able to turn things around if we are united in our efforts."

   "Mrs. Davis, I feel confident that with both of our efforts we can help Jenny develop more responsible homework habits."

9. **Tell the parent that there will be follow-up contact from you.**
   A parent needs to know that you are going to stay involved. Provide this reassurance by giving a specific date for a follow-up call or note.

   "Mr. Stein, I am going to call you next Monday evening to let you know how things are working out for John."

   "Mrs. Davis, I'll give you a call Friday night to let you know how the week went."

10. **Recap the conference.**
    Write down all agreed-upon actions. Whenever communication takes place, there is always the question of whether each party understands what the other is saying. To avoid confusion and assure that the message was clear, you may need to clarify all agreements. You can do this by restating and writing down what you are going to do and what the parent is going to do. Keep this information in your files. If you feel that it will be helpful to the parent, say that you will mail home a copy of this agreement in a day or two.

    Teacher: *We've agreed to a number of things today. I'll put our decisions in writing and send them home to you. Here's what I've agreed to do: I am going to change the disciplinary corrective actions for John. From now on, each time he fights he will be sent immedi-*

ately to the principal and you will be called. No more reminders. No more detention.

The teacher writes while speaking.

Parent: *And I've agreed to take privileges away from him at home anytime I'm called about John fighting.*

The teacher continues writing.

Teacher: *Okay, I've got it all written down. Mr. Stein, I'd like to thank you for helping me put this plan of action together. Now John will know that we're working together to solve this problem.*

Another example:

Teacher: *Okay, Mrs. Davis. We've agreed to a plan of action here today that will help Jenny do a better job on homework. Here's what I will be doing: I'm going to develop a behavior contract for Jenny. Every time she doesn't turn in her homework, she will have detention. Every time she does turn in her homework, she will receive a point. Ten points, and she will earn a bonus grade.*

To be certain that we both understand what will be happening, I'm going to write down what both of us have agreed to.

The teacher begins writing.

Now, what will you be doing each night to help Jenny handle homework better?

Parent: *Every night, I'm going to check all of Jenny's completed homework. And I'll sign each paper to show you that I've seen it.*

The teacher continues writing.

Teacher: *That's going to be really helpful. When you check her homework each night, Jenny will better understand that both of us are committed to her success in school. I'm sure we'll soon see a difference in her homework habits.*

11. Close the conference.

Thank the parent for coming in to meet with you. Let the parent know that taking the time to improve the child's educational experience is time well spent.

Conducting a Problem-Solving Conference

Reminders

DO

- Bring documentation with you to the conference.

- Be sensitive to a parent's feelings throughout the conference. Listen carefully and make comments to demonstrate that sensitivity.

- Consider whether or not you want the student to be present at the conference.

- Explain problems to parents in observable terms. Be specific.

- Listen to a parent's comments and suggestions. Show your willingness to incorporate them into your plan of action.

- Give parents the materials they need to support your plan of action: stickers, checklists, award certificates.

- Leave parents with hope and confidence.

DON'T

- Don't arrive at the conference unprepared. Make sure you have written down all the points you want to cover.

- Don't have a parent sit on a student-sized chair while you sit in the teacher's chair.

- Don't dredge up incidents from the past.

- Don't overwhelm parents by presenting too many problems. Two or three examples are enough.

- Don't make idle disciplinary threats.

- Don't be condescending. A parent may have a valuable perspective on the problem.

- Don't talk about other students if the parent tries to divert the conversation by placing blame on others.

Conducting a Problem-Solving Conference
Checklist

Refer to this checklist each time you prepare for a problem-solving conference.

HAVE YOU:

☐ Written down what you will say to the parent at the conference?

☐ Decided what you will do to help solve the problem?

☐ Decided what you want the parent to do?

☐ Reminded yourself to listen to what the parent says—to treat him with respect?

☐ Organized the documentation you need to bring to the conference?

☐ Reviewed effective listening skills?

☐ Decided whether or not to include the student in the conference?

If the conference involves more than one teacher, have you:

☐ Designated one teacher to be the facilitator?

continued on next page →

Conducting a Problem-Solving Conference

Checklist (Cont'd)

☐ Arranged to hold a preconference planning meeting with all teachers involved?

☐ Gathered documentation from all teachers involved?

☐ Decided, with the other teachers, on one or two problems to focus on?

☐ Written down what will be said to the parent at the conference?

Using a Home-School Contract

I t's one thing for a parent to agree at a conference to work with you to solve a student's specific problem. It's sometimes quite another to actually succeed at making this partnership work. After the conference is over, after the parent goes home, how do you ensure success? How do you make certain that you meet the goals you and the parent set during the conference? How can you make certain you get the support you need?

The best way to successfully structure a parent's efforts with yours is by using a home-school contract. This chapter will explain the nature of this contract and detail the steps for its construction and use as follows:

- What is a home-school contract?
- When should you use a home-school contract?
- Why is a home-school contract effective?
- How should you write and present a home-school contract?
- Daily communication is a must.

What is a home-school contract?

A home-school contract is a written agreement between teacher, student, and parent. The contract states that the student agrees to a specific behavior. If the student complies with the terms of the contract, she will earn praise and rewards from both the teacher and parent.

Be sure the student understands that both parent and teacher are working together in a team effort to solve a problem. The student knows that if she chooses not to comply with the contract, she can expect predetermined corrective actions from both school and home. The success of a home-school contract demands that both parent and teacher cooperate and consistently enforce it. A home-school contract is an effective technique to use with both elementary and secondary school students.

The examples of home-school contracts presented in this book are based on the behavior management techniques developed in *Assertive Discipline*. While the balanced system of supportive feedback for appropriate behavior and consistent corrective actions for inappropriate behavior established therein is extremely effective, your specific home-school contracts should reflect your approach to behavior management. You are encouraged, however, to establish a discipline plan that doesn't only discipline misbehavior but also rewards improved and appropriate behavior. Furthermore, it is important that the home-school contract you establish suits your personal teaching style and the parent's personal parenting style.

When should you use a home-school contract?

Use a home-school contract to correct behavioral, academic, or homework problems for any age level. A contract is warranted when you can answer yes to any of these questions:

- Have you tried to solve the problem through other means, without success?

- Could the student benefit from a structured system of supportive feedback and corrective actions?

- Does the parent need daily feedback regarding the student's behavior at school?

- Do you suspect that the student receives little supportive feedback at home?

- Have the student's parents asked for help from you in solving the student's problem?

Why is a home-school contract effective?

A home-school contract helps the teacher, parent, and student focus on a specific problem that needs to be solved. Vague comments like "He's always getting into trouble" or "Her behavior is just impossible" don't help a problem get solved. You need to pinpoint exactly what behavior you want from a student. The home-school contract will help you and the parent do just that.

A home-school contract is really a plan of action for helping a student improve his behavior. Parent and teacher decide together which steps they will take to solve the problem. You as the teacher may stress the importance of consistency when disciplining a child for inappropriate behavior. You may stress the value and benefit of supportive feedback and encourage the parent to frequently reward the child for appropriate behavior. You may not,

Sample Home-School Contract

Home-School Contract

Jeffrey Smith promises to stay out of fights on the school yard. Each day the student does as agreed, he can expect the following actions to take place.

From the teacher:

1. Verbal reinforcement
2. One point for each day of appropriate behavior—when 10 points are earned, Jeffrey may spend an extra hour on the computer.
3. A note home to parents telling them of Jeffrey's successful day

From the parent:

1. Verbal reinforcement
2. One point for each day of appropriate behavior—when 10 points are earned, Jeffrey may invite a friend to dinner and a movie.

Each day the student does not do as agreed, he can expect the following actions to take place.

From the teacher:

1. Fifteen minutes detention after school
2. A note home to parents telling them about Jeffrey's behavior that day

From the parent:

1. Loss of TV and phone privileges that night

The contract will be in effect from October 6 to October 17.

Parent's signature: _____

Teacher's signature: _____

Student's signature: _____

however, decide what the parent should do. The home-school contract has to be a true collaborative effort between teacher and parent, where both parties play a part in the outcome.

A home-school contract requires the parent to state, in writing, that she agrees to fulfill the obligations of the contract. Teachers' attempts to solve a student's problem often fail because parents don't carry through at home. The contract will help structure disciplinary responses for parents who don't know what to do to help their child. It gives parents a framework to follow and teachers a means of keeping track of what's going on at home. Once the parent signs the agreement, the teacher is within his rights to inquire if the parent is following through as planned.

Keep in mind that the effectiveness of the contract depends greatly on how it is composed. A home-school contract is not a prefabricated document to be used in any situation with any student and parent. It is a very personal agreement, custom-tailored to meet the needs of a particular situation. Its content is defined cooperatively by the teacher and the parent. A home-school contract is not a means to tell a parent how to raise her child and to impose your own discipline plan. It is not a forum for dispensing parenting advice and changing a parent's child-rearing practices. Instead it is an attempt to incorporate the parent's usual child-rearing practices at home into your disciplinary efforts at school to solve a very specific problem.

How should you write and present a home-school contract?

A home-school contract is a collaborative effort between teacher and parent and should be dealt with as part of a problem-solving conference. Here are the steps to explaining and writing a home-school contract.

Step 1: Introduce the concept of a home-school contract to the parent.

A careful explanation of the contract is vital. Chances are the parent has never even seen one before. Explain right away that the contract is an agreement between you, the parent, and the student and that the purpose of the contract is to help the student succeed in school. Be sensitive. Once again, put yourself in the parent's position and realize that this procedure at first might seem a bit intimidating. Let the parent know that you have successfully used home-school contracts before.

"I feel that the best way to help (student's name) *is for us to put together a home-school contract for him. A home-school contract is a written agreement between me, you, and your child. The contract will state that* (student's name) *agrees to a specific behavior. If he complies with the terms of the contract, he will earn praise and rewards from both you and me. If he chooses not to comply with the contract, he will receive predetermined corrective actions from both school and home.*

"The reason a home-school contract can be so successful is that your child will know that we're working together to help him solve his problem.

Whenever he misbehaves during the day, I'll let you know about it. Likewise, when he behaves appropriately, you'll know about that, too.

"I've used home-school contracts many times in the past and have found them to be successful.

"This is the contract form."

Show the contract to the parent, and let her look it over.

Step 2: Determine how you want the student to behave.

Work with the parent to focus on one or two specific areas of concern. (These should be the same problems you presented to the parent at the beginning of the problem-solving conference.) For example: "I'm concerned about Jeffrey's fighting at recess" or "I'm very concerned that Serena is still not completing her homework assignments."

"Let's begin the contract by focusing on exactly what we need your child to do at school. We've been talking about his problems with (state problem). *We will write down on the contract that* (student's name) *will promise to* (state desired behavior). *Do you have any questions about this?"*

Step 3: Explain the corrective actions you will provide if the student does not comply with the contract.

You must decide what you will do at school if the student chooses not to do what is expected. You should determine your disciplinary measures before the parent arrives for the conference. Explain to the parent that you will use corrective actions each time the student does not comply with the contract.

"I want your child to clearly understand that we cannot allow him to continue a behavior that's not in his best interests. Therefore, I want to spell out exactly what I will do if he chooses not to follow the promise he made in the contract. Here's what will happen at school: Each time he does not comply with the contract, he will stay after school for detention. In addition, of course, a note will go home letting you know what happened."

Write the corrective actions in the contract.

If the parent strongly objects to the disciplinary measures you choose, you need to pause to discuss this. If the parent's objections seem valid, be prepared to adjust your course of action.

For example, if the parent objects because staying after school for detention interferes with a student's need for medical attention, try to agree on a different corrective action. If, however, the parent objects because staying after school for detention will interfere with a social activity, explain that missing the activity will make the corrective action work.

In any case, don't just impose any part of the contract on the parent. The resentment that may ensue will endanger the effectiveness of the entire contract. Always invite, respect, and accept a parent's input.

Step 4: Help the parent choose the corrective actions to provide if the student does not comply with the contract.

The success of the home-school contract depends upon the parent's willingness to follow through at home. This means a parent must be willing to discipline the child if he does not follow the terms of the contract. Be aware that this is often difficult for parents to do effectively. Their disciplinary measures may be extremely inconsistent.

Parents must let their child know that they will not tolerate misbehavior at school. This part of the contract is vital. You must impress upon parents the importance of consistent follow-through.

"Next we need to spell out exactly what you will do at home if this misbehavior continues. You need to choose a corrective action that (student's name) *will receive each time he misbehaves. Choose something that you know he won't like. Parents often choose corrective actions such as loss of TV or phone privileges, grounding, or restricted use of a bicycle or other sports equipment. Think for a minute about what you might choose."*

Write down the corrective actions the parent will use. Discuss the options if the parent is unsure. Try to guide the parent to choose corrective actions that are not too harsh. It is not the severity of the disciplinary measure that ensures its success, but the consistency with which it is imposed. Strongly discourage the parent from using punishment that is physically or emotionally harmful. Make sure the parent understands that corrective actions are not meant to be punishment at all, but a reminder for the child to change his behavior.

Step 5: Explain the supportive feedback you will give to the student for appropriate behavior.

Motivating students to change their behavior requires supportive feedback. A home-school contract must specify the rewards that you, the teacher, will offer at school when the student behaves appropriately.

The best form of positive support, particularly for younger students, is verbal reinforcement. The contract must include that you will consistently reinforce the student when he complies with the terms of the contract. In addition, you may want to couple your verbal reinforcement with tangible rewards. Think about what the student would like to earn. What would motivate him to give that extra bit of effort? You may even want to ask the student what he would like to earn. The more involved the student is in this process, the more success you will have.

Decide on the tangible rewards you intend to use before meeting with the parent.

"I feel very strongly that it is important for your child to receive supportive feedback when he behaves appropriately. Here's what I plan to do: Whenever he does what we have asked him to do, I will let him know that I recognize and appreciate what he has done. I want him to feel proud of his achievement and to understand that appropriate behavior will earn attention. In addition, I will give him an extra incentive. I know that your son would like to earn extra time on the computer. Each day he complies with the contract, I will give him a point. When he gets five points, he will earn 15 minutes of computer time. I think he will want to work toward this reward. Do you agree?

Now let's fill in these provisions on the contract."

Sample Ideas for Tangible Rewards

Ideas for Tangible Rewards

In addition to verbal reinforcement, you may want to motivate students with small tangible rewards. Here are some ideas.

For elementary students:

- Healthy snacks
- Class monitor
- First in line
- Lunch with teacher
- Free reading time
- Extra computer time
- Choose PE activity
- Award certificate
- Stickers

For middle and secondary students:

- Extra computer time
- Gift certificate from a fast-food restaurant
- Free admission to a school function
- Right to be first to leave class
- Gift certificate to school store or another store

Should the parent offer strong objections to the particular supportive feedback you choose, discuss it. If a parent's objections seem valid, be prepared to adjust your plans accordingly. For example, a student may spend many hours at the computer at home, and thus the parent may not want him to earn any more time at the computer at all. Since it is not your place to suggest that the parent restrict computer time at home unless it interferes with your student's performance at school, it might be more effective to try and agree upon another reward. If, however, the parent objects to the fact that the student receives any reward at all for appropriate behavior, calmly explain that supportive feedback will help the student continue his efforts to improve his behavior.

Step 6: Help the parent choose the supportive feedback to provide when the child complies with the contract.

Parents need to understand that their words of praise and support are very important to their child. Emphasize clearly that the parent really is the most important person in the child's life and that her praise means a lot.

"I've told you about the supportive feedback I will give (student's name) *each day that his behavior improves at school. It's just as important that you give supportive feedback at home, too. He really does care about what you think of him. You can do so much to encourage his efforts. I would like to write down on the contract that each day your son behaves, you promise to give him lots of well-deserved praise.*

"In addition, you may find that it would help to give an extra-special reward for good behavior. Choose something that you know your child would like and that you are comfortable giving. You may want to do the same thing I'm doing at school. Each day he behaves appropriately, he will earn a point from you. When he earns five points, he receives the reward. Keep in mind that the gift of your own time might be the most valuable reward you can give. Lots of students really enjoy earning special time alone with Mom or Dad.

"Here are some ideas that kids often appreciate. (Give parent some age-appropriate suggestions. Be sensitive to the parent's financial circumstances.)

- *Going out for lunch with Mom or Dad*
- *Having a friend over for dinner*
- *Staying up late one night*
- *Going out to dinner*
- *Buying a new book*
- *Spending an hour of uninterrupted time with Mom and Dad*

Step 7: Decide on the duration of the contract.

You need to decide how long a contract will be in effect: 1 week, 2 weeks, or 3 weeks. Consider the age of your student and the behavior you are dealing with. Fill in this information on the contract.

Step 8: Sign and present the contract.

The home-school contract must be signed by all involved parties: student, teacher, and parent. At this point, the student may be included in the conference. Carefully explain the terms of the contract to him. Make sure that you and the parent present the contract together, clarifying the fact that you're working as a team.

Show a warm, positive attitude here. Let the student know that you regard the contract as an opportunity to change things for the better, not as a punishment.

"As you know, your mother (or father) *and I are very concerned about* (state the problem). *You have received detention many times, but the problem hasn't been solved.*

"We have put together a contract that will help you behave appropriately at school. This contract is an agreement between you, your mother, and me about what will happen when you do and do not behave.

"Let's read it together."

Read the terms of the contract, making sure the student understands every point.

"As you can see, when you sign this contract, you agree to (state desired behavior). *Each day that you behave according to the contract, you will receive* (state your supportive feedback) *from me at school and* (state parent's supportive feedback) *from your mother at home. On the other hand, on days that you do not comply with the contract, you can expect to receive* (state your corrective actions) *from me at school and* (state parent's corrective actions) *from your mother at home. Your mother has agreed to follow through with these corrective actions because she cares about you and wants you to succeed at school.*

"This is how the contract will work: Each day, I will be sending home a note to your mother telling her how the day went. If everything went well—that is, if you behaved according to the contract—I will tell her so. If the day did not go well, I'll tell her that, too. Do you have any questions you'd like to ask me or your mother?"

Before closing the conference, make sure once again that everyone clearly understands the terms of the contract. Reassure the parent that the next day she will receive a note from you updating the student's progress. End the meeting on a positive, enthusiastic note. Everyone should know that you expect success.

Daily communication is a must.

Once you've filled out and signed the contract, you need to decide how you will communicate with parents. In order to enforce the terms of the contract, you will need to be in daily contact with parents. The best method of daily communication is a home-school note. Each day the contract is in effect, send home a note letting the parent know how the student behaved in school that day. Include in your note:

- Date
- How the student behaved that day
- Actions you took (supportive feedback or corrective actions)
- What the parent needs to do at home (supportive feedback or corrective actions)

Sample Home-School Contract Daily Contact Sheet

Home-School Contract Daily Contact Sheet

Student's name _____

Date _____

Dear _____,

☐ Today your child behaved according to the terms of the contract. I have given the supportive feedback that we agreed upon. Please follow through at home with your supportive feedback.

☐ Today your child did not behave according to the terms of the contract. I have taken the corrective actions that we agreed upon. Please follow through at home with your corrective actions.

Please get in touch with me if you have any questions or would like to talk about the contract.

Sincerely,

Additional comments: _____

_____

_____

_____

Using a Home-School Contract

Reminders

DO

- Use a home-school contract when you want to ensure a parent's continuing involvement in solving a student's problem.

- Write the contract with the parent. Take all comments and suggestions seriously. If appropriate, change your course of action accordingly.

- Decide ahead of time which supportive feedback and corrective actions you will use.

- Prepare to give the parent guidelines and suggestions for choosing the supportive feedback and corrective actions she will use.

- Think carefully about how you will present the concept of a contract to a parent. Make notes on what you will say.

- Be sure to emphasize to the parent how important his praise and support is to the child. Consistent follow-through is the key to making the contract work.

- Send home a note each day telling the parent how the student behaved.

- Always follow through with your plan. When the student misbehaves, use the corrective action you agreed upon. When the student behaves appropriately, she deserves lots of praise.

Using a Home-School Contract

Reminders (Cont'd)

DON'T

- Don't feel that using a home-school contract is asking too much of a parent. This kind of structured involvement is exactly what many parents need to help them discipline their child at home for misbehavior at school. It will also help ensure that the student receives lots of positive attention at home for improvement at school.

- Don't hesitate to call a parent any time you have a question regarding follow-through at home. If you have a feeling that the parent isn't living up to the terms of the contract, give him a call. Remember that the parent's signature constitutes a promise of action. Likewise, don't hesitate to call with good news either. A parent will be most happy to hear from you when things are improving.

Using a Home-School Contract

Checklist

Refer to this checklist when you prepare to use a home-school contract.

HAVE YOU:

☐ Decided on the specific behavior you want from the student?

☐ Decided before the conference on the corrective actions you will include in the contract?

☐ Decided before the conference on the supportive feedback you will include in the contract?

☐ Reviewed the guidelines for writing a home-school contract?

☐ Made some notes about what you will say to the parent(s)?

Chapter 14

Providing Support for Parents' Disciplinary Efforts

No matter what efforts you make at school, without parent support, it will be very difficult for you to get some of your students to behave appropriately and improve academically. Unfortunately, the parents of many of these students are often unable to influence and discipline their own children. In other words, students who need assistance the most at home may get it the least—not because their parents don't want to help, but most likely because they don't know how. To increase these parents' ability to support you at school, you may need to give them some simple strategies to use at home.

Please note the following qualifications:

- Parents must want your help. Do not give parents advice on behavior management unless they have indicated to you that they want to hear your suggestions.

- Do not work with parents on your own if you suspect the child or parent has emotional problems. Keep in mind that you are not a therapist or counselor and that it is not appropriate for you to intervene on your own in circumstances that require professional help. If you suspect that a student, or a parent, needs counseling, involve the school psychologist, counselor, and/or principal.

Begin by once again impressing upon parents that the home environment is one of the most important influences on a child's academic performance and social behavior. A parent's influence can significantly increase a child's interest and success in school. This is true at any age and grade level. Parents need to take the time and make the effort at home to support their children's work at school. It is never too early or too late to get involved.

Make sure the parent understands that you do not want to dispense general parenting advice. Instead, what you want to do is increase the parent's ability to influence the child's performance at school. You are enlisting the parent's help for a specific problem because he is in the unique position to provide this help.

Your attitude has to reflect that you consider the parent the expert on his child. His expertise has been honed by years of experience. His expertise has raised a child with unique qualities beyond the specific behavioral problem you are dealing with.

You, on the other hand, have been trained to use certain behavior management approaches in the classroom. With your guidance, a parent can adapt these techniques for use at home.

Two experts working together can and will support the child to succeed in school.

In this chapter, you will find the following suggestions to help parents back you up at home by supporting your classroom disciplinary measures:

- Provide parents with skills to support your classroom discipline efforts.
- Help parents improve personal relationships with their children.
- Determine if academic assistance is needed.
- Make follow-up contact with parents.

The approaches suggested are simple and straightforward yet extremely effective. However, the following list is by no means exclusive. There are many more techniques available that may be equally effective. Be sure to use your professional judgment when deciding which technique you will present to a parent. In most cases, there's no need for the parent to change his approach to parenting. Present these strategies as helpful hints to be incorporated into the parent's personal parenting style to make it more effective and increase positive influence over his child.

Provide parents with skills to support your classroom discipline efforts.

When you speak with parents, explain that you will be working as a team to help their child improve her behavior. Make parents aware that this kind of teamwork sends a strong message to a child that her parents and the teacher are truly concerned about her success in school, at home, and in life.

Here are some techniques you can offer parents.

1. **Clearly tell your child exactly how you expect her to behave at school.**
   The first skill parents must learn is to clearly communicate how they expect their child to behave at school. Most parents who have trouble disciplining their children are not firm, clear, and direct about what they expect their child to do. Instead, these parents beg, plead, or use empty threats. Frustrated parents often lose their temper and end up yelling at their children. Emotional responses

do not get results. They do not help teach a child to behave appropriately, and they leave the child without clear direction.

Parents need to address the problematic behavior specifically, and impress upon their children in a firm yet calm manner that they won't allow their children to continue acting this way at school.

2. **Avoid arguments. Use the broken-record technique.**
Parents often fall into the trap of arguing with their child whenever they ask the child to do anything. Arguing is not useful. Nobody wins. Parents must stick to their point. A technique called the "broken record" will help these parents avoid fruitless arguments while remaining calm.

The parent keeps repeating what she wants. Every time the child argues, the parent responds with a calm but firm "I understand, but I expect you to . . ." If the child continues to argue after using the broken-record technique three times, the parent needs to postpone the conversation until later.

The broken-record technique can help a parent avoid being dragged into a pointless debate and can help focus the child on the desired behavior.

3. **Back up words with disciplinary action.**
Parents need to understand that simply demanding that their child behave at school may not be enough to ensure that it happens. Parents must learn to back up their words with actions to let the child know they are serious. This means a parent must be willing to impose corrective actions when the child chooses to misbehave. If the parent doesn't follow through, the child may not either.

As stated in chapter 13, the corrective action a parent uses must be something the child does not like, but it must never be physically or psychologically harmful. Suggest taking away privileges, such as watching TV, using the computer, or talking on the phone. Grounding is often effective. With younger children, grounding can mean being restricted to their room without TV for a short amount of time. For older children, grounding can mean not visiting with friends for a certain number of days.

The disciplinary measure must be used consistently. Each time the child chooses to misbehave, he must be given the corrective action. Make sure the parent understands that it is not the severity of a corrective action but its consistency that makes it effective.

It is vital that the parent remains calm when disciplining the child. The corrective action is not meant as punishment but rather to help the child choose more appropriate behavior in the future. Therefore, it is also important that the parent does not carry grudges. The matter must be over and done with once the disciplinary measure has been carried out.

4. **Know what to do when your child begins testing you.**

    When parents begin setting limits and backing up their words with actions, the child will often try to manipulate the parent into backing down by crying, getting angry, or becoming defiant. It's a good idea to prepare parents for this possibility.

    No matter how the child reacts to the chosen disciplinary measure, the parent must remain firm and follow through consistently.

5. **Acknowledge your child for appropriate behavior.**

    As a teacher, you know that corrective actions can stop an unwanted behavior, but that supportive feedback is the key to changing behavior. Parents need to understand that it's just as important for them to give supportive feedback at home as it is for you to give it at school. Unfortunately, parents who are frustrated with their children's behavior may behave negatively when they relate to their children. It is vital that parents understand that they must balance their disciplinary corrective actions with supportive feedback if they are going to teach their child how to behave in a more positive manner at school. This is a very critical point that must be explained carefully.

    Suggest to parents that they praise their child for appropriate behavior. Impress upon them one more time how important parents are to their children and how much their praise will mean.

    Tell parents how helpful it is to combine praise with special privileges or rewards, like staying up late one night, getting extra computer time, or going out to lunch.

    Whatever privilege or reward the parent picks, it must be given consistently. The child must know that just as he can expect a disciplinary action for inappropriate behavior, he can also expect lots of praise and support for good behavior.

Help parents improve personal relationships with their children.

Parental support of a child's work at school is important. Reaching out to a child to listen and learn about his life at school can improve a child's interest in and performance at school.

Many students feel that their parents show no interest in their performance at school and, in fact, don't really care about them at all. Obviously, this is not true. The vast majority of parents care deeply about their children and want to do whatever is in their power to help their children succeed in school.

Suggest to parents that they take 5 minutes a day to do any of the following:

- Ask about the day at school.
- Talk about special school events.
- Just talk about anything.

Advise parents to listen intently when the child talks and nod or ask questions to show interest. The child may begin simply by telling facts about a subject, but as parents demonstrate their attentiveness, the door is opened to increased understanding and sharing of the child's inner life.

Conversations like these can do wonders. They can make a child feel important and valued, they can improve the relationship between parent and child, and they can show that the parent cares.

Suggest to parents that they turn off the TV during dinner and just talk with their children so that they can listen and learn.

Determine if academic assistance is needed.

At the root of some discipline problems lies an academic weakness. For example, if a student comes to school unprepared, without completed homework, the student may easily stray off the task during class. If appropriate, you may want to suggest that the parent provide homework support in tandem with the disciplinary techniques you've recommended. This may take the form of structuring time for the student to do homework (see chapter 7) or considering after-school tutoring programs, either at school or privately.

Make follow-up contact with parents.

Be sure to give parents a follow-up call in a few days to let them know whether or not the student's behavior at school is improving. If problems are continuing, you may want to use a home-school contract (see chapter 13).

Providing Support for Parents' Disciplinary Efforts

Reminders

DO

- Let parents know that if they agree to it, you will provide suggestions for solving their child's behavioral problems.

- Clearly explain to parents how important it is that they follow through with both corrective actions and supportive feedback.

- Suggest that parents reach out to their children and take a more active interest in their children's lives.

- Put yourself in the parent's position throughout conversations with them. Recognize that it may not be easy to receive advice on handling one's own children. Above all, be sensitive to this issue.

DON'T

- Don't give parents advice unless you know they want your suggestions.

- Don't work with parents on your own if you suspect that the child has emotional problems. Involve the psychologist, counselor, or administrator in any efforts you make.

Providing Support for Parents' Disciplinary Efforts

Checklist

Refer to this checklist each time you plan to advise a parent on behavior management techniques to use at home.

HAVE YOU:

☐ Made sure that the parent wants your advice on disciplining her child?

☐ Determined to the best of your ability that the child or parent does not have emotional problems that should be dealt with by a counselor?

☐ Reviewed the guidelines for using the techniques presented in this chapter?

Chapter 15

Dealing With Difficult Situations

I f you haven't already, sooner or later you will encounter parents who make things difficult for you. They may be angry at you or angry at the school. They may be upset by years of perceived (or real) injustices. They may be frustrated by their inability to deal with their children, or they may just be overwhelmed by the stress in their own lives. Whatever the reason, these are parents whose roadblocks threaten to undermine your teaching efforts.

At first, these roadblocks may seem insurmountable. They may appear to be so established that you're sure you've come to a dead end with this parent. Not true. You may be detoured, but you can get back on track.

This book has stressed the importance of developing an effective attitude, holding fast to professionalism and confidence, and recognizing roadblocks. Make sure you are honest about your attitudes toward a parent. Once you recognize a problem that may stand in your way, it will be much easier to deal with the parent in a sensitive yet effective manner.

This chapter presents several ways in which your preparation and the right attitude will see you through even the most difficult situations. They are:

- Prepare in advance to handle angry or distraught parents.

- Use specific communication techniques for difficult situations.

- Use specialized techniques with the most difficult parents.

- Difficult situations *can* be handled successfully.

Now is when you will really see the benefits of what you've learned in *Parents on Your Side*. When you know that you can deal effectively with the most difficult situations, you will know you have learned your techniques well.

Prepare in advance to handle angry or distraught parents.

"This parent came in and just read me the riot act. I had lowered her daughter's grade on a term paper because it was turned in late. But according to the parent, I was to blame. She said I was such a lousy teacher that her daughter didn't know how to do the work. I didn't know how to respond. I was just shaking. And the worst part of it was that all of my students were watching!"

You can't avoid situations like these. You can't even anticipate them. When they occur, you have to be prepared to stand your ground and proceed with confidence. You have to show respect and practice sensitivity at all times, even if a parent does not. You have a lot riding on this moment, and you need to handle it carefully, professionally, and effectively. Your behavior toward the parent has to be exemplary. The well-being of your students depends upon your ability to reach the parent right then and there.

As you've probably told your students, the more thoroughly you learn your lessons, the easier they will be to apply. Those same words pertain to you. When a difficult situation arises, you won't have time to check this book for the right technique or the most effective phrases to use. You must have already learned the words, the attitude, and the techniques and made them part of your teaching style.

Use specific communication techniques for difficult situations.

The following communication skills will help you handle challenging situations. Learn these "how-tos" now, before you need them.

How to disarm criticism

"I do the best job I can for my students. So it's always hard when a parent criticizes my teaching or accuses me of not caring about a child. It hurts. All I can think about is defending myself."

One of the most distressing situations you may find yourself in as a teacher is to be on the receiving end of a barrage of criticism by a parent. It's usually unanticipated, generally uncomfortable, and almost always hurtful.

"You're the cause of my daughter's problem."

"If you knew what you were doing, my son wouldn't be in this mess."

"Your assignments are boring. Why would she want to study?"

"My son's never had problems before, so you must be doing something wrong."

Though comments like these may sting at first, don't become hurt or angry. Stay in control. Recognize that you're dealing with a very distraught parent and that you've got to keep a clear head. Maintain a professional attitude. Don't react in this way:

"Look, I'm doing the best job I can."

"I have 149 other students. I can't spend all of my time with your child."

"I've tried everything. You just don't realize how hard it is dealing with your child."

Reactionary statements like these are not the words of a confident professional. They inspire neither respect nor understanding from the parent. Defensive responses such as these will not help you break down a parent's anger. They only shut down communication and leave the parent no choice but to continue his criticism. And once this cycle begins, it's hard to break.

You need to know how to quickly disarm the criticism and get the parent back on a more productive track.

Follow these guidelines.

If the parent's concern and criticism are justified, accept your mistake.

Sometimes parents are justified in their criticism. Teachers, like anyone else, can make a mistake. It's difficult, however, in the face of an angry tirade, to sit back and think, "Wait a minute, maybe there's some truth to what this parent is saying." You have to take this step, though, if you are to turn a confrontation into a more positive relationship. Stop, think, and then answer the parent honestly and straightforwardly. Don't make excuses or place blame on others. Make your statement clearly.

"You have reason to be angry. I should have contacted you sooner about this problem."

"I feel you are right to be upset. I should not have become so angry with your son the other day."

"You have reason to be frustrated. I was unaware that your child had a problem with this subject, and I should have been."

Admitting your mistakes may make you feel uneasy, but just think about the effect your words can have on the parent. Your response may defuse the parent's pent-up anger and resentment and pave the way for further constructive communication.

If the criticism is incorrect, or only partially correct, follow these steps:

1. **Listen to the parent's complaints without defending or justifying yourself.**

   The parent is angry and needs to talk. Give her the chance to "let it out." Use the effective communication skills introduced in chapter 9. Watch your body language and make sure it reflects openness rather than defensiveness. Look at the parent while she is speaking and make it clear that you are paying attention to what is being said. Let the parent vent her anger or frustration, and show that you understand her point of view by using reflective listening techniques.

2. **Show your empathy and concern by asking the parent for more specific information about the complaint.**

   This is the most useful way to disarm a parent's criticism. By asking questions, you are showing that you care about what the parent is saying. In addition, you are showing that you are able to handle criticism and maintain control in the conversation.

   "That really concerns me. Can you explain more about what you mean?"

   "Can you give me some examples of what you are saying?"

   "Have I done something like this before?"

   Remember that, justified or not, the parent's anger is real. People who are angry need to feel that they are being listened to. Let the parent talk it out.

3. **Now refocus the conversation. Restate the problem behavior, and clarify why it is not in the student's best interests to act this way.**

   After listening, you must refocus the conversation on the child's behavior and move away from the parent's criticism.

   "I understand how upset you are, but we still must help your child get his work done so that he won't fall behind."

   "I hear your point, but your daughter must do her homework or her grades will drop."

   "I can see how frustrated you are with the situation, but we must help your son stop his disruptive behavior in class so that he doesn't continue to get into trouble."

4. **If a parent is still critical or angry, point out that conflict between the two of you is harmful to the student.**

   Be a peacemaker. Explain that continued antagonism is not in anyone's best interests, especially the child's.

"I hear your point, but our disagreeing will only harm Stuart and will not help him solve his problem."

"You have a right to be upset with me, but this won't help Tom."

"I know we don't see eye to eye on this issue, but we can't help Juliette unless we work together."

5. **Finally, if the parent is still upset, suggest that he talk with the principal.**

   Do not allow a critical parent to continue criticizing you. If it becomes clear that the parent is not going to calm down, it is appropriate to have the parent talk to the principal. Just bringing up this alternative may calm down the parent.

   "It seems as though you and I cannot resolve this issue, so maybe you should speak with the principal about it."

This kind of dialogue can disarm criticism.

Here is a conversation between a parent and a teacher who uses the techniques described to disarm the parent's criticism.

Teacher: *I'm concerned about Ted's fighting. He's had three fights with other students in the last 3 days.*

Parent: *He says the other kids pick on him and you don't do anything about it.*

Teacher: (listen, nodding head) *Uh-huh.*

Parent: *It's just not right. He's never had problems in school before. I just don't know what's going on in your class.*

Teacher: (ask for more information while, if appropriate, leaning forward) *Can you tell me more of what he says about how the kids pick on him?*

Parent: *He says Milo and Kevin tease him. He says sometimes you're standing right there and you don't do anything.*

Teacher: (avoid defensiveness in your body language—don't cross your arms, don't lean backward) *Are there any other problems he's had with students that he's told you about where he felt that I did nothing?*

Parent: *He said the same thing happened last week with Jeremy.*

Teacher: *Mr. Cole, I can understand why you would be upset if you were told he was being picked on and I watched and did nothing. I do not allow students to pick on one another. I would never condone this behavior by ignoring it. But we really have to discuss ways to help Ted stop fighting. We both want what's best for him, and if we work together, we can make that happen.*

How to keep the parent conference focused on your goals

"I feel prepared when I begin a conference, but with some parents, it just seems to fall apart. Usually these are parents who have something to complain about. When the conference is over, they've said it all, and I'm left thinking about what I didn't get a chance to say."

Too often, teachers lose control of a conference to a parent who takes over the agenda. Staying in control of a conference means keeping parents focused on your goals. This can be difficult when parents are upset or anxious. They may want to talk about the student's other problems, problems at home, or excuses for why the student is behaving inappropriately. When teachers get sidetracked and allow the parent's goals to divert the conference in a nonproductive direction, little is accomplished.

We will look at two very effective techniques for keeping a conference focused on your objectives. The broken-record and the wrong-person techniques are very effective for keeping a conference in focus. Both techniques can be used in a variety of situations that demand attention be paid to the issue at hand.

Bear in mind that neither the broken-record nor the wrong-person technique should be used in situations in which the parent honestly tries to help solve the problem by offering comments from his own perspective. Do not stifle or cut off communication. Always hear a parent out before you decide whether his concern may be legitimate or just an attempt to change the subject or place blame.

Use the broken-record technique.

You can keep from getting sidetracked by using the broken-record technique. When you use this technique, keep repeating your goals for the conference again and again, like a broken record.

Here's how it's done.

Clearly communicate to the parent that you understand her concerns and goals. Then restate your goal for the conference.

> **Parent:** *I wish somebody at this school would do something about the way the other kids are acting at recess. Every day, Ron comes home telling me about how all the kids are getting him mad and making him get into fights.*

> **Teacher:** (indicate that you understand the parent's concern) *Mrs. Evans, I understand you feel that the other children are picking on your son, but* (restate the goal) **we need to focus on how we can work together to help your son stop fighting at school.**

If the parent continues to focus on different goals, or argues with you, keep repeating your goal without being sidetracked by the parent's comments.

Parent: *But he comes home every day upset about what the other kids say. I want something to be done about this.*

Teacher: *I understand your concern about your child being picked on, but* (use the broken record) **we must focus on how we can stop him from fighting in school.**

Parent: *But he always says it's not his fault. Like I've told you, the kids won't leave him alone.*

Teacher: *At a later time we can discuss the children picking on your son. I understand how concerned you are about that. But our time here today is limited, and* (use the broken record) **we must discuss how we can help him stop fighting in school.**

When you use the broken-record technique, you are showing the parent not only that you recognize her concern, but that you have enough control and confidence to redirect the conference to the problem at hand.

Use the wrong-person technique.

Some parents will try to shift the responsibility for their child's poor behavior onto a teacher's shoulders. They will make it seem as though you, rather than the student, are the one causing the problem. The wrong-person technique can help the parent focus on the real situation. When using this technique, take great care not to sound hostile. Don't put the parent down. Keep your mind on the golden rule, and speak to the parent in the manner in which you would like to be spoken to if the situation were reversed.

Here are two examples.

Teacher: *If Evan chooses to continue to misbehave, I will be forced to keep him after school.*

Parent: *Wait just a minute. You can't do that. If you keep him after school, he'll miss the bus. Then I'll have to leave work to pick him up. If I don't work, I don't get paid.*

Teacher: *Mr. Curtis,* **I think you're talking to the wrong person.** *If you don't want to miss work, you'll have to talk to Evan about that. If he adjusts his behavior, he won't have to stay after school.*

Teacher: *Kristin broke a class rule three times today. That means she will have to stay 15 minutes after school tomorrow.*

Parent: *I'm sorry, but you can't have Kristin stay late tomorrow. She has soccer practice.*

Teacher: *Mrs. Kelly,* **I think you're talking to the wrong person.** *If Kristin does not want to stay after school, she will have to learn to follow the school rules. Otherwise, I have no choice but to keep her after school.*

As mentioned before, neither the broken-record nor the wrong-person technique is meant to shut down the lines of communication. In fact, it is extremely important that you always invite, listen to, and, if appropriate, accept a parent's input.

How to get a commitment from noncooperative parents

Getting support from a noncooperative parent may depend on more than disarming criticism or keeping the conversation focused. At some point, you will have to get a commitment from the parent to support you. This can be difficult, especially when the parent is still angry, upset, or overwhelmed.

There are specific steps you can take to motivate these parents to support you. You need to let parents know:

- Why it is in their child's best interest that they support you

- Why you, as a teacher, cannot handle a problem on your own

- What the outcome will be for the child if the parent does not work with you

Here's what to do:

1. **Emphasize that you cannot solve the child's problem on your own.**
   You must clearly explain to the parent that you are limited in your ability to motivate her child to improve behavior or classroom performance. Parents must understand that the greatest power to affect change lies with them.

   "I want to be very clear with you. As a teacher, there is only so much I can do to motivate your child to behave at school. I can promise you that I will do everything in my power to help your child. But you must understand that you are really the one(s) who can make the difference."

2. **Point out that the parent is the most influential person in a child's life.**
   Stress to parents that they are truly the most important people in their child's life.

   "You are the most important person in your child's life. What you say to your child and what you expect of him make a tremendous difference in how he looks at himself. You have the ability to turn things around for your child. But to do that you must be willing to support my efforts here at school."

3. **Present the negative outcome you feel will occur if the parent does not support you.**

   Sometimes you have to lay it on the line. A parent who won't get involved is jeopardizing the child's success in school—and needs to know what that can mean. Too often, teachers avoid letting parents know the potential negative consequences of their uninvolvement.

Here are some typical problems students have, and the potential short-term and long-term negative outcomes.

Problem: The student will not do homework.
Short-term negative outcomes:
The student will fall behind in class.
The student will fail tests.
The student will earn poor grades.
Long-term negative outcomes:
The student may be held back in school.
The student will never reach academic potential.
The student has greater potential for dropping out of school.

Problem: The student fights with peers.
Short-term negative outcomes:
The student will continue to receive detention at school.
The student will have fewer and fewer friends.
The student will face suspension.
Long-term negative outcomes:
The student's self-esteem will decrease.
The student will never learn to deal appropriately with conflict.
The student will face the real possibility of expulsion later.
The student will not get along with coworkers as an adult.

Problem: The student is chronically tardy or truant.
Short-term negative outcomes:
The student will fall behind academically.
The student may eventually be suspended.
Long-term negative outcomes:
The student may be held back.
The student may eventually drop out of school.

If necessary, here's what to say to parents.

"It's my responsibility to tell you what you can expect to happen if you don't support my efforts to help your child. Your child is not turning in any homework assignments or classroom assignments. Because he's not doing his work, he's not keeping up in class, and he's failing his tests.

Unless the situation changes, he will fail this subject. And that means a strong possibility of being held back next year.

"Mrs. Rey, those are just the short-term consequences he faces. I must also tell you that students who are held back for these reasons run a much greater risk of ultimately dropping out of school. And the long-term consequences of that are loss of self-esteem, poorer choices of jobs, and a life that just isn't as full of promise as it could have been."

Only present the negative picture of the consequences of uninvolved parenting if all else fails. Usually it is best to approach a reluctant parent with drawing the positive picture that you will create together if the parent gets involved and supports your efforts to help the child at school.

How to deal with a parent who makes an unscheduled visit to school

"I was standing in front of the class, giving a social studies lecture, when this parent roared through the door demanding that I talk to him right then and there. He was obviously ready to explode. I wasn't sure what to do."

Few incidents are as upsetting as having a parent barge into your classroom or stop you in the hall on the way to class demanding to discuss an issue with you on the spot. You are caught off guard, students are present, and the parent may be angry and impatient. This is a situation that you must handle skillfully, otherwise it may escalate and become extremely unpleasant for you, the parent, and the student(s).

Here are some very simple techniques to use when handling these situations:

1. **First, be sensitive to the parent's concerns.**
   Keep this in mind: No matter how inappropriate a parent's behavior may be, he obviously must be upset or anxious to have come to school in this manner. If at all possible, stop what you are doing and listen. Put yourself in the parent's place. Be sensitive to what he is saying.

   "Mr. Santiago, you must be very upset to come here today to talk to me."

   "Mrs. Burke, I can see that you are very worried about Tracy's grades, or you wouldn't be coming to school like this."

2. **Let the parent know that his concerns are too important to discuss at this time.**
   Defuse the parent's anger. Let him know that you, too, want to discuss the problem, but that you would prefer to schedule a meeting at a time that is more conducive to finding a solution.

"I hear how upset you are about Paul's suspension. This issue is too important to discuss now when I've got 25 students here. We need to find a time when we can discuss it in more detail."

"I hear how upset you are with how I dealt with your daughter. This is too important to discuss now when I have to be in class in 2 minutes. We need to find a time when we can meet and talk."

3. **Set a time with the parent to talk about the problem.**
   Be very careful not to let the parent feel that you're putting her off. Assure the parent that you want to discuss the issue further. Tell the parent exactly when she can expect to hear from you.

   "I will call you as soon as school is over today, and we can discuss it further."

   "Could you please wait for me in the office? I have a break in 15 minutes. I'd like to talk to you about setting a time when we can meet."

   "I will call you at home tonight. We'll make an appointment to get together and discuss this problem."

4. **If necessary, get administrative help.**
   If the previously mentioned techniques do not work, and the parent stays in the classroom or continues to follow you through the halls, get help from the principal or vice principal immediately. If necessary, give a note to a student to take to the office asking for assistance. This is especially important if a parent seems out of control and threatens you in any way. Under no circumstances should you stand there and allow a parent to verbally abuse or threaten you.

Here's a sample conversation with a parent who makes an unscheduled visit.

Below is an example of a teacher dealing effectively with an angry parent who has made an unscheduled visit to school.

The teacher is walking in the hall on her way to class.

Parent: *Mrs. Shelby, I want to speak with you right now. How in the _____ can you suspend my daughter? What is your problem?*

Teacher: *Mrs. Webster, can you explain what you mean?*

Parent: *Yes, I can explain what I mean. You sent Denise home. I had to leave work. I really can't believe this. You are on my kid's case every single day. I've had it with you and this school.*

Teacher: *You seem very angry and upset.*

Parent: *You're right about that. I've had it.*

Teacher: *Mrs. Webster, this issue is too important for us to discuss now. I'm on my way to class. I want to talk to you about this in greater detail, but we'll have to talk later.*

Parent: *I want to talk about it now.*

Teacher: *I understand, Mrs. Webster, but this is much too important for us to discuss now. I will call you as soon as school is out today at 3:30. Will you be home?*

Parent: *Well, I won't be home. I have to go to work and make up the time I've lost because you suspended Denise.*

Teacher: *Then can I call you at work?*

Parent: *No, you know you can't call me at work. I'm in enough trouble there already.*

Teacher: *Then what time do you get home from work?*

Parent: *About 7:00.*

Teacher: *Then I'll call your home tonight at 7:30.*

Parent: *You'd better do that!*

Teacher: *I promise I will call you at 7:30 tonight. I hear how upset you are and I want to help Denise as much as you do.*

How to handle phone calls from parents

"It's one thing for me to make the phone call to a parent. I can prepare myself and take charge of the conversation. It's a lot harder when I get a message that a parent wants me to call him. I may not know what the parent is concerned or upset about. I have to be ready for anything."

You've learned how to structure a conversation when you call a parent about a problem. But what happens when the parent calls you? Obviously, you can't plan exactly what you will say. Every phone call from a parent is different. You can, however, be prepared to handle the parent's emotional state as well as take steps toward solving the problem.

Here are some guidelines to follow.

1. **Listen to what the parent has to say.**
   If a parent calls you, she is concerned about something. At the beginning of the conversation, just listen to what the parent has to say. Don't interrupt or try to cut the parent's comments short. Listen carefully and take notes.

2. **Be sensitive to the parent's concerns.**

   You may feel that the parent is overreacting to something. You may feel that she is being overly protective. You may even feel that the parent is being manipulated by the child. That doesn't matter. What does matter is that you make sure that anything you say reflects an awareness of the parent's emotional state and her concerns about this issue. Under no circumstances should you make value judgments. For example, never say "It's ridiculous for you to be upset," or "There's no reason for you to be concerned." Comments like these will alienate the parent and hinder further productive conversation.

3. **Use "disarming criticism" techniques if necessary.**

   Review the techniques described earlier in this chapter. These techniques can be used just as effectively in a phone conversation as in a face-to-face conference. Listen to the parent's concerns, ask for more information, and be empathetic to her feelings. Under no circumstances should you become defensive, try to blame the student, or tell the parent she is wrong in calling. Handle the situation well and you may open the door to future positive communication with this parent.

4. **If you did something wrong, apologize.**

   If the parent has a legitimate concern, the best technique is to simply apologize for making a mistake. Don't become defensive. Don't minimize your actions. Apologize clearly to the parent and reassure her that such actions will not occur again.

5. **If the parent is misinformed, point out the facts.**

   Sometimes a parent may call because of something the child says about your classroom, your teaching, or other students. The student's reporting may be inaccurate, but it is still very important that you listen to the parent's concerns before gently but firmly pointing out the truth.

   "Mrs. Debs, I understand that Cleavon told you he has been given five worksheets to do in 10 minutes and that there's no way he can finish them on time. The truth is, Mrs. Debs, that he and the other students have been given two worksheets that can easily be done in the time allowed if the students stick to their work."

   "Mr. Lombardi, I understand that Benjamin said he was singled out and embarrassed in front of the whole class. I understand that he may feel that way, but here is what happened. He was shouting in class. I walked over to him and, very quietly and privately, told him that he had a choice to either stop shouting or sit away from the other children. He continued to shout, and so he was told to sit in the time-out spot."

6. **Do not make quick decisions.**
   When a parent is upset, she is likely to want you to make a quick decision to change something: your discipline methods, your teaching methods, your curriculum, your classroom organization, and so on. Unless you agree that the particular situation warrants immediate action, do not allow the parent to pressure you into making changes before you've carefully thought them through. Let the parent know you hear what she is saying and you understand the concern, but that you want to think about the situation before taking any action.

   "Mrs. Rogers, I hear what you are saying about changing Stephanie's reading group. I want to give this situation some thought. I will call you tomorrow to discuss it further."

   "Mr. Ikura, I understand you want Greg's seat changed. There's some merit to what you are saying. I want to think about the effect it would have on him, and I will talk to you about it tomorrow."

7. **If appropriate, ask the parent to come in for a conference.**
   If a parent raises an issue that cannot be easily resolved in a brief phone conversation, ask her to come in for a conference to discuss it further. This will communicate to the parent your concern and interest in what she has to say.

8. **Admit you do not have all the answers.**
   If the parent raises an issue regarding a student's academic performance or behavior that you do not have an answer for, do not hesitate to say so. You don't have to pretend to know everything. However, you should reassure the parent that you understand her concern and will look into the matter further.

   For example:

   "I hear what you are saying. I do not have an answer, but I will meet with the (principal/psychologist/counselor), and I will contact you again with some information that can help your daughter."

   "I hear what you are saying. I do not have an answer, but I will speak with the director of the after-school care program and get back to you with some ideas for helping your son."

9. **Thank the parent for calling.**
   Whatever the nature of the conversation, let the parent know that you appreciate the fact that she called. Try to end the conversation on as positive a note as possible.

   "Thank you for bringing this to my attention. I will look into it and call you with a response tomorrow."

"I understand that this is a difficult situation. I appreciate your telling me how you feel about it."

Use specialized techniques with the most difficult parents.

"I have one parent this year that I can't seem to reach, no matter what I do. She avoids me, won't answer my calls, and when I do get hold of her, she makes it clear that she wants nothing to do with me or the school. Unfortunately, her son is on his way to losing it all. I can't let that happen—not until I've tried everything I possibly can."

The ideas, suggestions, and techniques presented in *Parents on Your Side* will enable you to get 98% of parents on your side. The remaining 2% are the hardest of all to handle. You may need to employ additional techniques if you are to have any chance of successfully reaching these parents.

> NOTE: The methods presented in this chapter should only be used with administrative support.

Method 1: Take the child home or to the parent's place of work.

If calling the parent doesn't produce results, try doing what the principal did in the following situation:

> George Cotter was the classic fifth-grade troublemaker. He had been a problem since he had transferred to the school at the beginning of the year. His father refused to cooperate when contacted by George's teacher.
>
> One day, George threw a chair across the room and missed hitting the head of a fellow student by three inches. The principal, Mrs. Burns, was notified. George was removed from class, and suspension proceedings began. The principal phoned Mr. Cotter at work. She spoke first to his supervisor, who said Mr. Cotter couldn't come to the phone. Mrs. Burns would not be put off. She told the supervisor that there was an emergency at his son's school. Mr. Cotter came to the phone within 2 minutes.
>
> Here is the conversation that ensued.
>
> **Principal:** *Mr. Cotter, this is Mrs. Burns, the principal at George's school. Your son was involved in a serious incident today.*

We need you to come to school immediately and help us work out this problem.

Mr. Cotter: *Hey, why are you calling me at work for something like that? I can't come to school now. I've got to work for 5 more hours.*

Principal: *When your son causes problems during our working day, you will have to leave your job and help us solve the problem.*

Mr. Cotter: *I can't do that. If I leave the office now, they'll dock my pay.*

Principal: *Mr. Cotter, you're talking to the wrong person. Every time George chooses to disrupt his class, I'll have to call you and ask you to take him home. If you don't want to be called, I suggest you talk to him about following the rules. He's becoming a serious problem, and the school can no longer be responsible for him.*

Mr. Cotter: *Wait a minute. That kid is your problem from nine to three.*

Principal: *No, Mr. Cotter. George is your responsibility 24 hours a day. You have a choice. Either you come to school now, or I'll be forced to bring George to you.*

Mr. Cotter: *Very funny. I'm not leaving work, and I don't want you to call me here ever again.*

Principal: *You leave me no choice. Good-bye, Mr. Cotter.*

The principal took care of some last-minute details, ushered George to her car, and drove to the father's place of employment. It was a long drive, about 10 miles away, but Mrs. Burns was determined to solve the problem of George's behavior once and for all.

Mrs. Burns took George into the manager's office, explained the situation to him, and Mr. Cotter was summoned. Seeing his son and Mrs. Burns standing next to his angry manager was very upsetting to Mr. Cotter. He had no choice. He took his son home and lost a day's pay.

The father in this situation was so greatly inconvenienced that he realized the teacher and principal meant business, and he finally agreed to work with the school to change his son's behavior. At a meeting with the parent, teacher, and principal, a contract was formulated to improve George's behavior. Mr. Cotter agreed to provide discipline whenever he received notice that his son was disruptive in school. Rewards for good reports were also agreed upon. The principal, teacher, parent, and student all signed the contract. In addition, the school arranged for regular meetings between George and the guidance counselor. Within 3 weeks, the problem was solved.

NOTE: Whenever you need to take severe measures such as this to ensure parental support, have the guidance counselor follow up on the home situation. There is always the possibility that the child may be physically or mentally abused. Report any suspicion of child abuse to the proper authorities.

Method 2: Have the parent monitor student behavior at school.

Some parents simply will not believe their child is a serious problem at school. Others absolutely refuse to do anything about it. In these cases, offer parents a choice—either they come to school and monitor their child, or the school will have to suspend the child. If the parent agrees, have her sit in on every class with the student, including cafeteria and gym. (Note: Use this method with older students only. Younger students may find having Mom or Dad in class pleasurable.)

To have its greatest effect, the parent must continue coming to school until the student shows improvement or the parent agrees to help.

This method is successful because:

- The parent sees exactly how the student behaves in school.
- The parent is usually inconvenienced and eventually agrees to help.
- The student feels pressure from peers about having her parent at school and begins to behave.

Method 3: Detain students after school, and have parents sign them out.

A frequently used corrective action for students who severely misbehave is to detain them after school. Then, when the detention period ends, the parent is required to come to school to sign the student out. A parent who has to leave work to pick up his child may be inconvenienced enough to work with the school to improve the child's behavior. Always give parents 24 hours notice before using this method.

Method 4: Have parents escort truant students to school.

If a student is continually truant and the parent has not cooperated in solving the problem, offer a choice. The parent must bring the child to school each morning and sign him in, or the child will be suspended.

Method 5: Visit the student's home.

A home visit is an effective positive technique to use with parents. Going to a student's home to deliver good news or get acquainted with parents is one of the best means at your disposal to demonstrate that you care about a student and her success. A home visit is also a powerful technique to use with parents you are having trouble reaching or dealing with. A home visit gives you the opportunity to sit down with a parent in his own home and discuss the problem at hand. The visit shows the parent you care enough to go out of your way to solve a problem. The visit shows that you mean business.

Follow these guidelines:

1. Do not arrive at a student's home unannounced. Make every effort to set up an appointment. Ask your administrator for help if you are unable to reach the parent.

2. As with any other conference, be prepared. Write down all points you wish to cover with the parent and bring your notes and documentation with you.

3. Review guidelines for disarming criticism and keeping a conference focused on your goals.

4. Keep a positive and professional attitude. Listen carefully to the parent's concerns and be sensitive to what he says.

5. At the end of the visit, let the parent know that there will be follow-up contact from you. Once having made this effort, you will want to do all you can to keep this parent involved.

Difficult situations *can* be handled successfully.

Dealing with difficult parents may be unsettling, but when situations are handled with skill and confidence, you can move toward a productive outcome. As was stated at the beginning of this chapter, these situations are the ones that will really test your professionalism and confidence.

If you speak and act with confidence, if you've learned to recognize and deal with your own roadblocks, if you've practiced and honed your own communication skills so you can recognize and move parents past their roadblocks, then you have indeed achieved the ability to handle difficult situations with parents. Getting even reluctant parents on your side will greatly improve your students' chances for success.

Dealing With Difficult Situations

Reminders

DO

- Make sure you learn and review the techniques of this chapter frequently to make sure you have them at hand when the need arises. Preparation is key.

- Always show respect, practice sensitivity, and above all, listen to the parents' concerns.

- Disarm criticism.

- Keep conferences focused by using the broken-record and wrong-person techniques.

- Get commitment of reluctant parents by impressing upon them how important their involvement is to their child's success.

DON'T

- Don't be defensive when facing a parent's criticism. If it's valid, apologize and adjust your behavior accordingly. If it's not, gently explain your rationale to the parent and move her toward commitment to changing the child's behavior.

- Don't allow a parent to corner you in the hallway or during a class. If a parent is upset, set a time that's more appropriate for discussing the problem.

- Don't make rash on-the-spot decisions. Always allow time for you to think about the best course of action.

Dealing With Difficult Situations
Checklist

HAVE YOU:

☐ Learned and thoroughly reviewed the guidelines regarding dealing with difficult situations?

☐ Reviewed the communication skills presented in chapter 9?

☐ Discussed with the administration which procedures to follow should a parent come to school and abuse or threaten you?

☐ Made sure you've done everything in your power to help a student adjust his behavior, so it won't ever escalate to a difficult situation?

Conclusion:
Ending the Year
on a Positive Note

● ● ●

Throughout this book, we have presented many techniques to help you implement a positive parent involvement plan that will carry you successfully from the first day of school to the last. The end of the year is the time to put it all together and take those final steps that will put the finishing touches on a noteworthy school experience.

This chapter will show you how to take the opportunity to make final, meaningful contact with parents and students. You will learn how to do the following:

- Provide a positive conclusion to the school year.

- Take pride in a job well done.

Keep in mind that you're not just ending one year; you're opening the door for all the years ahead. The effects of everything you've done this year are cumulative. The roadblocks you've cleared won't be roadblocks to the next teacher. What a step forward that is for everyone.

Provide a positive conclusion to the school year.

What you do as the year comes to a close will ensure that your students and their parents move forward with the best possible attitude toward school, education, and teachers. Don't let your involvement with parents slide during this period. Carry through with the professionalism and care you have demonstrated all year long.

Make Open House a parent thank-you event.

Just as Back-to-School Night set the stage for a year of dynamic parent involvement, Open House in the spring can serve as a retrospective of all that's been accomplished. Traditionally, Open House is a time for parents to tour the classroom with their children, look at their work, and chat amiably with the teacher and other parents. Now that you have parents on your side, it's time to add a new component: a heartfelt thanks to parents for their support.

Let "Thanks to you, it's been a great year" be your theme. Carry it through on the invitations you send home and on signs or banners you place in the classroom. Have students write notes to parents thanking them for all their help. At Open House, present parents with small thank-you favors.

- Have a basket of apples by the door with a sign that reads, "An apple from the teacher to the best team of parents ever!"

- Have a friend serve as photographer and take an instant photo of each parent and child. Slip each photo into a construction paper frame that says, "Thanks to you, it's been a great year."

Above all, make sure every parent leaves with the knowledge that his help has been noticed, appreciated, and worthwhile.

Send end-of-the-year notes to students.

"It was 25 years ago, but I still remember the note my teacher Mr. O'Leary wrote to me. It made me feel terrific. Finally, after all was said and done, I knew he thought well of me, and that meant a lot. As a matter of fact, I still have that note somewhere."

—Parent

Your words can have a lasting effect on students of any age. At the end of the year, take the time to give your students the gift of a few thoughtfully chosen sentences.

Don't view this correspondence as a perfunctory duty. Get excited about it. You are launching your students into their future. Fuel their journey with the best, most encouraging words you can. Chances are, if you were able to look ahead 25 years, you'd find some of your messages tucked away in boxes and drawers. And that speaks volumes about how the child felt when he received it.

"My 7-year-old daughter came running into the house waving a letter addressed to her. She kept shouting, 'It's from Mrs. Montoya! It's from Mrs. Montoya!' And that's just what it was—a letter from her teacher 4 weeks after school was out. You should have seen the smile on her face. She must have read and reread that letter a dozen times. Now it's pinned up on her bulletin board."

—Parent

Send thank-you notes to parents.

You've enlisted their support all year long. Now let them know how valuable their involvement and interest have been. This final contact from

Sample End-of-the-Year Notes to Students

Roberto:

I've watched you work hard this year to achieve your goals. I know it hasn't been easy, but you have succeeded admirably. I am proud of you, and I am proud to have been your teacher.

Sincerely,

Mr. Gonzales

Dear Jessica,

Thank you for all the things you did this year that made life in Room 9 so pleasant. I love the big picture and the poem you gave me. It will always remind me of the fun we had planning our model community. You were such a responsible mayor!

You are a talented and creative artist, Jessica, and a hardworking student. It has been my pleasure to have been your teacher.

Your friend,

Miss Walker

you is exceedingly important. Remember that this parent will be a parent in someone else's class next year. Do everything you can to pass along a group of parents who feel that their involvement was appreciated and who are eager to continue that involvement.

Call parents with whom you've worked to solve specific problems.

Take a moment at the end of the year to think about those parents with whom you've worked to solve specific problems. These parents deserve an extra-special pat on the back for the efforts they have made on behalf of their children. Make sure they get recognition from you. Review the progress made throughout the year. If appropriate, give guidelines for continued success. Above all, thank these parents for working with you to solve their children's problems. Point out the difference their supportive involvement made.

Sample End-of-the-Year Notes to Parents

Dear Mrs. Marcum:

This year has been especially successful for Jeff. I hope you realize what a big part you've played in that success. Once Jeff began doing his homework assignments, he found that he could keep up with class discussions and do better on tests. You've seen the results on his report card. Thanks again for giving him the message that homework must be done! Hope your summer is terrific.

Sincerely,

Mr. Amaral

Dear Mr. and Mrs. Avery:

It's hard to believe this terrific year has ended. I have so enjoyed working with both of you. You've been generous with your time and expertise. Our World Bazaar wouldn't have been the same without the wonderful posters you painted for us. Have a wonderful summer. I look forward to seeing you at school events next year.

Sincerely,

Mrs. Pollard

Take pride in a job well done.

You have set a new standard in education. Through your conscientious efforts to form a partnership with parents, you have demonstrated that quality education is a shared responsibility. You have taken the lead with confidence and professionalism. Be proud of your accomplishments. Know that the parents and students you have worked with will move ahead with a more positive attitude toward education. You have made a difference in the lives of your students and their parents.

You are an effective teacher.

Ending the Year on a Positive Note

Reminders

DO

- Make Open House a thank-you event.
- Send end-of-the year notes to parents and students.
- Call parents you worked with regarding specific problems.
- Use the end of the year to further a positive relationship with students and parents that will last for years to come.

DON'T

- Don't underestimate the importance of a simple thank-you.
- Don't underestimate the work you've done to create a good relationship with parents. It is important to other teachers as well.

Ending the Year on a Positive Note

Checklist

HAVE YOU:

☐ Thanked all parents who helped you throughout the year?

☐ Sent a note to parents who didn't attend Open House?

☐ Called parents who helped you with specific problems?

☐ Sent a special note to each student?

Recommended Reading
and Bibliography

Barth, R. (1979). Home-based reinforcement of school behavior: A review and analysis. *Review of Educational Research, 49*(3), 436–458.

Bridgman, A. (1985, February 6). States launching barrage of initiatives, survey finds. *Education Week,* 11–29.

Bronfenbrenner, Urie. (1966). *A report on longitudinal evaluations of pre-school programs.* Washington, DC: Department of Health, Education and Welfare.

Brookover, W. B., & Gigliotti, R. J. (1988). *First teachers: Parental involvement in the public schools.* Alexandria, VA: National School Boards Association.

Bumstead, R. A. (1982, March). Public or private? What parents want from their schools. *Principal,* 39–43.

Canter, L., & Canter, M. (1985). *Assertive discipline resource materials workbook.* Santa Monica, CA: Lee Canter & Associates.

Canter, L., & Canter, M. (1988). *Assertive discipline for parents.* New York: Harper & Row.

Canter, L., & Canter, M. (2001). *Assertive discipline: Positive behavior management for today's classroom.* Bloomington, IN: Solution Tree Press.

Canter, L., & Hausner, L., (1987). *Homework without tears.* New York: Harper & Row.

Caplan, N., Whitmore, J., Bui, Q., & Trautmann, M. (1985). *Scholastic achievement among the children of Southeast Asian refugees.* Ann Arbor, MD: Institute for Social Research.

Cavarretta, J. (1998, May). Parents are a school's best friend. *Educational Leadership, 55*(8), 12–15.

Chavkin, N. F. (1998, Spring/Summer). Making the case for school, family, and community partnerships: Recommendations for research. *School Community Journal, 8*(1), 9–21.

Chavkin, N. F., & Williams, D. L., Jr. (1988). Critical issues in teacher training for parent involvement in education. *Journal of Sociology & Social Welfare,* 17–28.

Chavkin, N. F., & Williams, D. L., Jr. (1989, October). Essential elements of strong parent involvement programs. *Educational Leadership,* 18–20.

Chira, S. (1993, June 23). What do teachers want most? Help from parents. *The New York Times,* p. 7.

Clapp, B. (1989). The discipline challenge. *Instructor, XCIX*(2), 32–34.

Coleman, J., et al. (1966). *Equality of educational opportunity.* Washington, DC: Office of Education.

Collins, C. H., Moles, O. C., & Cross, M. (1982). *The home-school connection: Selected partnership programs in large cities.* Boston: Institute for Responsive Education.

Epstein, J. L. (1993). *Effects on parents of teacher practices in parental involvement.* Baltimore: Johns Hopkins University Center for Social Organization of Schools.

Epstein, J. L. (1995, May). School/family/community partnerships: Caring for the children we share. *Phi Delta Kappan, 76*(9), 701–712.

Epstein, J. L. (1996). Advances in family, community, and school partnerships. *New Schools, New Communities, 12*(3), 5–13.

Epstein, J. L. (1997, September/October). Six types of school-family-community involvement. *Harvard Education Letter.* [Online]. Available: http://www.edletter.org/past/issues/1997-so/sixtypes.shtml.

Epstein, J. L. (1999). *Family partnerships with high schools: The parents' perspective.* [Research Report No. 32]. Baltimore: Center for Research on the Education of Students Placed at Risk.

Farkas, S., & Johnson, J. (1999). Looking at the school: Public agenda asks African-American and white parents about their aspirations and their fears. *Arts Education Policy Review, 100*(4), 24–27.

Goodlad, J. I. (1982, May). An agenda for improving our schools. *Executive Review 2.*

Hanson, S. L., & Ginsburg, A. (1985). *Gaining ground: Values and high school success.* Washington, DC: U.S. Department of Education.

Harris, L. (Ed.). (1987). *The Metropolitan Life survey of the American teacher: Strengthening lines between home and school.* New York: Metropolitan Life Insurance Company.

Henderson, A. (1987). *The evidence continues to grow.* Columbia, MD: National Committee for Citizens in Education.

Henderson, A. (1995, March/April). Families and student achievement. *PTA Today, 20*(4), 12–14.

Herman, J., & Yeh, J. (1980). *Some effects of parent involvement in schools* (ED 206 963). Center for the Study of Evaluation, Graduate School of Education, University of California at Los Angeles.

Hewison, J., & Tizard, J. (1980). Parental involvement and reading attainment. *British Journal of Educational Psychology, 50,* 209–215.

Hispanic Policy Development Project. (1990). *Together is better.* New York: Author.

Institute for Responsive Education. (1982). *The home-school connection.* Boston: Author.

Institute for Responsive Education. (1990). *Equity and Choice,* VI(3). Boston: Author.

Kagan, S. L. (1984/1985). *Parent involvement research: A field in search of itself.* Boston: Institute for Responsive Education.

Krasnow, J. (1990). *Building parent-teacher partnerships: Prospects for the perspective of the schools reaching out project.* Boston, MA: Institute for Responsive Education.

Langdon, C. A. (1996, November). The third Gallup/Phi Delta Kappa poll of teachers' attitudes toward the public schools. *Phi Delta Kappan, 78*(3), 244–250.

Langdon, C. A. (1997, November). The fourth Gallup/Phi Delta Kappa poll of teachers' attitudes toward the public schools. *Phi Delta Kappan, 79*(3), 212–220.

Lombana, J. H. (1983). *Home-school partnerships: Guidelines and strategies for the educator.* New York: Grune & Stratton, Inc.

Lynn, L. (1997, September/October). Teaching teachers to work with families. *Harvard Education Letter.* [Online]. Available: http://www.edletter.org/past/issues/1997-so/teaching.shtml.

McAllister, S. S. (1990). *Parent involvement and success for all children: What we know now.* Boston: Institute for Responsive Education.

McLaughlin, M., & Shields, P. (1987, October). Involving low-income parents in the schools: A role for policy? *Phi Delta Kappan,* 156–160.

McLaughlin, C. S. (1987). *Parent-teacher conferencing.* Springfield, IL: Charles C. Thomas.

Moles, O. C. (Ed.). (1996). *Reaching all families: Creating family-friendly schools.* Washington, DC: Office of Educational Research and Improvement.

National Center for Education Statistics. (Ed.). (1996). Types of contact between parents and school personnel. Indicator of the Month. Washington, DC: Author.

National Education Association. (1983). *Nationwide teacher opinion poll.* Washington, DC: Author.

National School Boards Association. (1988). *First teachers: Parental involvement in the public schools.* Alexandria, VA: Author.

Rich, D. (1987). *Teachers and parents: An adult-to-adult approach.* National Education Association of the United States. The Home and School Institute.

Rich, D. (1998). *Megaskills: How families can help children succeed in school and beyond.* Boston: Houghton Mifflin Company.

Rich, D. (1995). Conference connections: How to make parent-teacher conferences a positive experience for all. *Instructor.*

Sanford, Dornbusch, et al. (1987). The relation of parenting style to adolescent school performance. *Child Development, 58,* 1244–1257.

Seeley, D. S. (1985). *Education through partnership.* Washington, DC: American Enterprise Institute for Public Policy Research.

Smith, M. B. (1968). School and home: Focus on achievement. *Developing Programs for Educationally Disadvantaged.* New York: Teachers College Press.

Storer, J. H. (1995, Winter). Increasing parent and community involvement in schools: The importance of educators' beliefs. *Community Education Journal,* 16–19.

Thomas, W. B. (1980, November). Parental and community involvement: Rx for better school discipline. *Phi Delta Kappan,* 203–204.

United States Department of Education. (1986). *What works: Research about teaching and learning.* Washington, DC: Author.

Walberg, H. (1984). Improving the productivity of America's schools. *Educational Leadership,* 41.

Welch, F. C., & Tisdale, P. C. (1986). *Between parent and teacher.* Springfield, IL: Charles C. Thomas.

Index

Make the Most of Your Professional Development Investment

Let Solution Tree schedule time for you and your staff with leading practitioners in the areas of:

- **Professional Learning Communities** with Richard DuFour, Robert Eaker, Rebecca DuFour, and associates
- **Effective Schools** with associates of Larry Lezotte
- **Assessment *for* Learning** with Rick Stiggins and associates
- **Crisis Management and Response** with Cheri Lovre
- **Classroom Management** with Lee Canter and associates
- **Discipline With Dignity** with Richard Curwin and Allen Mendler
- **PASSport to Success** (parental involvement) with Vickie Burt
- **Peacemakers** (violence prevention) with Jeremy Shapiro

Additional presentations are available in the following areas:

- Youth at Risk Issues
- Bullying Prevention/Teasing and Harassment
- Team Building and Collaborative Teams
- Data Collection and Analysis
- Embracing Diversity
- Literacy Development
- Motivating Techniques for Staff and Students

Solution Tree

555 North Morton Street
Bloomington, IN 47404

(812) 336-7700 • (800) 733-6786 (toll free) • FAX (812) 336-7790

email: info@solution-tree.com

www.solution-tree.com

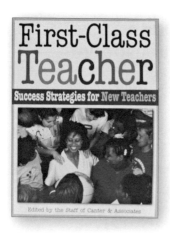

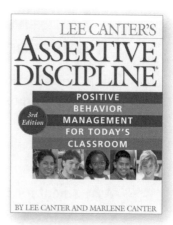

First-Class Teacher: Success Strategies for New Teachers
Lee Canter
This essential survival tool includes hundreds of strategies, lesson ideas, and activities, plus dozens of reproducibles. Whether you are a new or returning K–12 teacher, discover tips, techniques, and insights for handling overwhelming situations so you can thrive and stay focused on your goals. **BKF187**

Teacher's Plan Book Plus #4: Parents on Your Side®
Lee Canter
This 40-week plan book offers weekly tips and strategies for creating a powerful, positive parent involvement program. Introductory pages help teachers get started before the school year begins. The teacher-friendly design provides extra room to jot ideas and take notes. **BKF197**

Assertive Discipline®: Positive Behavior Management for Today's Classroom
Lee Canter and Marlene Canter
Third Edition! Employ a proven three-step approach for positive behavior management by creating a classroom discipline plan that includes: rules all students must follow; supportive feedback for students who follow the rules; and corrective actions for student who don't follow the rules. **BKF182**

Classroom Management for Academic Success
Lee Canter
This groundbreaking resource details effective management strategies you can implement from day one so that all students achieve in the classroom. Teacher-tested, research-based strategies create a classroom in which children learn free from the distraction of disruptive behavior. **BKF209**

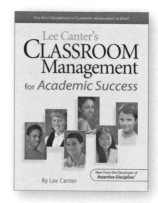

Solution Tree

Jafta's Father

Story by Hugh Lewin

Pictures by Lisa Kopper

Carolrhoda Books, Inc. / Minneapolis

My father, said Jafta,
is as tall and strong as a tree.

When he lifts me up to hug me hello,
it's like climbing to the very top of a bluegum.
When he laughs,
it's like poplars swaying in the wind.

When he carries me across the river on his shoulders,
it's like sitting in a baobab.

I'm sad when I think of him now
because he's not at home.
I wish he were.
He's in the city, working to make money for us.
I had a fight with Obed
when he said my father would never be back,
but my mother said of course he would come home.
Obed said, all right, he was sorry.

Once my father built us a hide-out
in the fallen willow, at the weir.
He fixed branches like stakes
around the trunk to make walls.

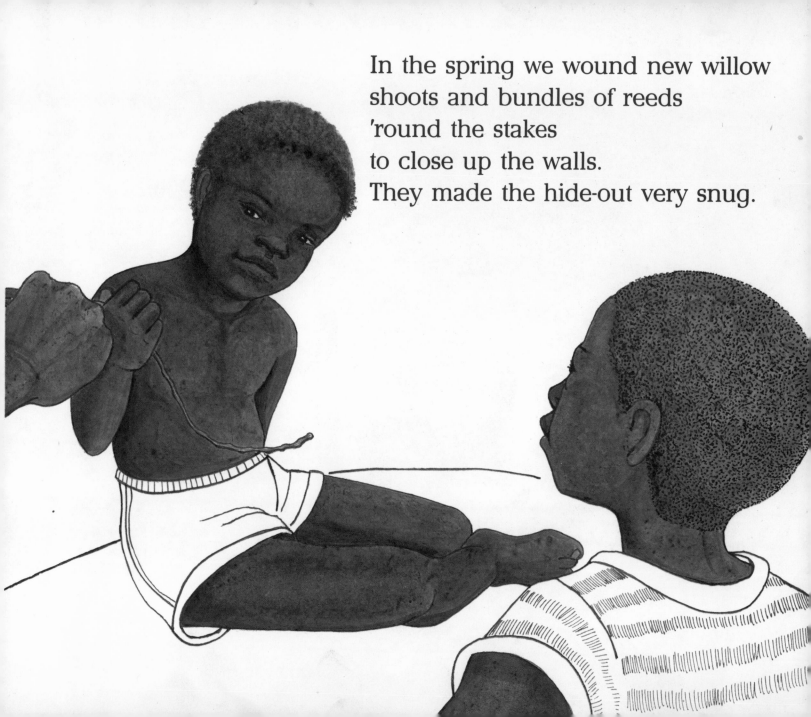

In the spring we wound new willow
shoots and bundles of reeds
'round the stakes
to close up the walls.
They made the hide-out very snug.

One day we found
that a wild sow
had moved in
and had her babies there.
They ran off squeaking
with their tails wiggling.

In the summer my father built us a raft out of logs.
We spent most of the long hot days of the holidays
sailing on the river
and only once got wet,
when Obed fell off trying to catch his goat.

When the trees began to turn brown in the autumn,
we collected a basket of leaves, twigs and logs
and invited the adults to a feast.
My father made a fire
and we cooked the meat
on the ends of sticks
and left potatoes
in the coals to roast.

We were allowed to stay up late that night,
watching the logs spit and splutter in the dark.
My father carried me home on his back–
I slept the whole way.

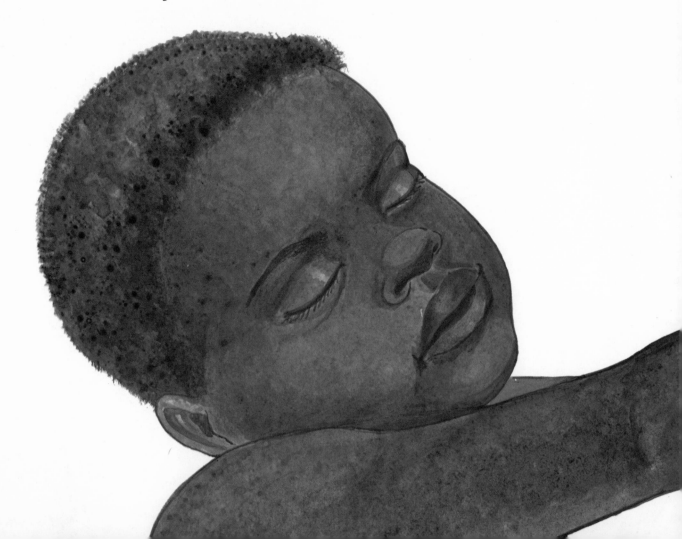

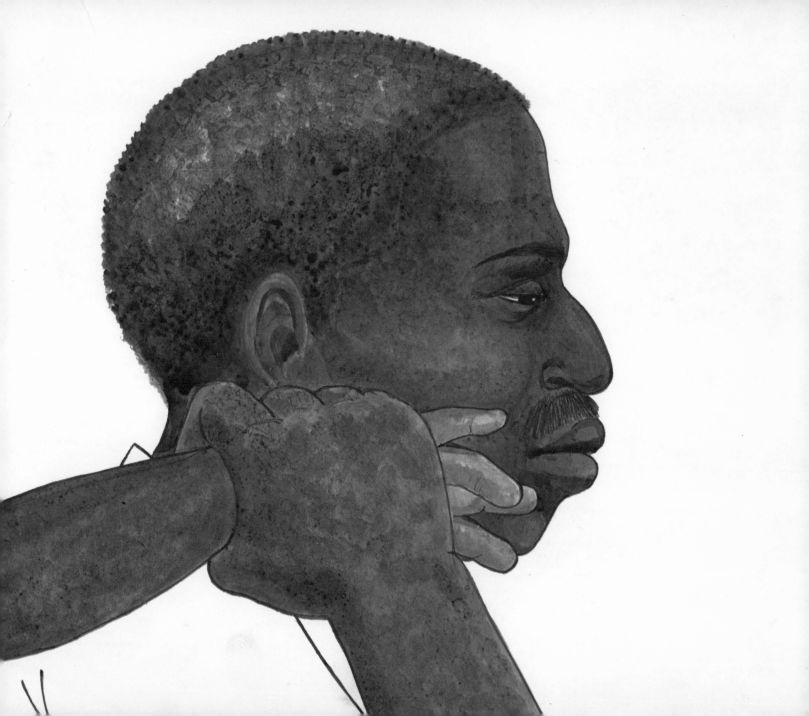

Soon it will be spring again.
Mother says my father will come home then.
I hope he does.

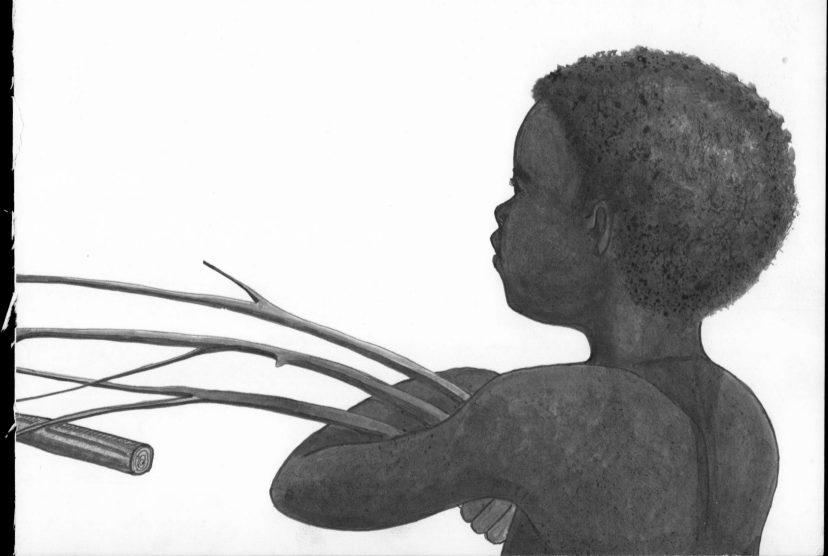

There are some words in this story that might be new to you.
Bluegum trees, originally Australian eucalyptus trees, are
common throughout southern Africa. They have long, elegant
leaves, and tall, very smooth trunks that shimmer blue/gray. The
baobab is a tropical African tree. Its huge, thick trunk and rather
out-of-proportion branches make it look a little like an upside-
down tree, with all its roots in the air. A weir is a small dam
across a river.

LIBRARY OF CONGRESS CATALOGING IN PUBLICATION DATA

Lewin, Hugh.
    Jafta's father.

    Originally published as: Jafta-my father.
    Summary: While his father works in the city
over the winter, a young boy thinks of some
good times they've shared and looks forward
to his return to their African home in the
spring.
    [1. Fathers and sons-Fiction. 2. Africa-
Fiction] I. Kopper, Lisa, ill. II. Title.
PZ7.L58418Jag 1983   [E]   82-12837
ISBN 0-87614-209-9 (lib. bdg.)

This edition first published 1983 by Carolrhoda Books, Inc.
Original edition published 1981
by Evans Brothers Limited, London, England,
under the title JAFTA-MY FATHER.
Text copyright © 1981 by Hugh Lewin.
Illustrations copyright © 1981 by Lisa Kopper.

Manufactured in the United States of America

1 2 3 4 5 6 7 8 9 10 92 91 90 89 88 87 86 85 84 83

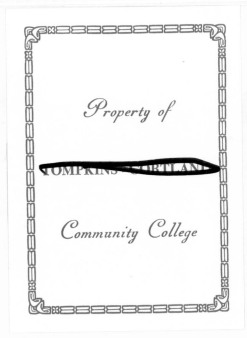

PEOPLES OF THE EARTH

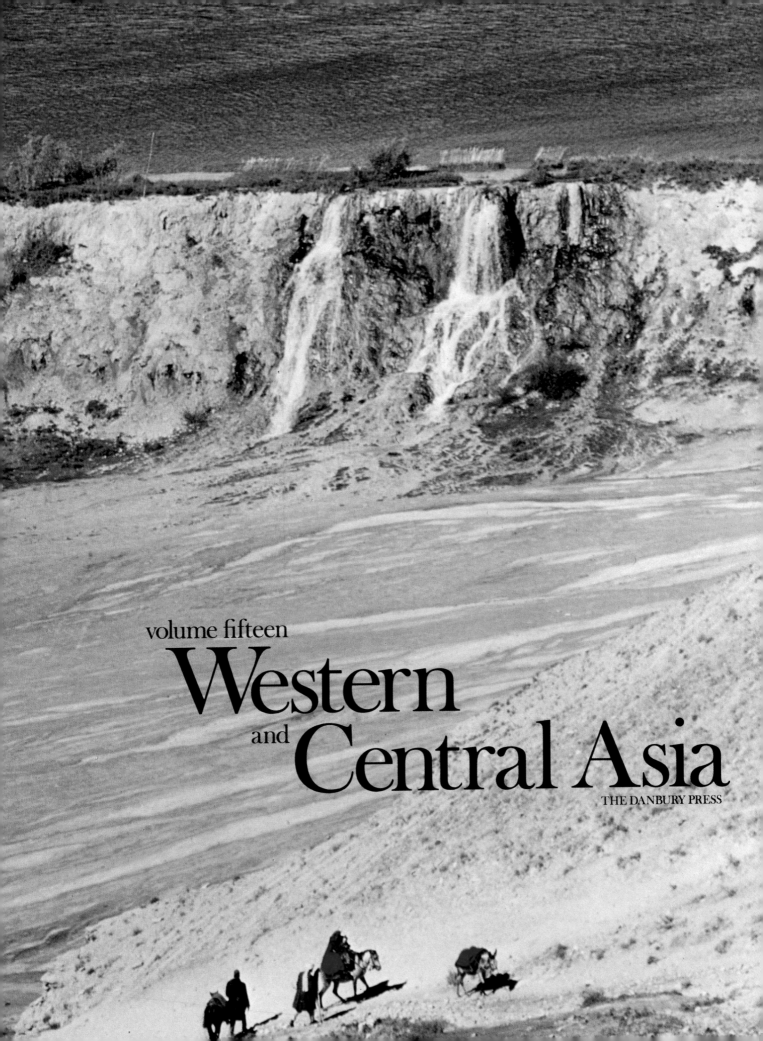

volume fifteen
Western
and
Central Asia

THE DANBURY PRESS

(Preceding page) Afghanistan
legend tells how the hero
Hazrat Ali flung down the
top of a mountain to build
the dams which form the five
lakes of Band-i-Amir in the
Hindu Kush.

Contents

Supervisory Editor of the Series:
Professor Sir Edward Evans-Pritchard,
Fellow of All Souls, Professor of Social Anthropology,
University of Oxford, 1946-1970,
Chevalier de la Légion d'Honneur

Volume Editor:
André Singer, BSc (Econ), B.Litt
Institute of Social Anthropology, University of
Oxford, joint editor of *Zande Themes: Essays
Presented to Sir Edward Evans-Pritchard*

284/28

The DANBURY PRESS
a division of GROLIER ENTERPRISES INC.
Publisher
ROBERT B. CLARKE

Library of Congress Catalog Card No. 72 85614

Printed in Italy by
Arnoldo Mondadori Editore, Verona

STAFF CREDITS
Editorial Director **Tom Stacey**
Picture Director **Alexander Low**
Executive Editor **Katherine Ivens**
Art Director **Tom Deas**
Assistant Editor **Elisabeth Meakin**
Project Co-ordinator **Anne Harrison**
Research **Cheryl Moyer**

Specialist Picture Research **Jeanne Griffiths**
Picture Research **Claire Baines**
Elly Beintema
Diana Eggitt
Carolyn Keay
Emma Stacey
Editorial Assistants **Richard Carlisle**
Rosamund Ellis
J M Marrin
Susan Rutherford
Pamela Tubby
Editorial Secretary **Caroline Silverman**
Design Assistants **Susan Forster**
Richard Kelly
Cartography **Ron Hayward**
Illustrations **Sandra Archibald, Ron McTrusty**

Production **Roger Multon**
Production Editor **Vanessa Charles**

The publishers gratefully acknowledge help from
the following organizations:
Royal Anthropological Institute, London
Musée de l'Homme, Paris
International African Institute, London
British Museum, London
Royal Geographical Society, London
Scott Polar Research Institute, Cambridge
Royal Asiatic Society, London
Royal Central Asian Society, London
Pitt-Rivers Museum, Oxford
Horniman Museum, London
Institute of Latin American Studies, London

PICTURE CREDITS
Cover: **Ian Berry** and **Bruno Barbey** (Magnum from the John Hillelson
Agency), **Tchekov Minosa, Roland and Sabrina Michaud** (Rapho, Paris),
Ross-Greetham. Ardea Photographics 33. **John Bayliss and Douglas
Botting** 72 t. **Jean Charles Bland** (Snark International) 93 tr. **Chris
Bonington** (Daily Telegraph Coll. from Woodfin Camp) 126 through
134. **John Bulmer** 34. **Franklin Cardy** 16. **Robert Cundy** 88 cl. **Maurice
Engels** 30 b. **Victor Englebert** 90 t, 102 – 103, 106 through 109, 111 cl,
112 tl & r. **Eriako** 90 bl, 93 br. **F.P.G.** 50 b, 53. **Philipp Giegel** 31. **Roy
A. Giles** 23, 97 t. **Sonia Halliday** 22 b. From the John Hillelson Agency –
Giles Sholl 54. Magnum from the John Hillelson Agency – **Eve Arnold**
2 – 3, 91, 92 tl, 98, 117, **Bruno Barbey** 46 bl & tr, 49, 51 r, 52, **Ian Berry**
20 br, 22 t, 24 – 25, 27, 28, 29, 30 t, 35 r, **Burt Glinn** 73, **Erich Lessing** 21,
Inge Morath 44 – 45, 46 tl, 50 t, 72 c, **George Rodger** 35 l, **Marilyn
Silverstone** 48. **Anthony Howarth** (Daily Telegraph Coll. from Woodfin
Camp) 58 through 67. **Anwar Hussein** 96. **Schuyler Jones** 118 – 119, 122.
Philip Jones-Griffiths 20 tl. **Peter Keen** 13. **Paolo Koch** (Rapho, Paris)
70 b, 71. **William MacQuitty** 55 b. **John Marmaras** (Daily Telegraph)
19, 20 tr. **Roland Michaud** (Rapho, Paris) 68 – 69, 70 t, 74 through 76,
78 – 79, 86 – 87, 88 tr, 89, 92 tr, 94 – 95, 99. **Sabrina Michaud** (Rapho,
Paris) 77. **Tchekov Minosa** 36 through 43, 56, 57, 104, 105, 110, 111 tl,
112 br, 113, 120, 121, 124, 125. **J. Powell** 100 – 101. **Ross-Greetham**
72 b, 88 bl, 114 through 116. **Hermann Schlenker** 47, 80 through 85.
Thomas Sennett (F.P.G.) 97 br. **Spectrum** 93 cr. **R. Waldkirch** (ZEFA)
26. **Jim Webb** (F.P.G.) 92 br. **Adam Woolfitt** (Susan Griggs) 55 t.

Key: **t**=top, **c**=centre, **b**=bottom, **r**=right, **l**=left.

Peoples of the Earth, volumes one to twenty

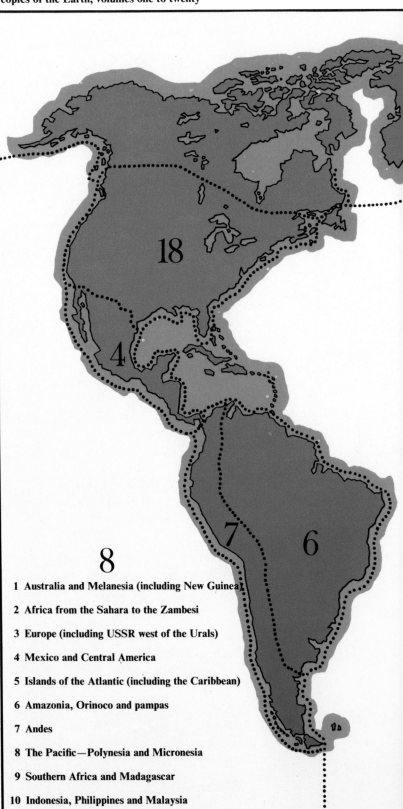

1 Australia and Melanesia (including New Guinea)

2 Africa from the Sahara to the Zambesi

3 Europe (including USSR west of the Urals)

4 Mexico and Central America

5 Islands of the Atlantic (including the Caribbean)

6 Amazonia, Orinoco and pampas

7 Andes

8 The Pacific—Polynesia and Micronesia

9 Southern Africa and Madagascar

10 Indonesia, Philippines and Malaysia

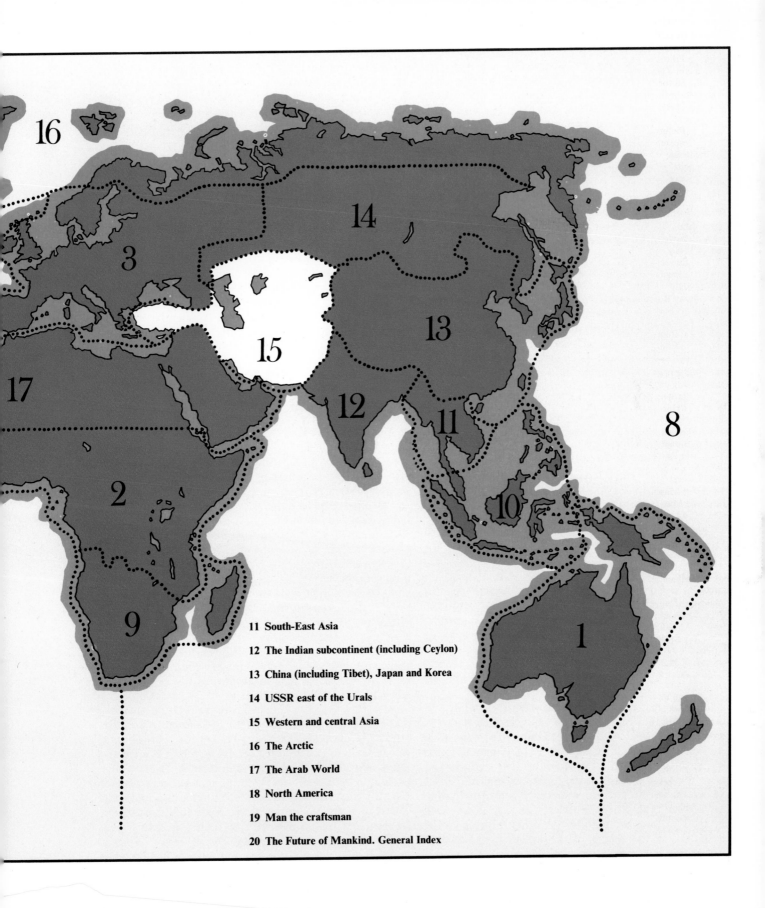

What is nomadism?

Pastoral nomadism is a way of life that has evolved in regions too dry, too elevated or too steep for agriculture. The nomad makes use of land that might otherwise be neglected. He moves regularly with his flocks or herds according to seasonal variations in climate. His animals, through their meat or their milk, provide him with a substantial part of his diet. He builds no permanent dwelling. His life is hard. He has very few material possessions as he is constantly on the move. He eats simple food. Often milk alone is his staple, for meat is too great a luxury since his animals represent his capital. To use them for meat is to destroy his livelihood. He must manage when water fails or if his flock or herd contracts an epidemic. Among many of the Beduin water is always scarce and can be used only for drinking. The Koran prescribes sand for daily ablutions, but many use animal urine for washing. When life becomes too hard for them many nomads die and others have to relinquish their way of life and take menial jobs in the surrounding villages or towns.

The world's nomadic population is undergoing increasing pressure. In the recent past forcible measures have been taken to settle nomads in permanent homes, in Iran and Turkey for example, and of course in Russia. Governments find they cannot control them and do not like the power they wield. Many nomads are under pressure from companies searching for oil in their natural grazing grounds. Yet it can be argued that many nomadic areas, especially areas where there are no natural resources, are unsuitable for any activity other than pastoral nomadism. The presence of nomads means that at least some products, like wool, meat and milk, are being produced from land that would otherwise be entirely barren.

Central and south-western Asia has traditionally been the home of probably the largest number of the world's nomads. Most of the rest live in northern Africa. There are others in central and southern Africa, southern Europe, northern Scandinavia and Siberia. In this enormous area—stretching from southern Africa to the Arctic Ocean, from the Atlantic to the borders of China —there are also many people who make their living largely or partly by keeping and exploiting domestic animals. But because they build permanent homes and have interests in the property they own they are not true nomads.

Some of them certainly have a way of life similar to nomads, for they migrate seasonally with their flocks or herds. In northern Africa, for example, there are such peoples as the Nuer. The Nuer move their animals in the dry season to the few water-holes in their territory and move them back again to the higher ground in the wet season. In the mountainous areas of southern Europe and western Asia are people who, with their flocks, seek the high pastures in summer and bring them down the mountains to the shelter of the valleys in the cold of winter. But their homes and the property they own give

these people attitudes towards their environment which are fundamentally different from those of nomads. They are called transhumant people.

Although what follows here concentrates on the proper nomadic way of life, much of it also applies to transhumant people in so far as they move seasonally to provide fresh pasture for their animals.

To catalogue the names and sizes of all these nomadic and transhumant people and give detailed areas of their distribution would be impossible, largely because groupings do not always correspond to a classification of their way of life. Many Turkomen, Kurd, Baluch and Beduin, for example, are nomadic. But these tribal names include many people who are not nomadic at all. Many are farmers and others live in towns. In fact it is rare to find entire tribes who are exclusively nomadic. Most areas tend to support two or more ways of life, each of which adapts to the environment in a different way. In the Middle East farming villages are frequently scattered through nomadic territory where, furthermore, the nomadic populations are not stable. The boundaries and size of nomadic groups and of the tribes with which they are associated are constantly changing. They change in response to fluctuations in climate and to factors like political security and the growth and decline in the populations themselves.

Although all nomads and most transhumant populations have traditionally lived so close to each other that their territories, which range over so much of Eurasia and Africa, almost overlap, they are not for that reason recognizably similar or related to each other. At a glance the various nomadic populations of the world have little, if anything, in common. They are nomads, that is all. Even within a single culture area like the Islamic Middle East, there are great cultural differences between the different nomadic groups. There are differences in their migration patterns, in the type of animals they herd, in what these animals produce, in their social and political organizations and in the relations they have with their settled neighbors. These differences may result from the ways different groups have adapted to widely differing environments. Underlying these cultural differences there are also certain similarities. These similarities result from the nomads' responses to the problems of adaptation to their environments.

Although the nomad depends on his natural environment for food he does not get his food directly from the land as hunting and gathering peoples do. He relies on his animals to produce his food for him. They eat the grass and other vegetables and turn it directly into protein as milk and meat. The nomad either consumes the milk and meat or he turns the animal products into cheese or butter, leather or skins. If nomads live close to farmers they may concentrate on selling meat or cheese to the villagers, because in return they may be given grain. But if they are isolated and have to live on what they produce themselves, they may keep their animals, so that they give a daily supply of milk. A nomad keeps the type of animal that is best suited to his environment. Each species of domestic animal makes different demands. Cattle, for example, need lusher grazing than sheep. Each species has a different life cycle and supplies different products. Which of those products the nomad concentrates on depends on whether or not he can sell them.

The grain crops on which nomads depend, as they do not generally subsist on animal products alone, change as one moves from south to north through the nomadic area. In the south millet is most important to the nomad's diet. In the Sahara, the Middle East and central Asia it is wheat bread, while in Siberia pastoral products are supplemented by fish and wild plants.

Nomadic people are also identified with different cultural systems. The most conspicuous distinction is between Muslim and non-Muslim people. But there are other distinctions—for example, between Arab, Iranian and Turkic groups – which involve quite fundamental aspects of the ways in which their societies are organized.

Just as the grain crops on which nomads rely change from area to area so do the animals they herd. South of the Sahara in Africa most nomads rely mainly on cattle to give them a daily supply of milk. They keep as many animals as they can so that even if only a few produce well, some at least will always be in milk. By having large herds they also lessen the chance of losing all their animals in an epidemic or drought. A large herd is like a walking bank account. When all else fails the animals may be eaten as they die.

As one moves from the lusher pastures of the savanna northwards the climate becomes more unfriendly. In the east African territories lying between the savanna and the Sahara, it is drier and the rainfall is more unreliable. But still nomads herd cattle.

Further north into the Sahara there is not only less rainfall; the rainfall also becomes even more irregular and unreliable. Gradually the nomads rely on camels rather than on cattle, for though the camel's endurance and its ability to go without water have been exaggerated, it is better adapted to an extreme desert climate than any other domestic animal. Goats, which desert nomads herd in small numbers come a close second. But they cannot travel such great distances in search of new pastures as camels can.

North-east of the Sahara on the Iranian Plateau in central Asia, and on the northern side of the Mediterranean where seasonal rainfall is more reliable and pastures are lusher sheep become the nomads' most important animals. Here on the Iranian Plateau, and in much of the Middle East and in the Mediterranean region, it is also characteristic of nomads that they live in relatively close economic contact with settled peoples. Here they pasture their animals in the open spaces between villages. In some of these places nomads have symbiotic arrangements with villagers: a villager may, for example, allow the nomad's herds to graze the stubble of his wheat fields in return for the droppings which fertilize the soil for the coming year.

Some nomads cultivate and produce their own grain which provides them with such an invaluable supplement to their animal-based diet. But as cultivation is often difficult to fit into the nomadic cycle a close economic relationship with grain producers provides a convenient solution. The villagers in return also need certain of the nomad's products, especially butter and ghee. On some parts of the Iranian Plateau, especially among the Baluch, some nomads have a close trading relationship with individual farmers. The farmers visit the nomads' camps in the spring when milk is most plentiful. And the nomads return their visits at the end of the summer. This is the hardest time of the year for them. The pasture is dried out by the arid heat of the summer. Surface water on which both men and animals depend is scarce. At this very time, however, the villager often has plentiful stocks of grain and, more important, it is also the time of the date harvest.

Dates are an important crop for the nomad throughout much of the Middle East. They are highly nutritious and are easy to store and transport. They might also seem an ideal crop for the nomad to cultivate since, compared to grain, they require little attention and a single tree produces large quantities of fruit. But although many nomads have a few palms here and there, all large date palm plantations, and almost all date palms, are owned and cultivated by settled people. A date palm represents a piece of fixed property; an investment that must be defended. It is therefore better for a nomad to maintain a relationship with settled people who cultivate palms and get his dates that way than to make himself responsible for palms he could not defend without modifying his way of life.

Defense of property and security have frequently caused major problems of conflict between farmers and nomads who live in close contact with one another. The farmer must defend his fields or plantations because he depends for his livelihood on them. The nomad is conditioned by his way of life not to respect such interests. He does not value such fixed resources because he himself does without them. He values his animals. He is not even very interested in conserving pastures. And so hostility, offset to some extent and in some cases by the economic relationship between them, has characterized the history of relations between nomads and settled populations. Even when economic relationships have been cemented by marriage they have tended not to last very long.

Although the two ways of life are ideologically opposed and have encouraged hostility there is evidence of economic contacts beteen farmers and nomads leading to farmers becoming nomads and nomads becoming farmers, especially in the Middle East. Nomads and cultivators may despise and mistrust one another. But since both nomads and farmers are affected by fluctuating resources there tends to be a continual movement of individuals and families between nomadic and settled populations who are in economic contact with each other. When cultivators, for example, suffer drought to the extent that everyone cannot be supported, they have no option but to leave the agricultural niche. Since most cultivators also keep some animals they usually move off with those animals and make them the basis of a new nomadic way of life. In times of widespread insecurity in the Middle East, as after the Mongol invasions in the 13th century, there appear to have been similar results and an increase in the numbers of nomads can be detected in historical records.

Nomads may also in certain circumstances become cultivators. A nomad whose flock is reduced so low by drought that he cannot live from it may drift into the nearby village as a day-wage laborer. Or, at the other end of the scale, a nomad whose flock grows beyond a size that he can herd himself may sell the excess animals and invest the proceeds in land. Having invested in fixed property he becomes interested in its welfare and so becomes attracted towards a settled life to ensure that he makes the most of his investment.

The option of settling down or becoming farmers is not open to all nomads. Where agriculture is not, as in most nomadic areas, a viable alternative the nomads survive by receiving animals from other herding groups. There is a complicated system of reshuffling so that all individuals have at least some animals. Animals are passed from one to another according to which people are related through their fathers' lines of descent. As a man's paternal ancestor is often remembered from many generations back he does have a lot of people – some very distant – related to him. The animals, which are his means of subsistence, also become a means of communicating with other members of his society, whom he might otherwise have nothing to do with. In this situation the nomad is not wholly dependent on his own herd or flock but on the herds and flocks of all his people.

In central Asia north of the Iranian Plateau where sheep are, as they are further south, the most important animals for nomads they also herd horses, the Bactrian or two-humped camel and, in mountainous regions, the yak. Here the severe central Asian winter demands special provisions for the animals. During the hard winter, when the animals cannot graze because of snow, the animals must be fed and sheltered. And there is a shortage of pastures as the growing season is so short. As the nomads have to cut hay for winter feed and, under Russian influence, build permanent winter shelters, they become diverted from a strictly nomadic way of life. Recently they have helped the Soviet programs for de-nomadizing central Asia.

In Siberia and northern Scandinavia, nomadic pastoralists herd reindeer in an exceptionally harsh environment that will not support any other domestic animal or plant. Here there are few alternative livelihoods open to them.

Having seen some of the obvious differences between nomads arising from the different ways they adapt to particular natural environments a number of similarities also become apparent. Nearly all nomads either own pasture communally or not at all. Individuals own animals. Nomadic herders do not purposefully change their environment in any way. They do not invest time, energy or wealth in their surroundings and so they do not individually own any fixed objects. Whereas non-nomadic peoples' social relationships tend to be dominated by their interests in fixed objects – a man who owns more land than he can manage himself might take on hired labor, so that a relationship of landowner and laborer emerges – they do not condition nomads' social relationships.

What influences nomads' social relations is something entirely different, although it is also an ecological factor. Studies of sheep nomads in the Iranian area, for example, have shown that many factors – how many animals the pasture can feed, the skill of the shepherd and the behavior of the animals – combine to determine the maximum size of a flock in any given place. Sheep seem to be more contented and produce better if they are kept in large numbers. If the flock drops below a certain number the sheep tend to waste away. But if the flock gets too big it is difficult to keep them together. The size of the flock is bound to change continually from year to year through the normal processes of birth and death, which are from time to time accentuated by drought, epidemic or an exceptionally fertile year.

Not only is there a maximum size for the flock; there is also a maximum number of people who can comfortably live off the flock. The number of people depends on what the flock produces and how many men, women and children are needed to look after it. As the flock changes in size so also the size of the nomadic group must be reshuffled with other groups. Only by this reshuffling can the right number of men – owning the right number of sheep and who bring with them the right number of women and children – assure the survival of the group.

Because of this, nomadic society must be homogenous. There must be no marked differences of status between members which would inhibit this constant reshuffling of people between one group and another. It must be a fluid society. There are exceptions. Some of the nomadic societies of northern Africa, for example, are clearly stratified into classes: the noble or upper class nominally controls all the pasture and grazing and employs everyone else in herding groups throughout the territory. But according to some studies made over a considerable period of time even these class distinctions are less rigid than they are claimed to be in native ideology. Furthermore, a man identifies less with his local herding group than with a larger social grouping based on his lineage and genealogy. Whereas cultivators tend to identify themselves by the name of their villages, nomads tend to identify themselves with an overall group, who might be dispersed over a wide area. There is constant movement within this group and within the territory which it inhabits.

Contrary to popular belief no nomads wander at random. The local groups with their flocks or herds move according to a definite seasonal pattern. The distance and range within which they wander seasonally is more restricted among some groups than others. There is always a definite seasonal movement, determined by the changes from a hot summer to a cold winter, or from a wet season to a dry season. As well as this movement of local groups, there are individuals who constantly move around independently. They leave their group to search for stray animals. Or they may go off to visit relatives in other camps, to attend weddings and other rites of passage, to trade, make pilgrimages to shrines, or to seek out government officials. Complicated codes of hospitality have evolved so that nomads may journey in safety. A stranger who comes to a camp is received into the tent of the senior member. This man feeds him and lets him rest there for up to three days without demanding any explanation. If the stranger stays for more than three days he immediately becomes a client of his host and is in a position of inferiority to him. He may perhaps be seeking political asylum. In Baluchistan in Pakistan, the expression 'to enter a tent' is synonymous with seeking asylum. A request 'to enter a tent' cannot be refused with honor. A guest's safety continues to be his host's responsibility for as long as his host's food remains in his stomach.

The characteristic fluidity and mobility of nomadic peoples on which their ability to reshuffle themselves to adapt to their environment depends is now on the decline, largely due to conflicts between farmers and nomads. The rise in recent years of nationalist governments, bolstered up by modern weapons, has also threatened many of the conditions essential to the nomadic way of life. For governments are promoted by settled people. They are staffed by settled people. And they are bound to want to control access to all the country's natural resources. Although nomadic people may be recognized as contributing to a wider national economy through their production of animal protein, they are generally viewed with suspicion. They are mistrusted because they remain independent, impossible to control, and because they have a long history of hostility with settled governments.

Peoples of western and central As

The people of western and central Asia, the people of Turkey, Iran, Pakistan, Afghanistan and Soviet central Asia, live in about one fifth of the Asian landmass. And although the area in which they live rubs up against, blends into and is influenced by four major cultural areas – eastern Europe, the Arab near east, south Asia and the far east – it has distinctive characteristics of its own.

Although modernization and industrialization have had varying degrees of influence on western and central Asia the peasant-tribal societies still dominate the cultural scene. The majority of the people spend most of their time engaged in basic food production, either by agriculture or by herding or, more commonly, by combinations of the two.

Farming and herding are both influenced by the availability of water, high mountains with heavy snowfalls – and subsequent melt-water and inhospitable deserts. Western and central Asia consists of a series of mountains and plateaux dividing north from southern Asia west of the Himalayas. The plateaux are separated by mountains which range out from two disembodied masses: the Pamir Knot in the east, and the Armenian Knot in the west. The land surface is overlaid with alluvial deposits of silts, gravels, clays and thick wind-born loess, particularly in central Asia. In most places above 14,000 feet, bare rock dominates. The high ground seldom falls to 1,200 feet above sea level.

There are few genuine irrigation systems in the mountains. Wherever possible the farmers use elaborate terracing or water-catchment areas to help cultivate the land. In the foothills and plains the people practise two types of irrigation. In the adjoining Irano-Afghan-Pakistani areas, specialists construct and maintain *qanat* (or *karez*) which lead water to the surface above the normal water table and allow large tracts of marginally arable land to be reclaimed. *Qanat* are tunneled-out underground canals connected by deep wells which, from the sky, resemble rows of anthills.

Along main rivers, such as the Indus, Hilmand-Arghandab and Karun open canals (main, lateral, feeder – plus the necessary drainage ditches) carry the water away from the rivers. In these and other areas the huge hydro-electric dams, generators and reservoirs have usually been western-inspired, if not partly western-financed. The Chinese, incidentally, are helping the Afghans in one such project. And in Pakistani Punjab and Sind, intricate tube well systems maintain a stable water table, often in conjunction with open canal systems.

As the irrigation systems vary regionally, so do the crops. Wheat-barley with rice and maize are cultivated wherever possible. And the farmers increasingly cultivate large varieties of vegetables, fruits (particularly fine melons in some areas), and nuts (pistachios are a major Iranian and minor Afghan export). Several varieties of cannabis and opium remain economically and socially

important crops. In passing it must be mentioned that south-west Iran has an additional resource. It virtually floats on a sea of oil.

There are two broad main categories of people in western and central Asia. There are the sedentary peoples of the cities, towns and villages. And there are the nomadic and semi-nomadic peoples who roam with their flocks. The sedentary people have settled in two types of places, all of which center on the availability of water and on strategic importance, as well as on historical accident. In the well-watered regions where the foothills meet the plains there is a nuclear settlement pattern; villages cluster about a town; a complex of villages and towns cluster about a city. But along the major rivers there is a linear settlement pattern: the villages are strung out like a necklace of beads.

Western and central Asian villages, whether they are in the highlands or the lowlands, are nearly always built on non-productive land. In the village people live and work for mutual protection in groups of people related by kinship. The styles of houses vary according to what building material is available. But the basic structure is usually square or rectangular and they are usually built of sun-dried bricks made in wooden molds and covered with mud and straw plaster. The flat roofs are made of pisé (rammed earth) interlaced with twigs and supported by mat-covered beams. Pressed mud walls of varying heights line the meandering village lanes and enclose the houses in small compounds. These walls traditionally ensured protection and privacy, and corraled the livestock at night. Some completely walled villages have watch towers to prevent surprise attacks: feuds are still common throughout western and central Asia. As one moves from the plains up the valleys to the mountains stones replace mud-brick and pisé as building materials. And in the more heavily forested areas of eastern Afghanistan, the Caspian coastal region and Anatolia the people build complicated, wooden, often multi-storey houses.

The villagers produce all the food they need. Except in times of war, famine, flood or epidemic, they are very nearly self-sufficient. Although there are few full-time skilled workers in the villages many farmers are also excellent builders and carpenters. The villagers do depend, however, on the town bazaars, on trading nomads, and on itinerant peddlers for such necessities as iron implements, tea, sugar and kerosene. And when the villagers themselves have local handicrafts, raw materials and surplus agricultural produce to sell they take them on donkeys, horses, camels or on their own backs and heads to sell in the bazaar of the nearest town.

Towns generally grow up where several major trails intersect, although the development today of asphalt highways has somewhat changed this. The town is the local commercial, communications and administrative center of the region. Here the lower grade civil servants –

Most Kazak live in the USSR. They are a fiercely independent people who used to roam the steppes with their herds. Now many of them are 'collectivized'.

the tax collectors, school teachers and quasi-military police – have their headquarters, and so, often, do absentee landlords or their agents. Telephone lines rarely extend beyond the town. And the town bazaar – particularly the tea houses and the caravanserais – are the places where visitors from the rural areas go to pick up information and news. In the town bazaar the villagers can buy goods and services from the ironmongers, weavers, dyers, potters, carpenters, masons, general shopkeepers, tailors, butchers, automobile repairers and caravanserai owners, who all work and live above or at the back of their shops. Some of the goods in the bazaar are finished products brought by lorry from the cities.

Where main roads meet cities develop. They are major commercial, administrative and communication centers linking the interior with the outside world. Large cities tend to be divided into an 'old city' and a 'new city'. The 'old city' is where large guild-like groups of artisans and skilled craftsmen live and work in separate sections of the bazaar. The 'new city' has usually developed in response to the imperialism of the past and the modernization of the present. Often the 'old' and 'new' cities are separated by a river. This is true even in the cities of Samarkand and Tashkent in Soviet central Asia.

The capital cities of western and central Asia are of course the center of government administration. Here partly elected, partly appointed parliaments meet to pass laws, and courts administer justice under new constitutions against a background of changing secular-cum-Islamic law.

Often villagers and nomads come to the city in the off-seasons for agriculture and herding to seek work in the rapidly expanding industries. Some stay only a little while, returning home when the planting starts or the flocks begin to move. But others settle permanently and frequently suffer all the pangs and pains of being economically urban-based while being emotionally and culturally rural-based.

The city grows rapidly, the town more slowly, but the village remains much as it has always been. Most villagers still prefer as little contact with city life and government authority as possible. They have a much closer relationship with the nomads and semi-nomads of their area.

Nomads are herdsmen who move as a group from summer to winter pasturelands and back again and have no permanent dwellings. They live either in black goats' hair tents or in *yurts* which are particularly popular in northern Afghanistan and north-eastern Iran. Most western and central Asian nomads take two months to reach the summer pastures where they camp for a time and then leave, taking another two months to return to the winter pastures. Few nomads move constantly. Most move only seasonally. They tend to keep livestock that adapts most easily to where they live. Sheep and goats suit mountain pastures. Camels and cattle adapt more easily to forest steppes and semi-deserts. Most of the camels are dromedaries, but in parts of Badakhshan and the Wakhan Corridor the nomads herd the two-humped bactrian camel and in the Pamir Knot, the yak. Some water buffalo are used in the wetter regions of northern Afghanistan, Pakistan and the Caspian coast. The most important beast of burden for the nomads throughout the entire area, however, is the donkey. Mules are used less frequently. And the horse is considered everywhere to be a prestige animal.

The relationship between the nomads and the villagers is often mutually advantageous. The nomads visit the villages and bazaars along their routes as they travel, gathering and passing on news. They also bring sheep and goats, skins, dairy products, wool, rugs and kelims which they sell or exchange for the farmers' grain, flour, vegetables, fruits and nuts. Trading nomads specialize in necessities that the villagers require: tea, sugar, kerosene, cloth, matches.

And the nomads are not, contrary to popular belief, parasites on the farmers' lands. Their livestock provides large amounts of fuel and fertilizer in the form of dung. Sheep and goats graze over freshly reaped fields constantly depositing manure. This, when it is plowed under, helps to replace nitrogen in the soil. In addition, the nomads have for generations maintained the 'marginal' grasslands. Because their flocks are constantly moving they do not overgraze the land like those owned by villagers. And again they add valuable fertilizing manure to the land. Without the flocks the hilly marginal grasslands would soon become semi-desert.

Some groups of nomads, particularly since World War II, have evolved into semi-nomads. This has happened when their traditional grazing lands have been

13

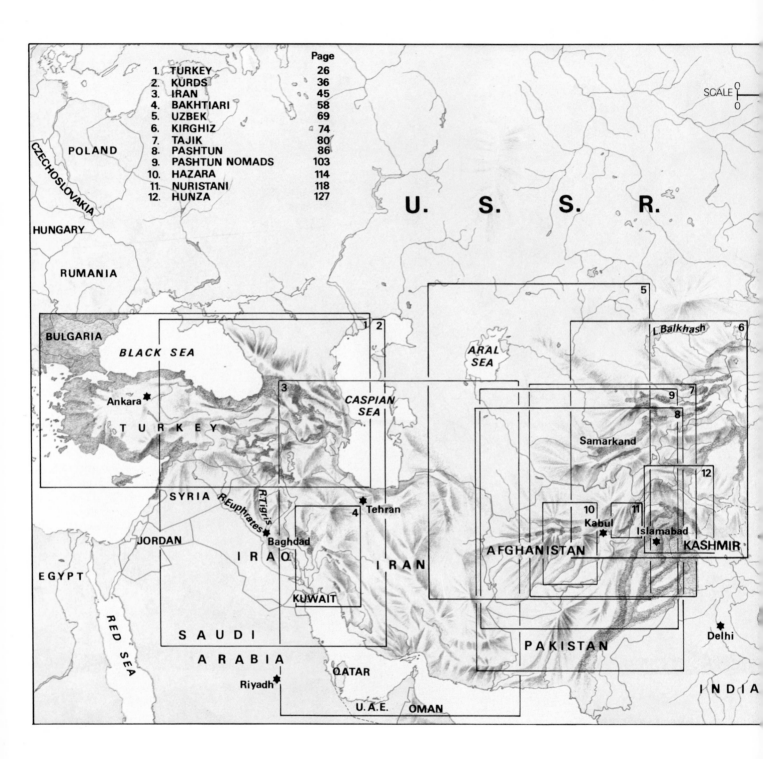

SCALE

taken over by the government in pursuit of a land reclamation project, or by farmers seeking better land – when fights have occurred. But the farmers have nearly always won as they have the support of well-equipped government armies. To maintain some part of their traditional way of life some nomadic leaders claimed or purchased lands from the governments involved. On this land they have settled. In these circumstances only part of the group goes with the flocks; the rest remain behind and farm. And as a group become semi-sedentary they build mud huts in their winter quarters. Few nomads – if any – however will ever become fully sedentary.

Islam is a dominant force in the lives of the people. It exploded into the region in the mid-7th century AD, and by the 9th century the non-Arab Muslim world of western and central Asia had come into being, enveloping early in its existence the formerly Christian Byzantine Empire of Anatolia, the Zoroastrian Sasanian Empire of Iran, the Buddhists and Hindus of Afghanistan, western India and central Asia. Islam split into two major divisions – Sunni and Shi'a. Sunni and Shi'a again divided into several sects. Most Iranians are Imami (or Ithna Ashariya) Shi'a, as are the Qizilbash, and some Hazara. Many Hazara, however, and most of the speakers of Indo-European dialects of the Wakhan and Badakhshan are Ismailiya Shi'a, followers of the Aga Khan. In western and central Asia, Islam must be considered both at a literate and at a non-literate level. Although there is a great body of literature in Turkish, Persian, Urdu, and Pashtu, the society is basically non-literate. They must depend on interpretations of their literature given by literate religious leaders. Much of the Islam espoused in villages and nomadic camps embodies many pre-Islamic beliefs. Even prehistoric folk-heroes survive locally with Muslim names: Gilgamish becomes the Sharif Ali, son-in-law of the Prophet Mohammad and dragon-slayer par excellence; in Christian iconography he becomes St George.

Non-literate, as well as many literate, Muslims and almost all westerners, consider Islam to be deterministic, anti-modern, and anti-progressive. Traditionalist religious leaders who interpret Islam encourage their flocks to accept the deterministic beliefs: all things happen because Allah has willed them; the moving finger writes. The strength of Islam, however, relates more to local than to universal doctrine as it is derived from its submersion in local cultures. The essence of Islam, particularly as it is interpreted by some modernists in western and central Asia, includes much free will. The modernists insist on the importance of beliefs parallel with Judaism and Christianity, the two other great religions which developed at the eastern end of the Mediterranean out of the same culture matrix. These important parallels are a belief in a Supreme Being and order in the universe; the equality of all men before Allah; social justice between men. True, Islam itself means submission, but

some modernists claim this does not mean blind, unquestioning acceptance of a predetermined fate, but rather a voluntary acceptance of a way of life after careful examination by the individual believer. The Islam of the village and camp, however, seldom approaches this idealized view of the faith. Some basic customs, such as the in-group blood feud, run completely counter to the essence of Islam, whether traditionalist or modernist.

Most of the people in western and central Asia are non-literate: in Turkey 80 per cent are non-literate, in Iran 80-85 per cent; in Pakistan 80-85 per cent; in Afghanistan 90 per cent; in Soviet central Asia about 50 per cent. And most of these are rural people: in Turkey 75-80 per cent are rural, in Iran and Pakistan 80-85 per cent; in Afghanistan 95 per cent; in Soviet central Asia 70 per cent. The peasant-tribal societies of western and central Asia are therefore, in contrast to the developed world, essentially rural and agrarian.

Literacy, *sui generis*, is not however the answer to precipitate change. Literacy, like a plow or a belief system, is simply a cultural tool and can be used to create and perpetuate a totalitarian régime as easily as it can create a favorable atmosphere for democratic institutions. And even if the bulk of the people were literate, linguistic diversity would still be a major divisive factor.

Turkey uses a latinized script developed almost overnight at the direct order of Mustafa Kemal Ataturk. The Soviet central Asian republics use a Cyrillic script. Iran, Afghanistan, and Pakistan retain a modified Arabic script. And locally oriented dress and ornaments continue to emphasize the special identity and pride of each group. The physical types, however, do blend from zone to zone. Varieties of the Mediterranean substock of the caucasoid group dominate in the west. There is much mongoloid admixture to the east and north-east. There are some australoid influences in Pakistan. And there are areas in Iran and Afghanistan where Brahui are found.

Usually, though not always, people's tribal or ethnic identifications and their languages tend to coincide. Modern Turkey is fortunate that almost all Turks speak Osmanli Turkish of the Uralic-Altaic language family. But in the rest of the modern states of western and central Asia there are myriad ethnolinguistic groupings which often slough across frontiers. Azerbaijani (Azeri) Turks live in north-western Iran and eastern Turkey, with their own Soviet Socialist Republic in the Soviet Union. The Shahsavan (Protectors of the Shah) live in the Moghan steppes south of the Russian border. The Kurdish people, who are also Indo-European speakers, live in Iran, Turkey and Iraq, and in small numbers in the USSR. South of the Caspian Sea towards the Elburz Mountains live several groups who speak Persian dialects: Gilaki, Gilani, Mazanderani.

In the Zagros Mountains, ranging from north-west to south-east, there are, in addition to Persian-speaking villagers (such as the Lur), nomadic and semi-nomadic 15

A Baluchi boy plays a *sorud*. His people live in Pakistan and Iran. Traditionally they are nomads who despise settled farmers.

groups of other Indo-European speakers (Bakhtiari, Kuh Galu, Mamassani), as well as the Turkic-speaking Qashqai. In north-eastern Iran various groups of Turkoman – Turkic-speaking, aquiline, mongoloid-looking people – live relatively sedentary modern lives compared to the past. There is a separate Turkoman Soviet Socialist Republic to the north, and other Turkoman live in the plains and foothills of north-western Afghanistan.

Along the Tangistani coast of south Iran many groups speak Arabic. Other Semitic speakers include the Assyrians, who are Nestorians, and Chaldeans of Iran and Turkey, with some Christian Armenians, who are Indo-Europeans, and Parsees or Zoroastrians who are Persian-speakers – further complicating the picture.

Persian-speaking villagers live on both sides of the Irano-Afghan frontier with groups interspersed among them of Berberi (Barbari) mongoloid-looking peoples who possibly have Aimaq antecedents. In the Sistan Basin of Iran and Afghanistan and adjacent areas of Pakistan live the Baluch and Brahui. A specialized group of Baluch hunter-fishermen called the Sayyad live in the Sistan swamps of the Hamun-i-Hilmand.

Pakistan has four major ethnolinguistic groups: Punjabi, Sindhi, Pushtun (Pathan), Baluch, all of whom are Indo-European speakers who use mutually unintelligible dialects. The Brahui speak a dialect of Dravidian, a language family concentrated south of the Narmada river in India. Urdu and English are the common languages among the intelligentsia.

Several thousand Kafir in Chitral still practise an old pre-Islamic form of animism and nature worship, but the majority live in Afghanistan and were forcibly converted to Islam in 1895-96. They are now called Nuristani, which means 'those who have seen the light'. Four major language families are represented in land-locked Afghanistan: Indo-European, Uralic-Altaic, Dravidian, and Semitic.

The Muslim republics of Soviet central Asia (the Soviet Socialist Republics of Azerbaijan, Kazakstan, Turkmenistan, Tajikistan, Uzbekistan and Kirghizia – and the Karakalpak ASSR) have been subjected to great pressures since World War I. Soviet armies subjected them to conquest in the 1920s. These years were punctuated by periodic revolts by the so-called *basmachi* (bandits to the Russians, freedom fighters to themselves). The 1930s saw collectivization of land and modernization, both equated with russification. After World War II ethnic and cultural consciousness increased. Islam, for example, in spite of vigorous anti-religious campaigns, was never stamped out. Islam is not merely a religion but a way of life. Many collective and state farms have mosques. The people prefer traditional clothing. Even in centers like Tashkent the women still wear the horsehair veil in the old city. Free enterprise continues to be important in rural society. Suppression led to large-scale migrations to the neighboring countries of Turkey, Iran, Afghanistan and China, and today the Soviet Union is faced with growing demands for 'Tajik power', 'Uzbek power', 'Kirghiz power' and so on.

Few governments in western and central Asia can begin to replace the delicate network of reciprocal social, economic and political rights and obligations which function in groups of kinspeople at the regional and tribal level. In these groups rights and obligations are tightly defined and include everything from the right to name a child to the provision of social welfare and the waging of warfare. Past contacts with the outside world, including central governments, has usually meant one thing to the villagers: extraction of rent and taxes, conscripts for armies, raw materials, labor for projects and women for the harems of the powerful and wealthy. This partly accounts for their constant resistance to change, even in Soviet central Asia.

Within the peasant tribal societies group survival comes before individual choice. An individual's role as leader or follower is determined by his position in his family. Primogeniture is not always the custom. Economically a man usually takes up the same work as his father. And when he marries his preferred mate is his cousin, or at least somebody from within his tribe. There are occasional exceptions to this – peasants have become kings; Pushtun men sometimes marry Uzbek women – but these are rare. People are bound to the land, which is often controlled by absentee landlords, because of a general lack of mobility. Even nomads, though they travel great distances, lack basic mobility, for they usually move from their winter quarters to their summer quarters and back again, year after year, generation after generation.

From the moment a child is born his position in the family is fixed. As the younger brother or sister he is pampered and loved. But this soon changes. At about the same time when children in western societies are just beginning to prepare for their future roles at school, the western and central Asian is already living his future role in life. Almost overnight he becomes an adult with a full range of social, economic and political responsibilities. There is no time for learning away from the family. The family is the way of life. In western and central Asian rural society the family is three-tiered. The old are respected, for they are the walking encyclopaedias of the society; fathers and mothers represent the economically producing unit (the present); grandparents (the past) teach the children (the future) about their history and customs. Folk-tales and folk-songs are important means of instruction, particularly since most of the people are non-literate. Unlike western folk-songs, the folk-literature of western and central Asia is meant to help perpetuate, not to protest. Again this illustrates the importance of the group over the individual.

Through folk-tales boys and girls learn the ideal personality type. For the male there is the warrior-poet. For the female there is the bountiful mother-helper. Children learn their economic roles from their parents, and from other brothers and sisters whose heavy-handed discipline quickly integrates the younger ones into a society graded by age and sex. Young people in the towns, many of whom are exposed to the individually oriented western education system, are rapidly moving away from the idea of respect for the old.

The kinship system can be described as basically patrilineal – as descent is traced through the father's side of the family; patrilocal – as the bride moves to her husband's house; and patriarchal – as authority rests in the hands of the elders. In reality, however, there are many matri-influences. Most marriages, for example, are endogamous. Although women have little formal public power, behind the mud walls of the compound they exert great influence. The levirate, a custom obliging the brother of a dead man to marry the widow, is still common in some areas. And there is a low divorce rate. Although polygyny is permitted by Islam monogamy is the general practice. Polygyny often has a cohesive social role – for the several wives of one husband tend to be close kin.

17

People of Istanbul
Turkey

The characteristic summer colors of Istanbul, as seen from a tall building, are still the green of trees and gardens and the soft brick-red of roof tiles. Many of the old wooden houses falling into decay or being swept aside for new buildings are of an intricate beauty in their fretted decoration. Thirty years ago the population of Istanbul was well below one million. Today it approaches 2.5 million, but the built-up area has not increased to anything like the same degree, presumably because many of the new buildings are blocks of flats put up on the sites and gardens of old houses. Little suburban centers like Bebek have greatly increased their population in this way, and by creeping up the hillsides overlooking the Bosphorus.

The population of Istanbul has always been mixed, even in Byzantine and early Ottoman days, not only because of the attraction of the ancient capital but because Byzantine emperors and Ottoman sultans moved populations about to suit their purposes. Aksaray, in the old city, is so-called because people brought from Aksaray in central Anatolia were settled there. Arnavutkoy, on the Bosphorus, is named the Village of the Albanians – who settled there long ago – but it now has a considerable Greek population. Balat has many Jews whose forbears have been there since the expulsion of the Jews from Spain and who speak Castilian Spanish today. There are still Armenians, in spite of the unhappy recent history of that nation, but whereas up to the early 1960s one often saw a newspaper in the strange Armenian alphabet being read or used to wrap up vegetables this is quite rare today. The Poles of Polonezkoy (*Koy* means village in Turkish) still speak Polish and cure bacon. There is still an old-established gypsy population, even though some of their shacks have been demolished in the cause of hygiene. Young gypsy boys play the fiddle at picnic places on popular holidays, whilst their sisters dance to the tambourine. Other gypsies, boys and men, teach the brown bear to perform the clumsy antics claimed to be dancing and look expectantly up to the balconies for coins. To move house the Istanbuli may call on one of the wiry, intense-eyed, dark-haired Kurd, who are the porters of Istanbul. They bend half forward with a sort of padded camel's hump of leather on their backs so that their huge loads won't cut into their skin. And Kurds do much of the laboring on new buildings. They rarely bring their families to Istanbul, but send money back to their mountain homes in eastern Anatolia. Except for the slant-eyed tribesmen who specialize in fur hats and gloves and have recently arrived from central Asia, the Turks who come to Istanbul are surprisingly European-looking. There has hardly been such a melting-pot of races as Asia Minor.

A boy will arrive and get a job as a grocer's messenger. He becomes known and trusted in the quarter, gets a job as a door-keeper to a block of flats, brings his mother from the country to look after him and eventually marries. Men establish themselves as car-washers, stake a claim in a street and make themselves useful in return for some sort of living. A man starts selling vegetables spread out on a big box off a boulevard in a side street – a stepped, cobbled street with no traffic – and he curls up inside the box for the night.

Since Ataturk's revolution all Turks are required to wear European dress. Middle-class men usually wear dark, unadventurous suits and go hatless; working-class men wear poorer suits and dark cloth caps. The newly arrived women, who in Anatolia would still wear their colorful traditional costumes, also conform, but cling to an old propriety by tying a scarf or colored handkerchief over their heads. Middle-aged Turks are silently shocked, whilst the youth of Istanbul openly jeer, at mini-skirted western girls, the long hair, untidiness and half nudity of young western men, and the open fondling of these young people in public.

The old crafts flourish in the city. There are gold and silver smiths and jewelers, coppersmiths, tailors, carpenters, mattress-makers and flockers. The knife-grinder comes to the door with his wheel to give knives and penknives a sharp edge for a few *kuruş*. There are plumbers and electricians, but these are much in demand in Germany and are not always easy to find in Istanbul. Half a dozen cheerful men now make buckets in a 16th century Turkish bath near the Küçük Aya Sofya Mosque and the gleaming new zinc of the stacked buckets catches the daylight from the central aperture in the dome. All these craftsmen have time to stop and talk about their work. Out along the Bosphorus there are fine boat-builders and, in the city, employment at an efficient ship-building yard. There are even market gardeners within the old city walls, for the walls were built to enclose a space which could make the city self-supporting over a long siege. Water was stored in great cisterns and some of the open ones are now gardens or football fields.

The new factories are mostly outside the city. They produce textiles, shoes, tires, medicines and a whole range of things in plastic. Tractors are assembled and cars are produced by building a Turkish body round an imported engine. Radios and sewing machines are made from locally manufactured and imported parts. Working conditions are good in the new factories.

Begging is illegal in Turkey and there are very few beggars in Istanbul. The most conspicuous begging of late years has been by young western Europeans, many of them British, who play the guitar and openly invite contributions towards their expenses. This astonishes and disturbs the Turk, who has been encouraged to look to western Europe for guidance in modernizing himself. The city is no longer tolerant of these young seekers for adventure or drugs. There is little observable prostitution in the city but there are, or were until very recently, some streets of strictly controlled licensed brothels, near the main shopping center, where the Turk will quite often

Behind the row-boats and a modern Bosphorus ferry rise the minarets of the Yeni Cami, a Byzantine church turned mosque in old Istanbul.

People of Istanbul

The Turk despises western ostentatious sexual freedom; but strip clubs have their clients as well as the more traditional licensed brothels.

The exquisite mosque of Eyup with its serpentine blue tiles is a center for Muslim pilgrims. Its brass gratings are 'kissed shiny by the devout'.

(Bottom) The revolution of Ataturk brought liberation to the young generation of Turkish women. Their mothers still follow Muslim tradition.

favor a middle-aged, motherly woman. There is crime, of course, mostly burglary and car theft for joy-riding, and there are some expert pickpockets and snatch thieves.

An Istanbuli with a few small coins in his pocket need never go hungry or thirsty for long, since, apart from restaurants and sandwich bars, there are small kiosks (a Turkish word) and itinerant vendors to supply him with a variety of refreshments. He likes his fruit drink really pressed from fruit, not colored or synthetic in any way. He buys bottled spring drinking-water at the grocers or queues to fill his bottle or jar at a tapped spring – perhaps with special properties. If he can afford the little extra money he drinks the bottled natural fizzy water, *maden suyu*. He loves and has great faith in *ayran*, yogurt beaten up with water. On a night out the Istanbul Turk will drink raki, a grape spirit distilled with aniseed and liquorice – before, during and after his meal. He regards beer and wine, both of which are good in Turkey, as rather effeminate drinks, but in mixed middle-class parties he will order them too. He has recently become a tea drinker, with sugar but no milk. Although the Turk introduced coffee drinking to the world today his country can produce plenty of tea but no coffee. High import duty has made coffee a prestige drink. In need of refreshment

20

(Right) Aya Sofia, now a State Museum, is a striking example of a Byzantine church which became a mosque with 20-foot Islamic inscriptions.

Istanbuli porters carry staggering weights and quantities on their backs, protected only by a leather-padded cradle.

Unemployment is a serious problem. Begging is illegal, and men who cannot find work often spend days in idleness smoking their nargilahs.

during the day and in the open air, a Turk will sometimes look for a vendor of pickle-water. This drink, *tursu suyu*, will be ladled for him with much ceremony out of great glass jars on a little push-cart. Until disturbed the pickled vegetables which flavour the liquid present a colorful arrangement. There are portable charcoal grills which will give him *köfte*, a hot meat rissole.

The Turk may not be as aware as a Frenchman that he eats in a great tradition, a tradition of cooking of which Istanbul has been the capital. The world has three great cuisines, French, Chinese and Turkish, and all round the eastern Mediterranean, from Greece through to Egypt and then along the north African coast, there are variants, usually inferior, of Turkish cooking. For the Istanbul Turk a meal is not a thing to be rushed. He may sit in the evening and not leave the table for two or three hours. No management will try to hurry him. *Mezes* will come first, a great variety of tasty little dishes as hors d'oeuvre with raki to drink, ordered by the bottle if he is not alone, and a Turk eating alone is a very rare sight. In good time he will order a grill, *şiş kebab*, gobbets of lamb grilled on skewers over charcoal, or swordfish, *kiliç*, if it is in season, grilled in the same way. The restaurant may specialize in *döner kebab,* cooked with proper ceremony behind a window near the entrance – sliced lamb pressed down on to a perpendicular bar and roasted in front of an upright, barred charcoal fire, the savory meat sliced off as it turns and cooks on the outside. His wife will probably have one of the sticky pastry sweets, *baklava* or *kadayif.* For lunch in the business quarters of the city he may turn in to a simple fish restaurant, possibly on a boat, near Galata Bridge, or reach down from the side ramp of the bridge for a sandwich of fresh tunny fried on a primus in a bobbing boat. The food of the worker, at least during the working day, is usually a loaf of bread flavored with *piyaz*, a salad or stew with chopped lettuce, beans and onions or with a raw onion or tomato.

The Turk likes personal service and the shops of Istanbul are still small. Young married couples will go to the great covered bazaar, Kapali Çarsi, a vast, roofed, traffic-less shopping area with lovely woven things, Turkish pop records, cheap shoes and a glittering street of gold. Couples of all ages will go to the Spice Bazaar, Misir Carsi, for the spices the wife needs in her cooking, for goat's milk cheese from goatskins and preserved meat, *pastirma*, from eastern Anatolia. And everywhere they will find fruit and vegetable stalls, with mountains of delicious oranges in the spring and huge peaches and apricots in summer.

Turks go often to Turkish baths, many of them very old. Some baths are used by both sexes, either on different days or in different sections. He may not be well off, but the Turk, even a struggling student, will have his shoes cleaned, either by boys – beginners who trail round the city with their makeshift boxes – or by established shoe-cleaners with a regular pitch and a beautiful box

In the Seref Stadium in Istanbul these Turks prepare to exhibit their powers and skill at the wrestling competitions.

(Bottom) Wrestling was once Turkey's most popular spectator sport. One of the western influences has been its replacement by football.

decorated with shining brass and colored pictures. Barbers ply a good trade and are to be found everywhere. A regular haircut and shave are necessities to a Turk.

For entertainment the Istanbuli will usually go to the cinema, either to a foreign film or to a melodramatic Turkish film produced on a shoestring. The theater flourishes too and a Turk of today can enjoy, translated into his own language, anything from *There's a girl in my soup* to Beckett's *End Game*. Opera, ballet and celebrity concerts are well attended and the Istanbul father may encourage his daughter to become a concert pianist, launching her, if he can afford to, in a recital with orchestra and bouquet.

But he will not go to see *Karagöz*, as his grandfather did. This ancient puppet show has been ousted, as a popular spectacle, by the cinema. Essentially a tent show, it was brought here from Asia by the Turkish invaders. In it images are projected from behind onto a screen of thin white material. The puppets, made of translucent animal skin and boldly painted, are worked with pieces of cane which cast no shadow on the screen. The sketches deal with everyday life, with touches of social satire but without any political or religious implications. The present-day Turk's grandfather saw grosser comedy than this century has seen, when Karagöz himself had a huge penis which was sometimes put to other uses than the erotic, as a post for tying up a donkey, for instance, and this had the audience rolling on the benches. Karagöz, the chief character, has recently been a poor countryman struggling to make both ends meet. His friend Hacivad has a townish air of pretense to refinement. Houses, mosques and bushes appear as scenery and extraordinary effects of fire and smoke are still produced by the few remaining practitioners.

Football has ousted wrestling as the popular spectator sport. Fishing is the pastime which gets most general participation, from small boys on Galata Bridge to well-to-do bourgeois couples who get their tackle out of their cars along the Bosphorus shore. Picnicking in the Belgrad Forest is another passion. Processions are popular, especially children's processions on appropriate holidays, when the children sometimes dance along the street to the drum and pipe. The revived janissary bands give a traditional note to such festivities. Political demonstrations occur as often as they are allowed by the government of the day and they can end in sudden violence if the police and army show partisanship. On Saturdays and Sundays people of all ages, but mostly young men, parade in the Istiklal Caddesi.

Marriage ceremonies are no longer what they were but are conducted in European dress in a municipal setting. The circumcision ceremony *sünnet*, however, still echoes the splendor and gaiety depicted in the colorful 16th century volumes of miniature paintings in the great libraries of Istanbul. The boys are beautifully dressed and wear round, felt-topped bonnets, bright with sequins, for

the customary visit to the mosque at Eyup before the operation at home.

Schoolchildren here are neatly and uniformly dressed to make less obvious the great differences in wealth which exist. Turkish boys are treated as adults from an early age and develop confidence and an independent outlook. Young girls are more strictly brought up and since they stay at home more in the evenings and do more homework are apt to do better than the boys in examinations. Even at university age many girls are not free to go out at night. But there is little discrimination against them in professional careers and several departments in Istanbul University are notably headed by women.

The people of Istanbul have learnt to tolerate a considerable swing from winter snow to summer heat. They are sensitive to winds from different quarters and their tempers are sorely affected by the *lodos*, the wind from the south. There always seems to be something going on in this lively city and – if there isn't – anyone with time to spare and a small coin in his pocket can take a ferryboat and visit his aunt or a mosque or a market at Uskudar, over a narrow stretch of water to another continent and another atmosphere.

23

Turkish villagers

Over 75 per cent of Turkey's
population are rural. This
Anatolian shepherd's
voluminous sheepskin coat
protects him in any weather.

In the more remote areas of Turkey, beyond the influence of the government and towns, are independent, self-sufficient villages, where the people grow all the food they need and use the rough natural wool of their sheep to make blankets and clothes. For these villagers the land provides all. They gather loose stones from the hillsides to build the walls of their flat-roofed houses. The wood they need to support the roof they cut down, or more often, because wood is scarce, cull from carefully tended stands of timber grown for the purpose. They transport both stone and wood, and anything else for that matter, in rough wooden carts. These carts have solid wood wheels which are attached to the wooden axles by wooden pins.

A Turkish village is such a jumble of streets and buildings that it looks as if it might have fallen out of the sky. It has however an order, an internal social order. The apparently haphazard clusters of buildings in fact represent different village quarters, each of which generally centers on a group of male kinsmen. The village is indeed a very special place for a Turk. Almost all his family live here, and it is by working cooperatively with his family that he obtains his livelihood. His wife probably comes from the same village.

There is no member of the village who does not belong to a household. The villagers describe a household as a group of people who eat from the same cooking pot. They are in fact a group of people who pool the fruits of their labor earned in the village or elsewhere, which revolves around a group of male kinsmen. Under the head of the household are all his married sons and their dependents, as well as his unmarried sons and daughters. When daughters marry they go to live with their husbands' families and become part of their households. The members of the household all live together under the same roof if possible. But if the household is very large they occupy several different houses preferably next door to each other. A villager explains it thus: 'We are three houses' he says, pointing at three houses in a street, 'but we are one house' – one economic unit, one household. The more successful and prosperous a household, the higher its position in the community. A man who marries a daughter of such a household will make a good match. Although the marriage will cost his family a great deal in bride-price, they will be more than compensated by the bride's family's contribution of clothing, furniture and other domestic items. The bridegroom will also be making an important alliance, likely to be very useful in his future dealings with the community.

A Turkish villager has not only great loyalty to his close kin, particularly the people who live in the same house, he also cares deeply about the welfare of the whole village. He is proud of the skill and enterprise of its menfolk. The virtues of the women of the village are jealously guarded and proclaimed in relation to other villages. Villagers who become prominent in national

25

Turkish villagers

The empire of Genghis Khan, the mighty ruler, stretched across all of Central Asia from the Pacific Ocean to the Black Sea.

The land's limited resources are used carefully. Lacking wood here in the Am-Tahier pass camel dung is collected and dried in the sun for fuel.

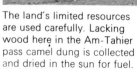

26

Motor vehicles belong to the cities of Turkey. In rural areas the camel and the donkey are still a man's best friends.

In the fierce winds of the Plain of Anatolia, this man with his cloak, cap and muffler is better protected than his sheepdog

affairs are remembered and talked about with pride.

Over three quarters of the population of Turkey are farmers who live in village communities. Each village is governed by a headman who is traditionally a man of wealth and power, and a council of elders. The headman is nowadays democratically elected every two years and paid by the government, who makes him responsible for duties. He has to assess and collect taxes, maintain the public buildings such as the school, and forward to the appropriate authority the names of all the young men eligible for national service. His signature must countersign all applications by his villagers for grants of money from the agricultural bank or for the supply of Government seed. He must also report anything untoward, such as an outbreak of an epidemic, to the authorities. Although Turkish law today requires a council to be elected with the headman, this formally elected council rarely meets. When a matter of sufficient public interest does arise it is debated, discussed and resolved by an informal council composed of all the senior householders. The government also demands that each village appoint a watchman or a policeman. His duties are not onerous, 27

Turkish villagers

These Mawlai dervishes, known in the west as whirling dervishes, stimulate themselves to a state of ecstasy by their continual whirling movement.

however, as all household heads are responsible for the behavior of their subordinates. The villagers appoint a couple of watchmen for the growing crops and herdsmen for the sheep and goats. These servants of the community, unlike the salaried, state-appointed officials, are paid in kind by each household they serve.

A household breaks up only when the head of the household dies. Then his sons set up their own households, although for a short time a group of brothers may keep the old household organization together, particularly if they have unmarried sisters to support or other responsibilities which require a corporate financial involvement. The danger when households break up and re-form is that one man may be left with too little land to farm and the possibility of being unable to provide food and clothing for his family and not being able to meet his other commitments – money, for example, for a son's wedding.

The increasing shortage of land is a problem which faces many villagers. Improved medical and maternity care in the rural areas result in people living longer. More people than ever before survive childbirth and the critical years of childhood. The population of the village grows and there comes a time when there is simply not enough land to go round. It is then that the men have to seek other work outside the village.

Fortunately this is relatively easy. The growing towns and cities are a ready market for labor from rural areas. Many farmers are also skilled builders and laborers and have no difficulty in finding jobs in the towns. The men are generally reluctant to leave their villages even temporarily, but they can do so happy in the knowledge that their small patches of land will be farmed by their brothers and their dependents will be well cared for. And with the money they earn the villagers buy manufactured goods and modern conveniences. The government is increasingly establishing factories and other enterprises in the rural areas to attract surplus labor from the villages. Better education today opens horizons for young people beyond the village and its traditional occupations. There are further possibilities of clerical, professional and administrative careers in the cities and towns. Nevertheless this is a particularly critical period for the village council whose responsibility it is to ensure that half the village arable land is left fallow each year to safeguard the harvests of the future, and that common village pasture is not encroached upon for crops.

Within the village, though, life continues much as it has for centuries. Only the seasons mark changes in village routine. In spring and summer the men tend their fields

Restaurant owners along the shore of the Bosphorus attract customers by providing belly-dancers for live entertainment.

The Turkish villager is a proud and hardy man. With all his kin around him he is part of a strong and reliable community.

(Bottom) Along the narrow cobbled streets of Ayvalik, on the Aegean coast, this old woman makes her way to the open-air market to buy fish.

which are usually some distance away from the village. The men go out with small animal teams and drag heavy wooden plows through the hard earth. Then they sow the seeds – mainly wheat and cereals – by hand. After that, apart perhaps from an early weeding and frequent prayers to Allah to send light rains to nurture the seed and lots of sunshine to ripen the grain, it is up to the watchmen to guard the crops and keep them safe from attacks by birds and animals. In small walled plots nearer home the villagers cultivate vines, fruit trees, melons and vegetables.

Every farmer concentrates on growing enough food for his household's needs. He makes sure that he stores some grain out of each harvest so that the family can have bread right through the winter and some seeds to plant in the following spring. If he has a surplus he sells it for cash in the market of the nearby town, or to the government warehouses.

The women spend their day cooking food for the household's daily needs. They also spend some time preparing food for storage for the winter. On baking days women sometimes make up to three months' supply of the flat hard bread made from wheat flour. Every day they milk the sheep and goats and every day they boil the milk immediately. They make yogurt by adding a little

29

Turkish villagers

After World War I an exchange
of populations took place
between Turkey and Greece;
all the Greeks then left this
small fishing town of Ayvalik.

of the old yogurt to newly boiled milk. The family eat yogurt either by itself or mixed with water to make *ayran,* a drink not unlike buttermilk. The remainder of the milk they put in a scalded calf's or goat's skin. The pores in the skin allow the milk to evaporate slowly and keep cool. When it has turned sour they remove it and separate the whey from the coagulated milk. They store the coagulated cream which has turned into butter for cooking. As a break from preparing and cooking the food the women go to the village fountain several times a day to collect water or wash clothes, and to meet, to talk, and exchange news.

Harvest time is the busiest time. Then the village hums with activity. Everybody who can hold a sickle goes out in the fields to help cut the crops. The grain then has to be winnowed, threshed and finally taken to the miller to be ground. The people who have a surplus of grain or flour hurry off to the market to get there early to take advantage of the higher prices early in the season. Then, after the harvest is over, the villagers have time to relax. Little work can be done when winter and the snows arrive. Households sit and talk around a fire far into the night in the long winter evenings. Then the young people listen entranced to the old people who tell stories of great and stirring events of long ago.

Men and women lead divergent lives in the village.

30

Although the Turks despise
their hippy western visitors,
these fields of poppy are
one of the world's main
sources of raw opium.

As good Muslims, these Turks take time off from their work, remove their shoes, and bow down toward Mecca in worship of Allah.

The men work outside the home on the farm. The women's work is in the home itself, preparing and cooking food and bringing up the children. In a large household the wife of the household head organizes and supervises her sons' wives and her own daughters. Her daughters stay with her until they are about seventeen when they marry. Her sons, however, leave at a much earlier age to join their fathers working in the fields. Only at harvest time, when there is a great deal to be done, do men and women work side by side. Even at mealtimes the men eat separately. Only when their men have had their fill do the women and children eat.

The way the houses are designed reflects this division between the sexes. Most are single-storey, flat-roofed dwellings made out of local stone and wood with roofs of hard-packed earth, in each of which there is a kitchen-cum-living room where the women spend much of their day. At night this becomes the bedroom of the head of the household. The biggest and best furnished room in the house is the men's living room from which women are barred except when they are required to serve the men coffee and food. In the houses of rich villagers there is also a separate women's room, possibly a lavatory and bathroom and a number of small rooms for the younger members of the household.

Marriage, against this background of separation in men's and women's daily lives, is based on other considerations than romantic love between the couple. The family decides when a boy or girl is ready for marriage and generally it is the boy's family who approach the girl's family to make the necessary arrangements. Apart from settling the all-important question of the bride-wealth the families also have to ensure that the kinship relationship of the couple is not too close. A couple who share a grandfather in common, for example, would not be permitted to marry. Even a couple whose grandfathers were brothers would find it difficult to get permission. Once these questions are settled the engagement is announced and the girl's parents begin to buy clothing and furniture for the couple with the money they have obtained from the boy's parents. With the rest of the money they start to amass food in preparation for the engagement party. After the party the wedding is solemnized in the village mosque and the legal papers required by the government are signed.

The couple are now legally married in Turkish law, but for the villagers there is still one important event that must take place before the couple begin to live together. About a month after the wedding ceremony in the mosque the girl's parents, with the help of the boy's female relatives, make preparations for a large feast to which the entire village is invited. Only after several days of feasting, dancing and storytelling, during which nobody except the women does any work, is the marriage recognized by the village and the young couple begin their life together.

31

The wheat fields are some distance away from Turkish villages. Ox carts with wooden wheels are a common means of transport.

Troglodytes of Cappadocia
Turkey

The spikey coned hills of the Goreme Valley, in Central Turkey's Cappadocia make one of the world's weirdest landscapes. Travelers have often called it lunar, yet now we know that the surface of the moon is far more ordinary than the jagged horizons of these Cappadocian hills that look like jumbled rows of dunces' pointed hats. The rock pinnacles were formed because the soft rock was protected in places by hard rock, so that erosion by the battering winds and vicious winters of Cappadocia made tapering columns with protective rock as a cap – until the cap fell off leaving behind a rocky needle.

The region has another unusual aspect. In the modern Turkey of new schools and skyscrapers there are Cappadocians who have shunned the right-angles and cemented security of smart houses. Like rotten teeth, the cones are riddled from top to bottom with holes – hewn from the soft rock by the owners. Inside them live Turkey's troglodytes.

Cave-dwelling is certainly not new to Goreme. The present inhabitants tell you that the first cave-dweller was Hieron (Hieronymus), an early Christian martyr fleeing from persecution in 300 AD. He ran from his vineyard into a cave and hid there till lured out by a trick and betrayed. Around 400 AD came St Basil of Caesarea (modern Kayseri, a thriving town about fifty miles north-east of the Goreme area). He thought cave-dwelling was conducive to holy life, and encouraged Christians to burrow into the pinnacles and live there. In the 13th century there were 30,000 cave Christians, and over 300 chapels. Cave-dwelling declined together with Byzantium and since 1500 AD there have been few cave-dwellers – although a few stay on, and almost none of them Christian.

The caves that open out at the very foot of the cones are usually for cows. To reach a cave inhabited by people you climb up a ladder to the dark aperture often twelve feet above. A family may own a whole cone, with caves carved here and there. Some are connected by chimney-like shafts, but most are isolated in the rock-face. One or two grander ones have rock staircases leading up. Others have entrances so small that you have to squeeze into them. Some have spacious balconies.

There are Cappadocians who still spend their spare time hacking away at the rock to make themselves another room, but most of the dwellings were made centuries ago by the Christians. Many of them were evidently chapels. It is remarkable how well they have stood the test of time, although vandals and Muslim fanatics have obliterated many of the frescoes that covered the walls and ceilings, and so has the harsh Cappadocian weather.

The chapels are mostly the size of an ordinary western living room. St Basil discouraged his disciples from becoming hermits – he thought few men were psychologically fit to live quite alone. But he thought the large monasteries of the Sinai desert were too big for the Superior to look after all the priests properly. So the Christians of Cappadocia probably lived in tight-knit communities of five or six to a cave.

The caves were punctilious replicas of the chapels of Byzantium, reflecting the rigidity of that Christian organization. In defiance of architectural need, they all had pillars, and high domes. Today many of the pillars are smashed clean away under the capitals, leaving the tops of them and the arches hanging like oddly formed stalactites. Sometimes the brittle rock face has dropped away to expose the stern bearded prophets and saints to the open air and sunlight. But in most of the cave chapels there is a twilight effect. St George (born in Cappadocia) and his dragon lurk in shadows or in darkness. Only with a torch can you see the rich colors that sometimes still remain – tomato-reds, deep blues and mellow golds.

The caves that are lived in are well-carpeted. Home-woven rugs are hung on the walls and lie on the floors and divans, which are of wood (a rare commodity in Cappadocia) or carved out of the stone. There are plenty of cushions, and guests, with shoes off, can recline comfortably in the family's best cave. Niches and shelves are carved out of the walls.

The kitchen and living room will often share a single, central chamber, but the sleeping quarters are not always connected. A family might have to descend a rickety ladder to the base of the cone and then climb another to a bedroom cave. Arched ceilings, raised altar and frescoes of the walls make some local farmers superstitious and they will speak of cave ghosts. Still more caves may intrude into the cone, above or below the main living places. Some are used as stables or storerooms, others are empty and dark and scattered with the débris of centuries.

At first, outsiders find it hard to see. The caves are smoky, and the eyes take time to adapt to the dim light and the sting of smoke. The cave-dwellers have drier abodes than their compatriots on the plains, and their homes never leak.

But in almost every way, the cave-dwellers' style of life is similar to other Cappadocian and Anatolian Turks. There are many families in the Goreme Valley who have some members living in caves, others in ordinary houses. Some houses huddle at the foot of a cone, and it is hard to see whether they merge with caves or not. Many people in Goreme have lived in both cave and house, and many own both types of dwelling – though it is true that of this category most people put their animals and stores in their caves, while they themselves live in the house.

Like all Cappadocians, the women and men wear baggy trousers, and the women have bright printed scarves with which they hide the lower part of their faces, leaving just the nose peeping out, when they see strangers. When it is cold, the people sometimes wrap rugs round themselves. (Goreme is famous for its weaving, and women spend much time making rugs, grainsacks and

Caves dug out of the eroded rock cones in Turkey's Goreme valley have been inhabited since paleolithic times.

Troglodytes of Cappadocia Turkey

Early Christians made the
Cappadocian caves into
chapels and monasteries.
Today walls can still be seen
covered with fading Byzantine
paintings.

saddlebags on their upright looms.)

Work is mostly agricultural. People rise at dawn and go off in creaking carts, with solid wood wheels, pulled by donkeys. Only on Friday do they rest. But there are long periods, especially in winter, when there is not much to do. The idea of day-to-day work is horrific. Nevertheless, the soil is poor, and so are the people. When there is an opportunity for work, it is grabbed. Many go off as migrant labor to the big towns. The wheat yield is low, and few men are rich. Cows and chickens add to the diet of cereals.

But there is fruit, too – dried apricots, raisins, grape-jam, apples. Everyone eats yogurt. And they make delicious mint salads. Shish kebab is the staple meat dish – sheep brains are a luxury. There is good white wine, and you can taste it before buying. Vodka, brandy and raki (an aniseed-flavored spirit) cheer you up in winter.

Troglodytes have the same village system as the people on the plains. They have common grazing lands, small (often fragmented) smallholdings of their own, and an elected headman. Some men own several caves, even several cones, and rent them out to others; but generally there are no great differences of wealth.

The family is the closest unit. Boys are almost all married between the ages of 16 and 22, girls between 14 and 18. But even after marriage, sons stay in the father's household till the father dies. Though the family is close-knit, fathers and sons often have bitter quarrels.

The troglodytes follow the same Muslim code as other Turks. To call a man *gavur* – infidel – is the worst abuse. Since the time of Kemal Ataturk's assault against religion, Mohammedanism has lost much of its fervor, but in Goreme the people fear the cave spirits as well as Allah. There is often hushed talk of wandering cave ghosts, and the wierd cones are sometimes called fairy chimneys.

As in the rest of Turkey, there is a conflict in the people's (especially the men's) behavior. On the one hand there is the need for 'morality' – you are respected if you know the Koran, are wise, gentle, kind and dutiful towards the *hoca* who leads the Friday prayers. On the other hand, 'honor' must be kept at all costs. It would be laudable to knife a man for soliciting your daughter. Violence is common, though strangers are treated with usual Turkish courtesy.

All in all, Turkish troglodytes differ little from their compatriots on the plains of Anatolia or Cappadocia. There are many more uninhabited caves than inhabited ones. But if you explore the cones and are lucky enough to come across a deserted old chapel, complete with painted prophets and St George, you do not have to be a romantic to think yourself back into the days of the caves' founders, who ate so little and prayed so much. And you feel that the spirits of those early Christians and their Byzantine successors are the true occupants.

Muslims live in the caves today. Even so, the people fear wandering cave ghosts and the cones are sometimes called fairy chimneys.

The Cappadocian soil is poor and so are the people. If there is a chance of work in the towns, the young men leave the valley.

(Bottom) Some people live in houses huddled at the base of the cones. They keep their livestock and stores in the caves at the back.

Kurds
Syria, Turkey, Russia, Iran and Iraq

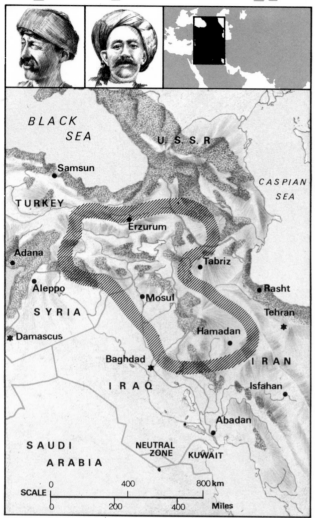

The Kurds have a reputation in literature as fierce, predatory mountain bandits. They admire courage and the qualities of leadership. Their ferocious reputation has probably arisen because not only have they always had to defend themselves from their neighbors but they are also divided from each other into isolated and opposing communities.

The Kurds are possibly Kardukai, descendants of the peoples who harried Xenophon's retreat in 400 BC. There are references to Kurds dating back to the Sumerian and Assyrian periods. Their history has been one of constant conquest and subjugation by others: by the Arabs in the 7th century, by the Mongols and Seljuks in the 11th century and by the Turks until the collapse of the Ottoman empire. Then, after World War I, their lands were divided between Syria, Turkey, Iran and Iraq. Ever since the Kurds' harsh, mountainous territories were first called Kurdistan in the 12th century they have persistently struggled for self-determination.

Kurdistan today is divided between five national

37

Since the 12th century the Kurds have been bravely fighting for autonomy in their mountain fastnesses — so far without success.

The finest turquoises in the world have been mined in Persia for over 800 years. Now the craftsman uses machines to grind and polish the stones.

lines of mounds, looming over flat plains like strange lunar craters and pointing the way to the village that awaits the *qanat's* supply of cold, fresh water.

The village, in the past, was defended against marauders by high mud walls with corner towers and a single gateway. Families lived in narrow rooms in the outer wall leaving central area clear for livestock. The walls, however, were easily broken down. And a determined invader could merely sit at the mouth of the *qanat* which was often some distance from the village, and cut off the water supply. Then the main defense lay in negotiation, isolation or, in the long term, assimilation. Today most villages have spread both inwards and outwards from the defensive wall, which remains only as a reminder of a more turbulent past. The village is a network of narrow lanes between high mud walls with low doorways which occasionally open out into courtyards. Each courtyard is the home of a family. For much of the year the villagers live outdoors and the courtyard is a bustling center for cooking, washing, talking and playing. On one side the animals are stabled – usually a donkey for carrying burdens, a cow for work or for meat and some sheep and goats for their meat and milk products. The women make yogurt (*marst*), sharp cheese and *dugh*, a refresh-

ing drink from goats' milk, to supplement the crops of the field. Chickens roam free, dropping their eggs on the baked earth where they are gathered by the children.

The male head of the family is a small king. The family is a self-sufficient unit which provides its members with a place in the economic and social life of the wider social unit, the village. A husband and his wife or wives live with their children and aged parents, unmarried brothers, sisters, aunts and uncles in a small complex of rooms where everything is shared. Although civil law now forbids polygyny, a man may, by Muslim law, take four wives, and it is still a sign of wealth and status in many villages. The wives live in separate rooms in the same courtyard. They often treat each other like sisters.

Children help to do adult work from an early age. The boys help their fathers in the fields and tend livestock in the grazing land beyond. And girls learn to wash, cook and sew. At the end of a long day in the fields the men return to their respective courtyards and, after washing from a jug poured by one of the children, they go to sit in the main room. This room is always kept clean and tidy. Rugs cover the floor which has been carefully swept with twigs. The mattresses and quilts that are laid out for sleeping at night are neatly piled away in a niche. And the samovar for boiling tea gleams bright in the corner. The men take off their pants and jackets and sit in loose pajamas on the floor. A cloth is laid out in the middle. The women serve plates of mutton stew, flavored with local herbs. Beside each place they lay flat ovals of bread, baked in a mud-brick oven in the courtyard. The bread serves both as staple food and as utensil for eating the stew. When the men have finished the women carry out the food that is left. They eat with their children in the next room. After the meal many go to visit neighbors or sit talking. The women sometimes join the men and discuss the state of the land and crops, outstanding events such as weddings or deaths and, in recent years, the career of a favored son who has gone to the town to be educated. In winter the family keep warm under a *corsee*. Charcoal embers are placed on a tray beneath a low table, a large quilt is spread across, often reaching the walls of the small room, and everyone crowds underneath with only their heads and shoulders sticking out.

Weddings create great excitement. As they are a public affirmation of relationships between family groups as much as individual relationships between two people they are arranged by the families. It is the boy and girl who are involved, however, who have the first say. When the boy has seen the girl and taken a liking to her, he usually approaches the girl's family with an offer. Although for much of their lives they will spend more time with members of their own sex than with each other, they are under considerable social pressure to remain together. For the Iranian villager marriage is the most important step in his life. It is the means of access to land, status and security. On the day of a wedding a drummer

Entire Persian families may work for months to produce a single carpet: the father chants the color pattern to his wife and children, also tying knots.

and a flute player arrive to play, and a large meal for many guests is provided. The bride and groom are taken in procession to their respective bath houses to be washed, shaved and newly clothed. The groom wears a neat suit. The bride wears a long flowered dress and a white, full-length veil. At night the mothers of the couple, having given the girl the appropriate advice, make the public announcement of her virginity once the marriage has been consummated. Wedding days are the gayest days in the village.

Many of the religious feasts tend to be sadder occasions. The Shi'a Islam of Iran developed to some extent as a means of expressing a local identity within a religion brought by a foreigner. Although the Iranians wholeheartedly embrace Islam – with its message of equality and its warrior heroes with their understanding of human weakness – they nevertheless resented the Arab peoples who brought it to them. In the conflict over the true line of succession after Mohammed's death the Shi'a Muslims favored Ali, the prophet's son-in-law, and his appointed successors, Hassan and Hossein. They broke away from orthodox Sunni Islam, which accepted the political as well as religious domination of Arab Caliphs in Medina and Baghdad. They await the return of the twelfth Imam who disappeared while still young and without a successor. They acknowledge no one after him.

Each year the villager recalls the events of those turbulent years after Mohammed's death. He mourn-

49

The poor man's Persian carpet is a Kalam-Kar printed cloth which can be made into clothes or hung up as a wall decoration.

By painting his horse and harnessing it in a special way this Tehrani hopes to keep his most valuable possession from the evil eye.

fully re-enacts the murders of Ali, Hassan and Hossein. All aspects of his daily life are based on the example and precepts of the prophet and his followers celebrated in the Holy Book, the Koran. His ritual reciting of prescribed prayer, alternate kneeling, standing and bowing on the prayer mat, which he performs in public five times a day, is only the surface expression of a deep faith that scorns the transitory world. It helps the villager cope with his poverty and gives him a sense of importance. The Shi'a Muslim villager, who sees himself as more 'advanced' than the followers of Christ, whose teachings Mohammed superseded, has a confidence and certainty that belie his poor material conditions.

The other major line of continuity in the Iranian village, one that enables foreign influences to be accommodated and then assimilated, is the villager's faith in the glorious Iranian past. The legends of that time when Iran was the founder of the world's first great empire were passed on through oral tradition and captured for posterity in the verse of Ferdowsi, a 12th century Iranian poet. His simple, easily remembered verse, which combines folklore and history, provides Iranians with a national epic accessible to all. In many teahouses in the towns and villages men earn their living by reciting from the epic, reaffirming a sense of identity, a common link with the past, a shared sadness in its loss.

Another major continuity factor in the Iranian village lies in the very physical conditions of life there and in the system that has evolved to cope with them. Five elements are necessary to grow cereals and grain crops in Iran's semi-arid plains: land, water, seed, draft animals or equipment, and human labor. These five elements have traditionally been shared between the peasant who works the land and the richer landlord who owns it. Each gets a proportion of the crop according to how many elements he provides. Thus the poorest peasant, who provides only labor, receives only one-fifth of the crop for himself and his family, while others get two- or three-fifths if they provide animals and seed. If a peasant reaches starvation level the landlord will usually lend him enough to survive. But this ties him even more irrevocably to the land. There are wheat and maize. As well as food, they provide stubble and stalks for animal fodder. The villagers also grow vegetables, grapes, and a few trees for fruit and nuts. Occasionally they plant a cash crop such as tobacco or opium. And then they collect wild plants and shrubs. Sheep and goats' wool provides yarn for village women, to weave rugs. In small mud rooms, with narrow doorways hardly admitting any light, women weave some of the world's most beautiful carpets on horizontal looms. They have learned local patterns from their mothers before them. They suckle children at their breasts as they carefully select the bright red and orange threads to be woven into symbolic flowers and geometric designs for merchants in the towns and, recently, the western tourist.

In some parts of Iran differences in terrain changed

Kinsmen join together to dig a new water channel for their fields. Stones must be levered away with the help of a two-man spade.

Civil law now forbids polygyny, but among the older generation in the villages it is still a sign of wealth and status to have more than one wife.

this general way of life. The two main mountain ranges form a large inverted V with its apex in the north-west and enclose the desert like the extended claws of a crab. They provide a more secure, more healthy livelihood for the inhabitants of the valleys. Water is more abundant here than in the plains and it supplies fresh fruit crops that are sold in the towns. Villages cluster on the steep southern side of the valley. The houses of mud, timber and stone climb the hillside on each other's backs, the flat roof of one providing the courtyard of the one above. Each family, rather than a common landlord, owns the orchards. As the towns expand and the demand for fruit increases these mountain villages, especially in the north, become richer, while the favorable climate and the abundance of water and shade make them popular picnic places for urban dwellers. In a country that is two-thirds desert this garden is idealized as a Paradise. Streams, trees and flowers are extolled in poetry and exquisitely represented in miniature paintings. The mountain peasant, who lives among the blossoms of spring, the cool shade of summer and the rich apple and pear harvest of autumn, is very aware how much more fortunate he is than the peasant of the plains.

Along the shores of the Caspian Sea in the north the physical conditions are again very different. High rainfall has created an area of lush green marsh and 'jungle' which vividly contrasts with the baked brown and yellow of the bare and arid plains. Here rice is grown in abundance and small hamlets, with orchards and trees, stand out from the flat green fields. The houses are different from both the mud domes of the plains and the flat roofs of the mountains. They are protected by steep-sloping roofs from the rain above and by high stilts from the swamps below. The frameworks are made from wood and the roofs are covered with rice straw. These houses are clustered in small groups, a collection of hamlets forming a village, unlike the closely-knit communities found elsewhere in Iran. Some landlords have recently brought to the area large-scale factory farming for cotton.

In all three areas, in fact, the influence of the modern technological state is beginning to be felt. Government schools bring new techniques of farming, machinery and medicine. And a land reform has attempted to take the land from the big landlords and give it to the peasant farmer to work in co-operatives. Many villagers no longer work by hand but hire tractors for sowing and reaping. And western goods such as washing powder, transistor radios and plastic household implements are a common part of daily life. These changes, however, have not undermined the traditional importance of religion and the family in the villages.

In the towns and cities of modern Iran change goes deeper. Increased trade and western influence has led to the growth of business quarters away from the old bazaars and many towns now boast an old and a new area. In the new area there are modern buildings of brick, cement and steel in European fashion. And here youths in tight trousers and flowered shirts, girls in mini-skirts and businessmen in smart suits and ties work in air-conditioned offices and take lunch in clean-tiled rice kebab restaurants or hamburger bars. In the old quarter the bazaar remains the same. It is divided according to professions. There is a street of copper-beaters, another of jewelry, another of spices and another of carpets. The beating of hammers, the glint of jewels, the aroma of spices and the comforting mellowness of the carpet shop continue to provide the excitement and atmosphere that Europeans associate with the eastern market. Men in turbans and women in full-length veils jostle with Arab traders and American tourists. Trading is conducted over a glass of weak tea in an informal atmosphere of polite bargaining which can, in the case of a rich carpet, take days rather than hours.

In the same area as the bazaars are the great mosques. The Koran stresses the necessity for prayer and early in the history of Islam the mosques, public 'places of prostration', took on a special character and importance. The essential elements were an open courtyard with 51

Iranians

Iranian farmers keep cows
as draft animals as well as
for their meat and milk.
Women make yogurt, cheese
and refreshing drinks from milk.

arcades on one or more sides and a covered sanctuary area which was the prayer niche, placed so that worshippers would face towards Mecca. One of the first things a Muslim is bound to do when he arrives in a strange city is to find the mosque. The high domes, often decorated in blue mosaic with even higher minarets from which the faithful are called to prayer, make his task easier, and contribute to the character of Iranian cities.

A distinctive aspect of the Iranian town for the foreigner is the open water system. *Jubes* or channels carry water from *qanats* down the sides of the streets, between lines of poplars and other trees and into side channels which are alternatively fed and blocked off by water foremen. Women gather at the *jubes* with their clothes and household pots and pans while children splash around them and men divert the water into gardens. Here it nourishes the cherished rose beds, shrubs and trees that provide the Persian with a daily glimpse of Paradise behind the protective wall of his courtyard. These *jubes* still run through both the old and the new parts of towns. In the capital, Tehran, *jubes* flow from the foothills of the Alborz, passing through the rich northern section of the city in cemented channels until they arrive in the poor south where the pollution in the water rises as the quantity falls.

The division between east and west and old and new apparent in Tehran is reflected elsewhere in Iran. In Meshed, the Holy City where two million pilgrims came to the shrine of Imam Reza in 1972, the bazaar and guest houses cluster around the magnificent courtyards and

In the mosque courtyard
villagers commemorate the
death of a local holy man.
Men and boys beat their
chests to the rhythm of dirges

(Bottom) The *tazie*, a passion
play, re-enacts Husain's death.
Here his assassin lashes out at
the Imam's children who were
later sold as slaves.

Iranians

With one of the hottest climates in the world, the citizens of Taheri, on the Persian Gulf, work from dawn and rest during the midday heat.

54

A traveling acrobat entertains in Kangan, another Gulf town. As well as jumping through burning hoops, he does brisk trade in good luck charms.

Iranians who live on the shores of the Caspian Sea have four varieties of sturgeon to choose from. Caviar is made by beating sturgeon ovaries.

golden dome of the shrine, while the modern city is developing some distance away. Isfahan, a tourist center with its grand royal square and mosques, and Shiraz, an oasis in the southern desert, famous for gardens and poets, adapt more gracefully to the new influences. But many smaller towns wear the western façade uneasily.

The parts of the town and city where new styles most often come into contact with traditional ways are the bus stations. Here men carry immense rolled mattresses containing most of the family possessions up ladders to the roofs of sleek, luxury buses, as their heavily-veiled wives wait below in a sea of children, students, traders and Coca-Cola sellers. The bus is decorated inside with hanging bobbins and balls, plastic gardens, pictures of the prophet and Ali, magazine advertisements for western goods and the driver's pin-ups. Sweeping across the vast deserts at 70 m.p.h. the buses provide a way of life as much as a journey, an Iranian adaptation of modern transport to the camel trains of old. The luxury coach has become the new 'ship of the desert'.

The other important meeting places are the parks. On public holidays the men stroll up and down the paths talking. And the families sit along the edges – as if holding court – with their blankets and mattresses spread out, samovar bubbling, pots of rice being distributed among the dozen or so relations, portable record players blasting out Tom Jones and other western favorites. Some youths wrestle in the traditional Persian manner, copying the styles of national heroes who still provide models of strength and virility like the Pahlavans of old. Professional wrestlers continue to present public performances and teach schoolchildren and win medals in the Olympic Games. Other youths pore over books as they prepare for all-important exams, the key to success in the developing world. Today the high schools and universities are, to some extent, replacing the old *zurkhana* where wrestling and religious values were taught, with the new symbols of degrees and exams. The educated youth of Iran are the tools of the 'White Revolution', the plans made by the Shahanshah to modernize the country. They carry education to outlying villages as members of an army 'Literacy Corps'. They staff the offices of numerous ministries working to 'improve' the conditions of rural and urban life. And they fill the cinemas, British Councils and Iran America Societies across Iran for a mixed and modern social life that is still difficult to find. They are providing the foundation for a new Iran, very different from the old Persia.

However, the traditional institutions of the family and religion continue to provide the foundations of life in town and village alike, despite the introduction of western influences. In the bazaars, the picnic grounds and the bus stations of modern Iran can be seen how Iranians are coping with the latest invasion in the time-honored way – by assimilating the new life-style to their own, uniquely Persian way of life.

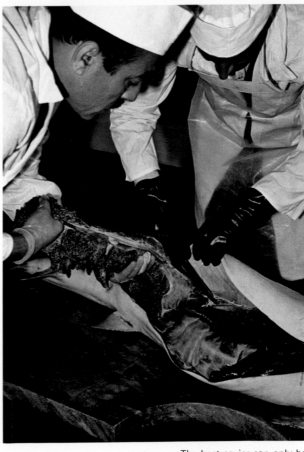

55

The best caviar can only be made in winter and is difficult to preserve. It has been known in Europe as a delicacy since the 18th century.

Dervishes

In the middle of the 19th century John P Brown, in a classic account of Turkish dervishes, described the following ceremony as performed by a group of Rifa'i dervishes after they had gone through several stages of ecstatic ritual:

'Several cutlasses and other instruments of sharp-pointed iron are suspended in the niches of the hall, and upon a part of the wall to the right of the Sheik . . . two Dervishes take down eight or nine of these instruments; heat them red-hot and present them to the Sheik. He, after reciting some prayers over them, and invoking the founder of the Order, Ahmed Rufa'ee, breathes over them, and raising them slightly to the mouth, gives them to the Dervishes, who ask for them with the greatest eagerness. Then it is that these fanatics, transported by frenzy, seize upon these irons, gloat upon them tenderly, lick them, bite them, hold them between their teeth, and end by cooling them in their mouths. Those who are unable to procure any, seize upon the cutlasses hanging on the wall with fury and stick them into their sides, arms, and legs.'

In other parts of the Muslim world different groups of dervishes practise their own rituals. In Turkey the

famous Mevlevi or Mawlawi dervishes, known to us in the west as the whirling dervishes, stimulate a state of ecstasy by a continual whirling movement. The Rifa'i, known as the howling dervishes, eat snakes, swallow hot coal and glass or cut themselves with knives. Groups of Naqshbandi dervishes in Persia, Afghanistan, Iraq and Pakistan follow a form of silent religious devotion. Chishtis in India retire from the world in solitary contemplation.

But what is it all about? What do they achieve by what might appear to us as outlandish stunts but to the dervishes are essential steps in their religious process? And above all, who or what are dervishes?

The first thing to understand is that the dervishes are mystics. Just as Christianity and Judaism have had great mystic movements or individuals, so has Islam. By their Islamic mysticism they believe that through one process or another it is possible for an individual to have direct experience of God. The theory and doctrine for this belief within Islam was laid down by the many writings and preachings of the Sufis. One meaning of 'Sufi' derives from the fact that the Arabic word *suf* means wool and so was used by the original ascetics in imitation of Christian hermits who wore woolen robes. And so it was the Sufis who provided the theory and the dervishes who provided the practice, which meant that many individuals were – and are – considered as both dervish and Sufi.

Unlike Christianity and the organization of the church, Islam had no form of corporation around which to organize the faith, and no fixed hierarchy of leadership from a Pope down to a priest. Up until the 12th century Islam relied upon the individual searching for a link between God and himself, perhaps through meditation or at most through his links with a religious teacher. Obedience to the teachings of a sheik or *pir* (religious guide) was set down during the 12th century as of paramount importance by one of the greatest Sufis of all, al-Ghazali, who, for example, wrote of the disciple: 'let him know that the advantage he gains from the error of his sheik, if he should err, is greater than the advantage he gains from his own rightness, if he should be right.' So at first the main group disappeared soon after the death of the holy man. Only after the 12th century did the teachings of certain Sufis bring about the creation of sects and holy orders the members of which were later known as dervishes. The main purpose of the dervish sects was, and still is, to help the individual relate to God through instruction, initiation, discipline and experience. The problem in understanding and explaining this was aptly put by the poet Robert Graves who once wrote of Islamic mysticism that 'whoever understands it is himself a Sufi.'

In different parts of the Muslim world many groups of deeply religious mystics belong to orders of dervishes who all believe in the same goal but follow different paths

(Above) This dervish who has impaled his cheek is a mystic believing that self-mortification is possible because of his direct experience of God.

to reach it and interpret the sayings of the founder of each group in different ways.

What do all seek so earnestly? 'Tis Love.
Love is the subject of their inmost thoughts
In Love no longer 'Thou' and 'I' exist,
For self had passed away in the Beloved.
Farid Al-Dim 'Attar

This excerpt from the poem of a great 13th-century Sufi, Farid Al-Dim 'Attar, is typical of the ideal behind dervish activities; an ideal that could be attained as much by lacerating the body with irons as by total seclusion and meditation. The orders are sometimes organized in a monastic form centered in one place but they can as easily be spread over as broad an area as that incorporating Africa, India and Indonesia. All the orders however trace a spiritual link with the respective founder of the order and it is in fact by the techniques of the founder that the dervish is characterized. Another common characteristic is that each separate dervish order has a particular distinctive garb worn by all its members. And so we see that the whirling dervishes of Turkey (the Mevlevi) wear tall hats, the Badawi of North Africa wear red turbans or the Haidari of Khurasan wear

The novice trains to conquer pain and unite with God by endlessly reciting 'Yah Allah' with breathing exercises, dancing or self-immolation.

iron rings on their necks, ears and fingers.

To become a dervish always involves a long and arduous period as a novice and even when the new member is fully admitted, the rituals are long and need total commitment. The main ritual of the dervishes is the *dhikr* or 'remembering' which can mean interminably reciting aloud a phrase *(dhikr-jali)* such as 'Yah Allah' or 'Yah hu' accompanied by breathing exercises, dancing or self-immolation; or it can mean mental recitation *(dhikr-dhafi)* and meditation. The purpose in every case is to achieve a state whereby the body loses all importance and the soul becomes all-important. Many Sufis believe that the attainment of a state of ecstatic trance is a sign of the degeneration of Islamic mysticism and that it is only necessary as a means of showing the ordinary man the heights that can be reached in searching for unity with God. The state of *hal* (ecstatic trance) is very like a religious drug for the soul that is administered by a unique form of physical or mental action.

The aims of most dervish orders were and are religious – towards a communion with God; but various groups have had political or educational purposes. The Sanusi of Cyrenaica for example aimed at restoring a pure Islamic society by political means and the order stood for a while as a strong political as well as religious movement – for example, the sheik of the order became King of Libya (Sayyid Idris) before oil and modernization led to a final collapse of dervish power. This political role occurred also in Turkey and among the Kurds and finally led to Ataturk abolishing dervish orders after 1925. The orders still exist there, but in common with most of central Asia, their numbers have been substantially declining.

The main dervish orders of central Asia still of some importance in the Muslim world are the Mevlevi, the Naqshbandi, the Bektashi and the Chishti. Groups of Chishti are found mainly in India but came originally from Khurasan in Persia and are characterized by their wandering habits and their use of music in their ritual exercises. The Naqshbandi have a reputation for piety and are the largest of the central Asian dervish groups found among the Kurds, in Anatolia, in the Caucasus and in Afghanistan and India. The Rifa'i and Haidari were for many centuries the most influential of all dervish groups, possibly because of the extremity of their *dhikr* acts, performed using fire and snakes. They are to be found in the Arab world as well as in central Asia, but after the 15th century they gradually declined in importance and now although they exist all over the Muslim world, they are largely banned by authorities who feel that their rituals are barbaric and do not conform to the current image of modernization. Mevlevi and Bektashi are two orders that have lately replaced the Rifa'i in importance.

Bakhtiari
Iran

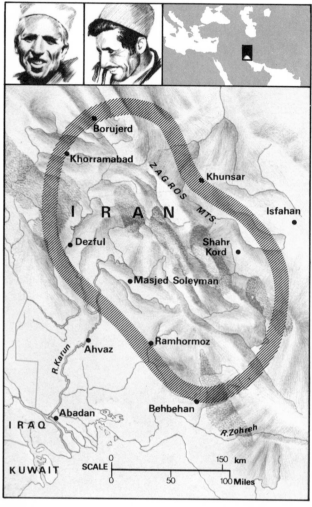

For the Bakhtiari, the great migrations which belong to the history of so many of the nomadic peoples of western Asia are still part of the present. The Bakhtiari are among the last of the mountain nomads for whom the yearly migrations from winter to summer pastures, with flocks of sheep or herds of goats, often cover 200 miles and take up two or even three months of every year. These migrations through the high passes and rocky gorges of the Zagros mountains of western Iran are precarious journeys which frequently take their toll of both animals and men. To the people, living in black goat-hair tents in encampments of no more than 15 families, the migrations can be a matter of life and death. If they do not move from the pastures of winter, their animals may die of starvation; and if they do not return here from the summer pastures, the animals are likely to die of the cold. Without their animals the Bakhtiari themselves cannot survive.

The Bakhtiari live in a region covering some 30,000 square miles in the central part of the Zagros mountains. The region is formed by a series of fertile plateaux and

59

Spring is the time for the
Bakhtian to move with their
flocks from the winter camps
across the great mountains to
high summer pastures.

Bakhtiari Iran

Women, both old and young, must walk throughout the long migration. The march may take a month and cross 250 miles of rough, mountainous land.

(Right) Maneuvering sheep along a precipitous rock path, the nomads file across the mountain face like a thin line of ants.

mountain valleys in which hundreds of villages have been built. On the valley floors there is extensive cultivation; but the upper slopes of the foothills are used to graze the flocks and herds, and it is here that the Bakhtiari nomads live through the winter months.

Between November and January the winter rains are expected, though like everything else they are unreliable. If the rains do not come, or fall late, then crops fail and the grazing withers. In some places one valley will have heavy rainfall while its neighbor nearby suffers a drought. Every year is unpredictable and brings its own problems for nomads and farmers alike. Sometimes it is a plague of locusts or an epidemic which destroys the crops and decimates the flocks.

In late spring the 'warm country' of the winter pastures begins to dry up and the grazing grows thin, denuded by the flocks. Then it is time to move to higher summer pastures in the east. For the Bakhtiari nomads, this journey means crossing some 200 miles of rugged mountainous country before reaching their summer quarters on the eastern side of the Zagros ranges. These summer pastures, called the 'cold country' are in high valleys where the air is cool and animals can be grazed until the late autumn. In the late summer months they slowly move down to the valley floor to graze on the stubble of harvested fields.

The spring migration is slow and the animals are grazed on progressively higher pastures. But in autumn,

Traveling for five hours, the sheep grazing like locusts along the mountainsides, the nomads halt, raise the black tent and light fires.

(Center) A market town is filled with excitement for the impending migration. Men fill saddle-bags with flour, dates and rice — all bought on credit.

(Over page) Animals and dry provisions have to be ferried across the swirling rivers. Women and children are followed by men and flocks.

The hoof of a mule is cut back before being shod. These animals do not represent wealth, but they are indispensable to the nomads.

(Bottom) The wealth of the Bakhtiari is in their sheep. From rough wool a woman spins yarn which is woven into *chogas* – woolen coats.

By midday the day's work is over for the men. Settled in a valley with grazing for the sheep, there is time to rest and to smoke.

(Bottom) In every valley there is a cemetery; graves are outlined with stones and engraved with accounts of the deceased's bravery.

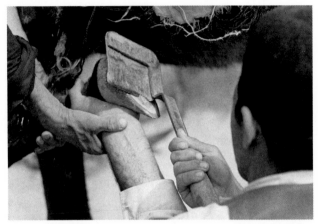

after the hot sun of the summer months, there is little grass even high in the mountains. This migration is faster, a time of privation with only thin pasture for the animals.

It is wild country which they cross during these migrations, spectacular and hazardous. The young and the old, the healthy and infirm climb on foot over higher and higher mountain ranges, through windswept rocky gorges, along precipitous cliff faces, across fast icy rivers and over freezing snow-bound mountain passes. But between the mountain ranges there are valleys, lush with grass in the spring, and here the nomads can rest their animals before tackling the next mountain.

During the spring the weather increases the difficulties of migrating through an already difficult land. Lack of water, intense heat and frequent duststorms hinder the start of the journey. Gale force winds, rainstorms and occasional electric storms sap the energy of the animals and make the going treacherous underfoot. In places the pathways along cliff faces are only a few feet wide. Pack animals panic and collapse under the weight of their loads. They have to be encouraged with a hefty whack and much screaming by irate tribesmen to move along in single file, nose to tail. The path and tracks are worn as

smooth as glass by centuries of traffic, often slippery with rain or the blood of animals with wounds and cuts on their limbs. Frequently the animals slither over the cliffs and crash to the ground hundreds of feet below. The loss of a donkey with its stores, household equipment – or even worse, the tent – spells disaster for a family.

Snow storms and sub-zero temperatures are common in the highest ranges. A sudden overnight drop in temperature can wipe out whole herds. To be suddenly caught by a blizzard while only halfway over an exposed mountain pass, unable to go forward or back, may mean death for the people as well as for their animals. There are many tales of nomads discovering whole families frozen to death. Fingers and toes in particular suffer from frostbite. Swollen with melting snow the rivers are another severe hazard to the nomads and their animals. The herds have to be swum across and hundreds if not thousands of sheep and goats are drowned annually. Until recently when bridges were built, in bad years the only way of crossing the Karun and Bazuft rivers was by *kalak* or rafts built on the spot by lashing branches to inflated goat skins.

The weather conditions vary from year to year. Even nomads traveling the same route, but a few days or weeks later, often encounter very different weather. There are crucial decisions to be made: when to start the migration, whether to cross a particular pass at once in spite of threatening weather, at what point to swim the animals across the river. The Bakhtiari nomad has no control over severe ecological and climatic conditions except through his own knowledge of the mountains and his skill, acquired by long experience. Good judgement is essential for efficient herding; the successful nomad learns to negotiate the physical hazards of the environment with minimal losses to his flocks. But misfortune strikes the efficient and inefficient indiscriminately, and luck plays an important part in the nomadic life. Poor judgement can steadily erode a flock over the years bringing a gradual impoverishment; sheer misfortune can wipe out a whole flock, a man's wealth and livelihood, at one time. It takes years to build up a new flock of sheep.

Severe animal losses are important in inducing some Bakhtiari to turn to cultivation and settlement. An alternative method of adjusting to catastrophic losses, yet remaining within the nomadic style of life, is to become a contracted shepherd, working for a wealthier tribesman in return for sheep. These contracts usually last for several years. Since the possibilities of such employment are limited, however, many Bakhtiari are forced to accept a sharp drop in their standard of living, some may be forced to rely on their kinsmen for help.

Animal wealth is precarious and unstable and most of the wealthier nomads invest in agricultural land. Some nomads may own over 1,000 animals, split into smaller herds under the care of shepherds: a flock of more than 200 sheep is unmanageable for one shepherd.

But there are also many Bakhtiari who migrate with fewer than a dozen sheep. And this number is not enough to support a family. Such tribesmen survive with difficulty and are finally forced out of the nomadic way of life.

Of some 600,000 Bakhtiari there are possibly 200,000 who still migrate regularly. These nomads live and migrate in camp groups of between four and fifteen tents. The same families do not necessarily migrate together every year, but at any given time the members of a camp group will either be close patrilineal kinsmen, related by marriage, or of the same descent. They form a co-operative group and are bound by mutual kinship obligations. Nomads are dependent on their kin for help and perhaps food when they have lost the pack animal which is carrying the food supplies. The size of a camp group tends to increase in times of insecurity, when threatened by marauding tribesmen or because of feuds between different sections of the Bakhtiari. Thieves abound in the mountains, particularly in the central, more isolated, regions. They must take great care to protect the flocks. At the turn of the century most carried rifles but now the Bakhtiari, like most of the Zagros tribes, have been subject to sporadic and successful 65

Beneath the awning of a black goat-hair tent, the men sit around camp fires in the company of the *maal* – the smallest tribal unit.

In the afternoon goats are brought to the tents by young shepherds who are no more than boys. Goats are milked only by the women.

attempts to disarm them by the Iranian Government.

The size of any camp will also depend on the total number of sheep owned by the individual members. The availability of water and grazing limit the number of sheep which can graze together. In the winter quarters camps are often smaller than the size which is best during a migration.

Daily life in the camps has a strikingly different tempo between the time of the hectic, strenuous activity of the migration and the leisurely, stable weeks in summer and winter pastures. Men are responsible for the herding and protection of the animals, and patrol the flocks during the night when on the move. Loading and unloading the pack animals, and pitching the heavy tents is also done by the men. At the end of the spring migration, the sheep are sheared, a task which all the men share. Men are also responsible for buying and selling sheep. Ewes lamb in the early spring and are only sold after they have ceased to produce lambs. But all rams of about a year old are sold to the peasants and townsmen. Only a few, usually no more than one ram for every 50 ewes, are kept for breeding purposes.

The Bakhtiari use the money from the sale of wool and sheep to buy wheat flour for bread, rice, tea, sugar, salt and clothes. They buy and sell in the peasant villages on the edges of their tribal territory and prefer to trade with specific merchants. Long-standing debts owed to merchants are paid off by the sale of young animals. But if the nomad has lost his animals he falls deeper into debt and buys on credit at a high rate of interest. After several weeks crossing the mountains, provisions of food are always low and the nomads are in a weak bargaining position. Some nomads will travel on to more distant towns in order to get better prices.

Women do all the domestic chores. They organize the tent, arranging the baggage to form a wall over which the tent it pitched. They collect water in goatskin containers, milk the sheep and goats every day, make yogurt, cook the meals and bake mounds of paper-thin unleavened bread over an open fire. Bread and yogurt are the staple foods with rice and an occasional piece of meat – except for the poorest. Meat is however only eaten on ceremonial occasions like funeral feasts, wedding celebrations and when entertaining guests. The people are

A young Bakhtiari girl carries a kid. The tribe's children are well-behaved, are often married at 13, and consider themselves old at 25

Beyond the highest slopes, after weeks of traveling, are the cool summer pastures where already the snow has melted. The end of the journey.

strict about the rules of hospitality. Food, or at least tea, is offered to every visitor. The more prestigious and honored is the guest the more lavish is the hospitality. Sometimes an animal will be sacrificed as a mark of esteem. Women never eat with the men if there are any strangers or guests in the tent. As is common to most Muslim societies the world of women is separated from that of the men. Yet tribal women enjoy more freedom than peasant women. They are not veiled and under nomadic conditions the seclusion of women is not feasible. While excluded from much of political life tribal women can exert considerable influence. They do not hesitate to fight alongside their men when the occasion demands. Some women have played important political roles in tribal life. They are called lion women.

The Bakhtiari are divided into many tribes, and more numerous sub-tribes, or *taifeh*. The *taifeh* is the most relevant social and political unit for the Bakhtiari. These *taifeh* groups have their own territories in both summer and winter pastures. The leaders of the *taifeh* are both arbiters of relationships within the *taifeh* and represent-atives of their *taifeh* in all relationships with other *taifehs*. These relationships are often antagonistic. Blood feuds persist between many groups for generations. Members of a *taifeh* think of themselves as descendants of one distant ancestor – although this is often a political fiction. Marriage is rare between different groups, except in the case of leaders who marry women from other *taifehs* for political reasons. Most marriages within the *taifeh* are made between close kin, and traditionally a boy will prefer to marry the daughter of his father's brother.

The *taifehs* are further subdivided into smaller descent groups so that a family's neighbors are also its close kin. Camp groups are made up of these small descent groups. The smallest of these groups, with communal rights to land – is called a *korboh*, which means literally 'sons of the father'. Reliance on kinsmen's help and co-operation is necessary to all nomads. But as more nomads turn to a settled way of life and agriculture this reliance becomes less relevant.

67

Uzbek
Soviet Central Asia and Afghanistan

68

On bazaar days this sleepy
little town in northern
Afghanistan becomes crowded
with fierce Uzbek tribesmen
from villages in the hills.

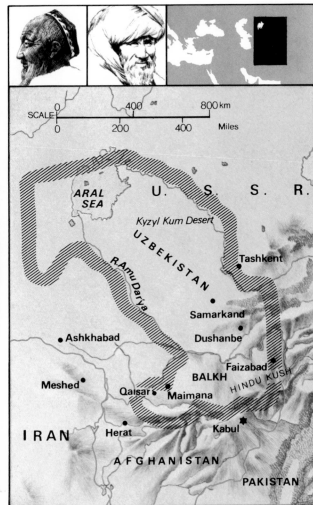

The Uzbek have never forgotten they once ruled the central Asian steppes and, as notorious warrior horsemen, invaded Russia with the Golden Horde and the legendary Genghis Khan.

The great horse-riding nomadic culture of Central Asia began to develop about 1000 BC among the Indo-European peoples who were then dominant – the Scyth, the Kushan and others. They spread from the borders of China to Asia Minor and eastern Europe. The peoples of Mongolia adopted the same nomadic way of life and first spread to the west in the 6th century AD, at the same time as Attila and the Turkic-speaking Huns were surging westwards.

Turkish tribes proper began to move into central Asia during the 6th and 7th centuries and by the 10th they were masters of the grasslands of the eastern Caliphate, and Turkish Muslim dynasties replaced the Persian Muslim dynasties which had converted them to Islam. The Mongols, the Golden Horde under Genghis Khan, returned in great strength in the early 13th century, sweeping away kingdom after kingdom as they moved

A caravan of straw-laden camels is owned by an Uzbek. Formerly nomads, all the Uzbek are now farmers or skilled bazaar artisans.

70

The proud Uzbek have never forgotten their past when they ruled the Central Asian steppes and invaded Russia with Genghis Khan's Golden Horde.

Uzbekistan is Russia's cotton producer and large amounts of food must be imported while the state farms are devoted to the cotton crop.

ever westwards. Genghis Khan was a brutal, brilliant military tactician on a scraggy Mongol pony leading an army which seemed to be part-horse. He made history by destroying the finest civilization of his day, and carved an empire from the China Sea to the Caspian Sea. But it was a transient empire; its ruler slept in a tent instead of a palace and his monuments were many ruined cities and silted canals. The Uzbek joined the Mongol hordes and reputedly Uzbek contingents accompanied the Golden Horde into South Russia in the 13th century; and in the 14th it was an Uzbek Khan who ruled the Golden Horde. Finally Uzbek conquered much of the steppes north of the Amu Darya and controlled them until the beginning of the 17th century.

By the 18th century the various principalities of central Asia were all controlled by one Uzbek ruler or another, and endlessly warring with each other. But the balance was upset by British and Russian imperialist competition in India and by the 19th century the Tsar of Russia had absorbed almost all the Uzbek khanates into his Asian empire. The Uzbek formed the backbone of many

basmachi – bandits to the Russians, freedom-fighters to themselves – groups which actively fought against the Bolsheviks until at least 1924. Many Tajik, who had been discriminated against by dominant Uzbek for generations, fought the Uzbek simultaneously. As for the Uzbek opinion of the Tajik, they have a proverb saying 'When a Tajik tells the truth he has a fit of colic.'

Collectivization in the 1930s destroyed Uzbek and Tajik hopes of independence; a second wave of *basmachi* revolts swept central Asia. But the proud nomads with their tradition of domination now had to submit or to flee: those ethnic leaders who would not accept collectivization and centralization under Moscow were purged and many of the defeated Uzbek, Tajik and others fled to northern Afghanistan and other neighboring countries.

About a million Uzbek now live in Afghanistan, and about six million in the USSR, scattered throughout Soviet central Asia. One quarter of the population of the area, 500,000, live in Soviet Tajikistan. In Soviet Uzbekistan they form over 60 per cent of the population – about five million. Tashkent, the capital, is their great center. Most Uzbek live on collective and state farms in the USSR. The distinctive Uzbek dwelling is a rectangular mud-brick house with a long front-porch veranda supported on columns – a style of house adopted by many Tajik in north Afghanistan. Most Uzbek in northern Afghanistan are tenant farmers where the Tajik are dominant, but the reverse is true in the western extremity of Uzbek distribution of Qaisar and Maimana. Often the Uzbek tenant will pay his landlord up to three quarters of a grain crop.

Where the Uzbek and the Tajik live alongside each other the two groups usually live in separate sections of a village or town and seldom intermarry – although they now do so increasingly in the larger towns and cities. The usual pattern is for a man's first wife to come from his own ethnic group; later wives can come from other ethnic groups.

As with the Tajik, Uzbek cuisine owes much to Iran. But the Uzbek, incongruously enough, have a whole range of pasta dishes including a soup resembling minestrone, *ash* (a noodle dish sometimes mixed with yogurt) and *ashak* (ravioli filled with meat, cheese or leeks). Pasta cooking may have been introduced from China, or from Italy, both at the ends of the great Silk Route of trade between ancient Cathay and the classical Mediterranean world during the first five centuries AD. The Uzbek also cook *munto*, a steamed meat dumpling, probably originally a Tibetan dish.

The classic central Asian bazaar exists in the Muslim areas of the Soviet Union as well as in northern Afghanistan. Town bazaars are usually held one or two days a week. Some towns actually bear the names of bazaar days, and when the Russians renamed Stalinabad, the capital of Tajikistan, they chose the pre-revolutionary name of Dushanbe, which means Monday, the former 71

Muslims pray in Samarkand despite Soviet disapproval. Far more ancient beliefs — magic, shamanism — survive today among them.

(Center) The valleys of the Hindu Kush provide water and pasture for the Uzbek and serve as routes for passing nomads in the summer.

bazaar day of the town.

The Uzbek have become bazaar artisans, shopkeepers and caravanserai owners in north Afghanistan. They are goldsmiths, tinsmiths, potters, jewelers and leather workers. However, in the areas where Tajik dominate, the Tajik perform most of this prestige work and the Uzbek have lowly jobs as butchers and ironmongers. Most of the handicrafts are women's work, including spinning wool and silk, embroidery, weaving, tailoring, felt-making and similar crafts.

Nomads and semi-nomads pass seasonally through many of the north-south valleys of the Hindu Kush, but none of the Uzbek are now fully nomadic. Some are seasonal shepherds and farmers and move to nearby alpine pasturelands with the local flocks or to highland wheat and barley fields for the reaping, threshing and winnowing periods each summer.

The Uzbek are all Hanafi Sunni Muslims but, with typically Uzbek disregard for authority and uniformity, retain many central Asian shamanistic and animist beliefs. Shamans can still be found who place themselves in trances and converse with spirits and receive answers to specific questions. Often a man will consider himself the soulmate of a particular animal, usually a horse or mountain goat, which will appear in dreams to warn or predict future events. Black magic exists, practised by witches – usually old women – and their spells may be countered by white magic. Uzbek lay curses on one another by sticking objects in clay or straw dolls. The Uzbek *mullah* is sometimes a combination of a Muslim religious leader, a shaman-diviner and a white magician. Even during the periods of the most virulent anti-religion campaigns in central Asia, the resident Uzbek never gave up Islam, and underground *mullahs* held services for the faithful.

Uzbek women, like their Tajik neighbors, prefer clothing made from brightly colored tie-dyed silks or Russian chintz in flowered designs. The men usually wear brightly embroidered waistcoats or vests, and the pajama-type clothing popular over most of Afghanistan. The Uzbek men's clothes were originally designed for their nomadic herding life. Their boots for walking and working are of open boat-shaped leather shepherds' shoes laced with home-made string or leather thongs. Several other types of boots are worn, such as horsemen's boots cut above the knee with hard soles and high heels. Their clothes reflect their central Asian origin and most things are quilted for winter wear (and often worn by modern Tajik as well), such as a long-sleeved coat of many colors draped over the shoulders; women sometimes drape one instead of a veil over their heads when visiting friends outside their own compounds.

Games often characterize a culture (baseball for the Americans, cricket for the British, soccer for the French). For the Uzbek the game is *buzkashi*, though other people of north Afghanistan – especially Turkomen and Tajik –

Uzbek opinion of their close neighbors and ancient enemies the Tajik, is expressed in the proverb – 'When a Tajik tells the truth he has a fit of colic' also play it. *Buzkashi* literally means goat-grabbing, but players now commonly use calves. According to tradition the game developed on the steppes of Mongolia and central Asia where nomadic Uzbek and others are said to have used prisoners of war instead of calves or goats.

At the end of the summer's wheat cycle many Uzbek practise *buzkashi* on the freshly plowed fields. When snow comes the games cease, but the horsemen renew their contests after the spring planting, especially near *nawruz*, the first day of the Afghan year.

The rules are informal. The headless carcass of a calf is placed in the center of a circle and surrounded by the players of two opposing teams, which sometimes exceed 1,000. Naturally only a few *chapandaz* (master players) ever get their hands on the calf. The rest ride spare horses, and from time to time a *chapandaz* darts outside the play and remounts.

Scoring a goal can be simply described, not so simply executed. At a starting signal, traditionally a rifle shot, the first *chapandaz* push their horses rearing and snorting in formation towards the center of the circle. Each man attempts to lift the calf to his saddle. Horse and man function as one being. The sport is dangerous, but serious injuries are rare because of the excellent training of the horses.

After a. rider has grabbed the calf, he lifts it to his saddle and secures the calf's leg between his leg and the pummel, and he heads for the turning point, carrying his whip in his mouth. He must circle this pre-determined spot, sometimes two to three miles away, but more often under a mile, then return and drop the carcass inside the original circle or one near it.

The other riders attempt to snatch the calf from any opponent clinging to the carcass. Minor injuries are common as whips flail, striking opposing players as well as horses. For this reason, *chapandaz* wear heavy fur and skin hats and cloaks. When a rider picks up the calf, the action begins anew. Strung out like cavalry after an initial clash of arms, the riders dash across the landscape, exhibiting breathless skill. Teamwork supposedly plays an important role in *buzkashi*, and the game does characterize the main themes in Uzbek culture: close co-operation within a framework of fierce, individual competition. Informal horse racing and local forms of wrestling are also popular.

The Uzbek are endlessly independent and resistant: although they are the minority group in Afghanistan, they are the largest group of Turkic speakers and since the beginning of the new period of constitutional monarchy (1964) the Uzbek have tried to get the Turkic languages accepted on a par with Indo-European Dari and Pashto. The Uzbek have also taken the lead in demanding more regional autonomy for the Muslim Soviet Socialist Republics of Soviet central Asia. The Uzbek are one of the world's minorities which make themselves felt.

Uzbek women, as proud as their men, wear a *chapan* when they leave their compounds ready to hide their faces from the gaze of strangers.

73

Kirghiz
Soviet Central Asia

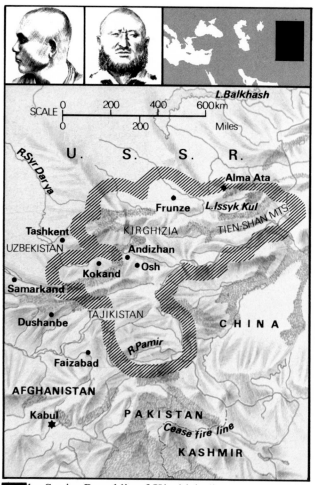

The Soviet Republic of Kirghizia lies entirely within the mountain region of central Asia, running from the Tien Shan region in the north-east, to the Alai range in the south. The higher parts of Kirghizia lie above 10,000 feet and are only accessible on foot or on the backs of animals. Here in the mountains there are highland deserts, desert steppe and steppelands which can support little agriculture. Here, traditionally, the Kirghiz people followed the life of nomads, herding horses, yaks, cattle, sheep, donkeys and even camels, ranging through the mountains and mountain passes on yearly migrations to new pastures. Even today, since their land has become part of the Soviet Union which in the early years discouraged nomadism, the Kirghiz have preserved many of their old ways. Their nomadism is now described as 'roving'; but the nomadic family is hardly changed. Collectivization has barely disturbed the old pattern of life which gave the Kirghiz people close ties with each other and in which they were dependent on their herds for most of their needs. Only the raids against oasis settlements and the wars with other tribes which inspired epic poetry and bred heroes are now past.

74   About a million Kirghiz live today in Kirghizia. There

75

A Kirghiz boy sits with one
of the famed shaggy-haired
horses of his people. Horses
have always been important
to these nomads.

Here on the mountain steppes nomads live in *yurts* — felt covered tents — and graze horses and sheep, goats, yaks and camels.

are also 100,000 or so who live in neighboring Uzbekistan and 30,000 in Tajikistan; still others live in Afghanistan. They share with the Kazak and with other central Asian peoples not only a nomadic way of life but also their Mongol appearance and a Turkic language – the outcome of centuries of intermingling with the tribes who descended on the central Asian steppe.

It was only as recently as the 19th century that these peoples had sorted themselves out into six major ethnic groups, each of which represent a mixture of elements – Tajik, Uzbek, Turkomen, Kirghiz, Kazak – and it was largely in relationships with outsiders that they became conscious of being members of an ethnic group. Otherwise the major distinction between them was in their way of life. Either they were sedentary farmers or they were nomadic herdsmen. These two patterns of life have endured in central Asia since prehistoric times. Among both the Kirghiz and the Kazak, horses have always been the center of attention while sheep and cattle are the mainstay of the herding economy. But unlike the Kazak, who were open-steppe pastoralists roaming a hundred miles from winter to summer pastures, the Kirghiz were mountain-meadow pastoralists who migrated only short distances each year.

The Kirghiz have not always lived in the mountains. Originally they lived around the headwaters of the Yenisey river in southern Siberia, and their history cannot really be separated from the history of other peoples in central Asia.

The earliest known inhabitants of the area were of the Caucasoid physical type. Gradually other peoples arrived. Some paused, either for a few decades or for centuries, before moving on. Others remained to blend with the earlier population. It was around the 6th century AD that Turkic tribes began their sweep into central Asia. The Mongols followed the Turks. In the 13th century Genghis Khan invaded the west and set the stage for Mongol domination through his sons. The Mongols who remained in the west, far from their homelands, drew many Turkic tribes into their ranks, with the result that their language became so Turkicized that Mongol speech finally disappeared from central Asia. By the early 16th century Babur, who was descended from Genghis Khan, looked on the Mongols in his army as foreigners with strange customs. The Mongol armies of Genghis Khan and his successors were the last of the great tribal movements which flowed westward through western central Asia for more than 2,000 years.

The nomadic tribes within the steppelands, however, churned around for several hundred years longer. Timur, a Turko-Mongol descendant of Genghis Khan, conquered an empire that extended from China to the Mediterranean. In the 15th century Muscovite power expanded into southern Russia and caused a reverse movement of the Turko-Mongols. The old Mongol empire became divided into the Golden Horde, which

Inside the *yurt*, beneath the smoke hole in the roof, the Kirghiz eat, sit and sleep on the floor with little other furniture.

centered on the Volga river, and the White Horde, which extended eastwards into the steppelands of what is now Kazakstan and parts of southern Siberia. It was in these wars and the later passage of Oryat (western Mongols) as far west as the Volga, that the Kirghiz nomads were driven to the Tien Shan region.

Much of the spirit of those early Turko-Mongol nomads, the struggles and the victories of those turbulent years, can be recalled today in the epic poetry and folklore of peoples like the Kirghiz and Kazak. The heroes, the cultural ideals of honor and prestige, chivalry, love and war, all live on in the legends. There is, for example, a story which tells of the struggle and final victory of the Islamic Kirghiz over the Buddhist Uighur (Mongols) on the Orkhon river in 840 AD:

> *Like a wild mountain stream we ran down, against the cities we moved, we destroyed the idolatrous temples and laid our excrements on their idols.*
> *At night we attacked them, on all sides we lay in ambush, their locks we cut off . . .*
> *We laid our insignia on the horses . . . against the miserable dogs we flew like birds.*
> *The red flag rose, the black dust rose . . .*

A more recent epic song, belonging to the tradition of the Kazak, tells of a hero's single-handed victory over the Kalmuk (the Oriat who had been forced across central Asia during the 18th century). The hero fought for twelve days and nights, and at the end of the twelfth day he and his proud horse present a sad picture:

> *When he looked at his gray-white horse,*
> *from the hoofs, large as a fire site,*
> *only something of the size of a thimble remained,*
> *of the lips, large as two coat tails,*
> *only the width of two fingers remained,*
> *of the ears which looked like cut reeds,*
> *only a hand's width remained,*
> *of the flowing mane*
> *only a yard's width remained,*
> *of the tail which you could hardly embrace with both arms,*
> *only a handful remained.*
> *When he looked at his own body,*
> *he was wounded in seventeen places.'*

It is an epic tradition which inspired passages like:

> *We shall fight like stallions!*
> *We shall dip the string of the yellow bow*
> *into the red blood,*
> *and we shall draw it until it tears.'*

In 1916 the Kazak and Kirghiz rose against a Tsarist decree which drafted tribesmen into the Russian army. There were bitter reprisals from Russian settlers. How many tribesmen were killed or died of starvation through the loss of their animals is not known. But it is estimated that some 300,000 fled to China. An uneasy peace was soon followed by the Russian Revolution when many tribesmen fought against the Bolsheviks. There were three years of bitter fighting before the Russians imposed 77

Kirghiz nomads have never made very long migrations from winter to summer pastures. Here they ride yaks across the steppelands.

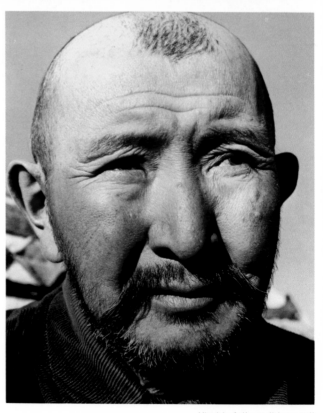

their power.

It was not until 1936 that the republics of Kirghizia and Kazakstan were accorded full status within the Soviet Union. The Soviet government showed very little hesitation in introducing changes. They began with a firm belief that agriculture was a more desirable way of life than pastoral nomadism – and were also aware that nomads were difficult to control. Soviet policy emerged with the intention of settling the nomads as quickly as possible, destroying the tribal kin ties, redistributing both land and animals. Thousands of nomadic families were forced into collective encampments where their animals often starved to death for lack of adequate grazing. Men who resisted were labelled 'reactionary *bays*' and either liquidated or expelled, their animals confiscated. At the same time, mining and industry were developed in regions which had been pasture lands or winter quarters of the nomads.

It seemed unlikely that the pastoral nomadic way of life of the Kirghiz could survive. Yet it has survived. It has even been accepted as the most efficient way of exploiting grasslands, deserts and mountain regions. The herders have now become 'specialists' skilled in the care of livestock. The nomadic family has become a 'brigade' in which each member holds an official title. But they are still nonetheless pastoral nomads. They still move according to the seasons to find pasture for their

78

Kirghiz folk traditions tell of heroes as invincible as the one who 'when he was four years old already swung the lance of fir-wood'

For centuries, the wood-framed *yurt* covered with felt has been transported during migrations — and it has always been women's work to erect it.

animals. Although less suited to the extremes of climate cattle are now promoted as more suitable animals for herding than horses.

By the 1960s the great drive to settle the nomads of Kirghizia and Kazakstan had passed. There has even been official concern for the welfare of roving herdsmen and their families, or brigades. In 1961 there was a call for the mass production of synthetic materials for *yurts* (the nomads' traditional tent) which would be more durable than the traditional felt coverings and wooden frames. The newspaper *Pravda* suggested that since mass production of synthetic *yurts* had not been organized, some sort of mobile dwelling on wheels might be provided, and the harsh living conditions of herdsmen and shepherds be alleviated by portable gas stoves and warm sleeping bags. This interest in mass-produced alternatives to the traditional – and much preferred – tents might, however, be interpreted as an attempt to control the independent Kirghiz and Kazak herdsmen more firmly.

The collectives, or *kolkhozes*, permit a Kirghiz or Kazak family to own a few animals of its own. In Kirghizia, for example, restrictions limiting workers who were regularly engaged in livestock-breeding to one cow, one milk mare and five sheep have been relaxed – even though on many occasions the collective's animals have been neglected in favor of the herdsmen's own animals. And although each *kolkhoz* usually has a center with a miller, a blacksmith, a carpenter, an elementary school and a cultural club, many of these places have no year-round residents. The regional centers, with all the other services like libraries, schools and hospitals largely serve as links with the rest of the Soviet Union.

The *yurts* in which most of the *kolkhozniks* live from spring to autumn are constructed in the traditional way. As in the old days women make the felt and carpenters make the wooden frame – although carpenters are now paid with money or grain instead of livestock. Setting up and dismantling the tents is also still the work of women. As they have always done, the people eat, sit and sleep on the floor. Different clothes and staple foods are among the changes of recent years among the Kirghiz, especially for those who have turned to industrial work like mining. But for the nomads, or rovers, kinship which was the basis of traditional tribal society has retained its vitality. The *kolkhoz* brigades are still family groups, and the *kolkhoz* itself is composed of members of closely related families. In many places it seems that the tradition by which Kirghiz married only outside this group of closely related families has only been replaced by a new tradition by which members of a family group *kolkhoz* marry only outside this group. Even the Kirghiz miners remember their tribal genealogies five or six generations back. Sovietization, it seems, has not destroyed the enduring spirit of the Kirghiz: 'The hero, paying no heed to the armies which were outside, stormed into the inside of the fortress.'

79

Tajik
Soviet Central Asia and Afghanist

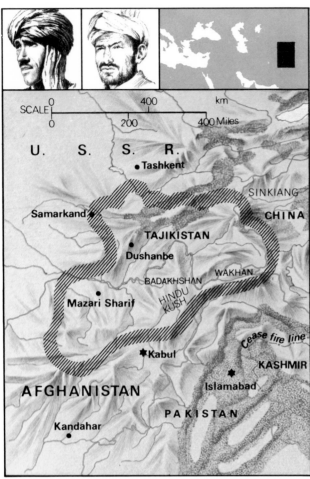

Tajikistan, on the Soviet-Afghan border, is a land of spectacular mountains. The snow-capped peaks of the great Pamir plateau in the east rise to 22,485 feet above sea level. From the mountains turbulent glacial rivers rush down deep rocky gorges to fertile valleys. This land is the home of about 2·5 million Tajik, whose ancestors have probably been around central Asia since at least the fourth millennium BC.

The word Tajik probably comes from the Old Persian term *tazi* which meant Arab. Gradually the term came to refer to all Muslims in central Asia, and was later used to distinguish Persian-speakers from Turkic-speakers. The Tajik themselves, while accepting the name, usually refer to themselves by the name of their valley or home – such as Panjsheri or Andarabi.

They are a Mediterranean people of caucasoid stock, in whom intermarriage with Mongols, especially with the Uzbek, has produced very mixed features, such as a combination of straight black hair, blue eyes with epicanthic eyefolds, high cheekbones, and relatively tall stature. In fact it is often difficult to distinguish them from the Uzbek. Further south, in eastern Hindu Kush toward Kabul, they have fewer Mongol traits.

In Tajikistan valleys and
orchards are high above sea
level. The rushing rivers are
spanned by bridges improvised
from tree trunks and boulders.

Tajik Soviet Central Asia and Afghanistan

Tajik villages are often surrounded by an outer wall — a relic of the Tajik's history of wars with Uzbek and Central Asians.

(Bottom) The turban is the traditional Tajik headdress. Men's clothing is often a mixture of local and western goods and improvised material.

Kulala village is well known for the pottery made by its women. The more money they make, the more they inlay their wares with gold.

Young Tajik children help at home and mind livestock. As they grow up they join their parents in the fields. The old people mind the babies.

They live across a tract of land which stretches from Chinese Sinkiang, through the Wakhan Corridor and Badakhshan, across the foothills and plains of Afghan and Soviet Turkestan, and up into the mountainous Tajikistan and neighboring Soviet Republics. They are the second largest ethnic group in Afghanistan – about 2·5 million to the Uzbek's one million. About 4·5 million Tajik live in the USSR. Only about half of these live in Tajikistan; the rest are scattered.

There are three distinct Tajik areas in northern and north-eastern Afghanistan: Badakhshan and the eastern Hindu Kush, Wakhan and the central foothills and plains of Afghan Turkistan. Only in the first two are there still relatively pure Tajik villages with minimum Turkic linguistic and Mongoloid physical influence. The Tajik speak Persian dialects of the great Indo-European language family. Their modern language probably developed from Arab influences on the Iranian Dari in the 9th and 10th centuries AD. Today the few Tajik who can read or write use Cyrillic script in the USSR, and a modified Arabic script in Afghanistan.

Along the easily accessible Afghan foothills leading to the Turkestan plains Tajik and Uzbek have intermingled a great deal, with the Tajik dominant towards the east and the Uzbek towards the west. In the north Pushtun and Baluch nomads and villagers have also intermingled with them. There are, as well, other groups who move through the mountains seasonally, call themselves Arab and speak an Arabicized Persian; most are ethnically Tajik.

Tajik and Uzbek certainly cannot be distinguished from each other by their clothing. The Tajik wear the distinctive, embroidered turban caps of the Uzbek, and the Uzbek wear those of the Tajik. The influence of whichever group dominates locally tends to be strongest. Both Tajik and Uzbek men wear long-tailed cotton shirts which slip over their heads and button at the right shoulder over wide-waisted, pajama-like pantaloons. They tuck the shirt in at the waist when they are working. They wear local sandals, often made from old automobile tires, or embroidered shoes or, increasingly today, Russian-made rubber overshoes and boots. As much of the second-hand clothing of the western world ends up in the bazaars of Afghanistan towns and cities Tajik often wear sports coats or suit jackets with their pantaloons. Most popular are surplus uniform jackets, especially of the British forces.

Tajik women, however, wear traditional clothing of floral cloth and the famous tie-dyed cloth of central Asia, little modified by the influence of the west. Most Tajik women who live in the country wear head shawls which they draw coyly over their faces when strangers approach. Few wear the *chaudry,* a sacklike garment which completely covers the body from head to toe. Only limited vision is possible when they wear this, through an embroidered lattice work, which is usually worn by women who have had extended contact with the urban world. The veil and isolation of women (*purdah*) were originally city customs of the Byzantine Christians and Sasanian Persians which were adopted by the conquering Arab Muslims as they became urbanized.

The Tajik areas are mountain oases, north-south valleys separated by passes. In broad lower valleys the Tajik practise dry agriculture growing wheat, barley and millet. Where the foothills meet the plains some irrigation (including underground tunnel-canals) is possible and here they cultivate onions, cucumbers, turnips, carrots and eggplants in irrigated fields near rivers. And nearer to the village farmers cultivate fruit and nut trees in well-watered orchards: mulberry, apricot, apple, peach, fig, almond and walnut. The wheat and barley are harvested in the summer; the vegetables in late summer and the fall. The higher valleys are mainly alpine pastureland for summer grazing.

The Tajik in Soviet central Asia have been more widely dispersed than those in Afghanistan and subject to the great pressures of collectivization and russification, which have weakened, though by no means shifted, their culture. Their basic economy has changed from subsistence farming to large-scale cotton farming, but there are still privately owned and maintained garden plots and the bazaar is still an important feature.

In many Tajik areas of Afghanistan more than half the families own their land. Tenant farmers, often Uzbek in Tajik-dominated areas, and Tajik in Uzbek-dominated areas, work under modified systems of land tenure. The landlord and tenant supposedly get one fifth of a crop for each of the five elements donated: land, water, seed, draft animals and labor. However, a good tenant farmer on a long-range contract will seldom get less than half 83

Rock drawings are evidence of the Tajik's ancestors of 4,000 B.C. Then as now the agile ibex was the hunter's favorite prey.

(Bottom) Soviet and Koran schools work side by side, but education has hardly improved since two generations ago when few Tajik were literate.

a charcoal fire. Occasionally they also eat chicken and beef and, more rarely, camel. They kill these animals by cutting their throats. This makes the meat *halal* – clean; animals not butchered in this way are *haram* – unclean and forbidden. For breakfast a Tajik farmer usually eats only bread which he dips in green or black tea. And for lunch or dinner he will very often eat *shurwa*, a thick meat and tomato soup eaten with side dishes of meat. He eats rice, either local or imported, with most meals. The Tajik are also fond of yogurt, dried curds, curds boiled in butter or in the fat from the tail of a fat-tailed sheep, and other dairy products. However, vegetable oil from India, Iran and Europe is replacing animal fats in many places. Like all Muslims, the Tajik eat using only the right hand. People eat from a communal dish or platter while sitting cross-legged on the floor or on a high wide wooden bench.

The Tajik's houses reflect a mixture of Irano-Afghan plateau and central Asian influences. Nearly all Tajik live in rectangular mud-brick or *pisé* huts built inside a walled compound. The more eastern Tajik families, however, prefer domed bee-hive huts.

The Tajik and Uzbek also use the *kherga* or *oôee*, a kind of portable tent, for two purposes. During the warm months many Tajik put up *kherga* and live in them as summer huts. And farmers – who with their families, donkeys and camels move to their highland fields for reaping, threshing and winnowing – also use the *kherga* as a home until the end of the agricultural cycle in late summer.

In Tajik families it is the women, helped by grandparents and older paternal aunts and uncles whose active working lives are usually over, who are responsible for bringing up and disciplining children. Fathers pamper their sons and daughters. Older children help to look after the younger ones and by the time a child reaches eight or nine, he or she is expected to watch over the family livestock as well. By their early teens boys are working full time with their fathers and girls with their mothers.

Early in their teens Tajik children get married – usually to a relative or to a local person. The Tajik prefer their sons to marry cousins, although they often have to accept more distant relatives. Some Tajik men do marry Uzbek women, but this is looked on with disfavor. The boy's family gives his bride's family a specified number of sheep and goats. In return the girl brings complete sets of clothing and household goods to her new home. This is an exchange rather than a bride-price: the bride's family in compensation for losing labor gains livestock.

It is at mosque schools, where they exist, that young Tajik receive formal religious training. Although government-sponsored secular schools have, since World War II, become increasingly important in the cities and larger towns, few have reached the villages.

Most Tajik are orthodox Sunni Muslims, although the

of a crop. This system often revolves around mutual agreement and respect rather than exploitation, though it does not always work so equitably in areas where one ethnic group is dominated by another.

For the Tajik, as for all western and central Asian peoples, lightly leavened bread is the staff of life. The Tajik are fond of eating goat and mutton which they make into *korma*, a stew with vegetables, or as kebab, meat cubes threaded on skewers and then cooked over

Although Tajik hunt
ibex with rifles, anything
they kill must have
its throat cut to be clean
enough for Muslims to eat.

Pamiri groups are mainly followers of the Aga Khan and local beliefs permeate Islam. Wany shrines (*ziarat*) to Muslim holy men are obviously pre-Islamic and sometimes even prehistoric in origin. Although in principle saints are forbidden in Islam they in fact proliferate, and brotherhoods arise around some shrines. Here amulets are sold which guarantee everything from curing rabies to fertility in sterile women. Some Tajik, although they seldom talk about it, believe in witches and witchcraft. Old women past the menopause are most liable to be suspect. Some *mullahs* admit that they know of counter-rituals to the black magic of the witches.

Certain groups of Tajik claim to be descendants of the prophet Mohammed, through his daughter Fatima and his nephew Ali, who many non-Arab Muslims believe is buried in Northern Afghanistan, not in Iraq. For the Tajik who live in Soviet central Asia Islam survives as a way of life although most of the Five Pillars have been abandoned.

In the rural world of the Tajik, formal entertainment, except for the ceremonies of birth, marriage and death, is rare. National holidays, the Afghanistan Independence in late August, for example, and various revolutionary celebrations in the USSR, are becoming popular and are replacing the more traditional end-of-harvest festivals. To the Tajik music is important, both in work and play. They sing folk-hero songs, songs ridiculing other groups, and love songs – some with homosexual motifs.

Homosexual and extramarital affairs are very common. As adulterous couples may still sometimes be put to death if they are caught – thus removing two economically and biologically functioning individuals from the group – adultery is usually met with a blind eye.

Tajik villages are generally governed by councils made up of the heads of all the traditionally important families. The council of elders, who are often called 'White Beards', effectively insulates the villagers from the outside world, which constantly tries to develop or exploit their rural way of life. In many areas in Soviet central Asia and in Afghanistan, when young men return home after serving in the military or working on development projects and new industrial complexes, a new informal power group has developed. This sometimes includes members of several ethnic groups – Tajik, Uzbek and Pushtun – and competes with the extended family and each of the ethnic groups for loyalty. Out of these new groupings grow workers' unions and political parties.

85

Kabul and the Pakhtun
Afghanistan

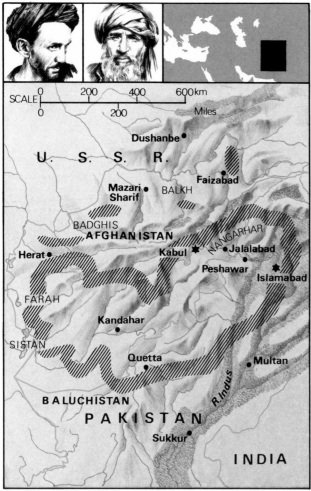

Kabul, over 5,000 feet above sea-level, is made beautiful by the contrast of its rich gardens and fertile fields with the barrenness surrounding it and the backcloth of high mountains on the sky-line. 'The climate is delightful and in this respect there is no such place in the known world' wrote the Mogul emperor Babur long ago. Once it was a walled city close to the Kabul river and protected by mountains, swamps and its magnificent citadel, the Bala Hissar. And once its capture was a vital step to the conquest of Hindustan.

Now Kabul, essentially a cosmopolitan city, is thriving and expanding. Its houses and industrial areas stretch into the surrounding farmlands and grazing areas. Kabul and countryside are merging as more and more people move in. It has 450,000 inhabitants and more are coming all the time. There is no proper old town in Kabul and few old buildings. In 1842 its famous covered bazaar was destroyed by the British in retaliation for the slaughter of an entire military force during the first Anglo-Afghan War. The traditional town center has, since the end of the 1940s, been gradually replaced by new roads, squares, parks, grand government buildings, hotels and shopping

87

Crossing the barren mountains
which surround the gardens
of the city of Kabul are
caravan routes to
India Iran and Turkistan.

The Pakhtun are rugged nomads who live in the mountains of Afghanistan. Their myths tell of their descent from the ten lost tribes of Israel.

centers, cutting through the remnants of the old town.

Wandering through Kabul one comes across small restaurants where tea is always available, bakeries where flat wheat loaves are made and sold, butchers, fruit and vegetable sellers, milk and cheese shops and street hawkers. The traditional bazaars are open streets lined by single-room shops, with 'serais' or courtyards behind. At one time there were covered streets. The older shops are usually just a single square room open to the street by day and shuttered at night. The old craft workshops are the same. There are additions to some shops like glass windows, doors, tables and chairs, so that they range from the purely traditional to the truly modern as might be found in any western city.

But Kabul has kept its own characteristics from earlier times and earlier purposes. There are still specific quarters for the different peoples living there. The Qizil Bash and the Hazara, both of whom are Shi'a Muslim, live in one area while the Chandawul, the Hindus and Sikhs live in another. Both these areas are on the edge of the city where most activities are dominated by Tajik, who are Sunni Muslim of the Hanafi sect, the state religion. There are different quarters too for copper-smiths, silversmiths, shoemakers, pottery, salt and sugar dealers, for example. The few remaining Jews are cloth dealers and money changers. By tradition the Pakhtun,

the most numerous people in Afghanistan, are not city dwellers at all. In Kabul their jobs are connected with their old caravan and transport occupations, so that they dominate lorry transport and mechanical workshops. They are now becoming more influential under the Pakhtunization policy of the government. Merchants and craftsmen are organized into bodies rather like guilds. They have elected leaders representing them to the city council. The artisans too, have guilds, and each trade has a saintly character as patron or *pir*, the founder and protector of the trade.

Traditional houses in Kabul are built of sun-dried bricks and are one or two storeys high. Towards the street bare walls are broken only by a wooden door, protruding pipes for waste and rainwater and a niche from where sewage can be emptied. Down the street runs an open ditch, a hazard to pedestrians. Occasionally a beautiful carved window opens from the guest-room on the first or second floor towards the street. Otherwise all the houses are entirely inward orientated towards the courtyards where the women are busy working.

This inward-orientation of the houses corresponds to the old ideal of the seclusion of women, so that the house walls and the *chaudry,* the outdoor veil worn by women,

Russia, China and Britain have all been involved in conflicts and wars centering on Kabul. This cannon dates from the Afghan wars, 1848.

(Top) The famous covered Chahr Chatta bazaar was destroyed by the British Army in 1842. Many shops and stalls have since been rebuilt.

Qizi Bash and Hazara live in
one part of Kabul — Chandawul,
Hindus and Sikhs in another.
Smiths, cobblers and potters
have their special quarters.

Mazar-i-Sharif is famous for its spectacular mosques. The Sunni Muslim population worships at the Shrine of Ali, son-in-law of Mohammed.

Centuries of constant wars and feuds have given Afghan soldiers high prestige. The 80,000-strong army is now equipped by the Russians.

serve the same purpose. But in 1959 it was decreed that unveiled women might be seen in public. Before this only applied to some of the tribal people and female servants. Consequently since 1959 women have increasingly entered the man's world. More women are being educated and some now hold top jobs including ministerial posts in the cabinet. As women become liberated so the house walls are gradually becoming lower and lower as one moves into the new parts of the city. In the modern apartment buildings it is impossible to build a wall which would serve the old purpose of keeping women hidden.

In a household there is either just husband, wife and children or it may be an extended family including their

In the boutiques of Kabul wealthy women buy fine shoes and stockings; outdoors they will be modestly concealed by their heavy veils.

The capture of Kabul was an important step in the conquest of Hindustan. The riverside districts always suffered the heaviest war damages.

close relations as well. On the floor of a one- or two-roomed house are plaited mats and rugs. A quilt with a couple of cushions is arranged along the walls for sitting on. Sometimes an oven heats the house or else there is a *manqal* which is a kind of pan holding hot charcoal and placed under a small table covered by a quilt. People sit around the table with their feet under the quilt.

The modernization of Kabul and Afghanistan causes problems. Traditionalists on the one hand, and modernists and even revolutionaries on the other tend to be mutually opposed. Imported goods and ideas bring in a variety of new cultural manifestations and values, while at the same time the old ones are still viable. Cultural conflicts result and these often become personal. Students, for example, often find a double cultural heritage, one in the capital and another when they return to their country homes.

Kabul has not always been a mere city. At one time it was synonymous with all Afghanistan. The 'Kingdom of Kabul' has been described in what is in many respects an unsurpassed account by Mountstuart Elphinstone, published in 1815, after his stay in the Afghan King's winter capital, Peshawar. Before the British arrived Kabul was much larger even than present-day Afghanistan. It included what is now the North-West Frontier province and the northern Baluchistan area of Pakistan. It had dependencies as well: the Uzbek-inhabited Balkh, the Aimaq and Hazara regions, Herat, Sistan, Lower and Upper Sind, Multan and the Kashmir.

The Pakhtun people in Iran and other neighboring countries are usually called Afghan. They are called Pathan in India and Pakistan. The real founder of modern Afghanistan was a Duranni, Ahmed Shah, who became king in 1747. His son, Timu Shah, moved the capital to Kabul in 1776, and it has since then been the seat of the Duranni kings, who are sometimes known as *Amirs*. This change in the position of the capital was important for Afghanistan's future. It was no longer in the midst of internally competing and quarreling Pakhtun. It was at the edge of their country in a densely populated oasis, peopled by Tajik. Furthermore it was even then a flourishing commercial town which controlled the most important road and caravan routes connecting India with Persia and Turkistan. It was a cosmopolitan city, where the ruling language was Tajiki or Persian, known today as Dari. The Pakhtun kings found in the Qizilbash, the Turkish-Persian troops left behind by the Persian king Nadir Shah, reliable soldiers and competent administrators. The state machinery became Persianized. This was probably vital for the consolidation of the Afghan state and may be the background for the multi-ethnic city of Afghanistan today, where the Pakhtun influence has recently been regaining its strength through an active national policy.

The Pakhtun are the biggest ethnic group in Afghanistan. They number 7 to 8 million people. In east Afghani-

The game of buzkashi is a test of virility and horsemanship played with a goatskin, filled with sand, weighing over 150lb.

The skin is placed within a chalk circle. Two opposing teams on horseback attempt to pick it up by the limbs and carry it to the goal line.

stan they live roughly south of the Kabul river, east of the Kunar river and east of a line drawn from Kabul to Kandahar, from where some 6 to 7 million extend into Pakistan, in the areas west of the Indus, and into northern Baluchistan. Their country is mountainous and rugged. Towards the east it stands like a wall overlooking the Indus lowland. Towards the west it gradually merges into the high barren mountain plateaux, leaving the Nangarhar-Laghman and Khost fertile lowland behind as remnants of the Indus lowland. The climate is dry subtropical in the lowlands and dry temperate in the highlands. In both areas there is a low rainfall in winter and steppe-like grasslands. Between are mountains exposed to the Indian summer monsoon rain, with magnificent forests of fir and cedar.

Most of the Pakhtun are settled farmers but on the traditional subsistence level and they use less than 10 per cent of the total land area. There is room for nomad sheepherders, called *kuchey* or *powindah* (pages 100-111) too. The Pakhtun farmers grow as their main crops wheat, maize, barley and sometimes rice, and in east Afghanistan grapes, apricots, peaches, cherries and pomegranates. The Pakhtun have rarely engaged in crafts and trading. They had few cities and those that were there were dominated by Hindus and Sikhs in the east and by Tajik in the west. But recently, as a result of the ongoing Pakhtunization policy in Afghanistan, they are coming to the cities as administrators and govern-

92

The rules of this wild game vary: often the riders carry short lead-tipped whips in their teeth with which they lash out at their opponents.

Competitive sports of all kinds
appeal to the people of Kabul.
Dog fights are especially
popular and often end in the
deaths of both animals.

(Center) Large sums of money
are wagered on the favorite
to win this cock fight. The
birds are bred and trained to
draw blood and kill.

ment employees.

Lower Laghman is a heavily populated fertile plain on the fringes of the Pakhtun area 18,000 to 24,000 feet above sea-level where farming is entirely based on irrigation from a tributary of the Kabul river. Here the Pakhtun are still expanding and establishing themselves as the dominant class of landowners. Tajik and Pashai – an old Indian-speaking people, largely confined to the mountain valleys – have various subordinate jobs in the villages. Lower Laghman was once dominated by a single Pakhtun tribe but now there is hardly a tribe which is not represented there. The old tribal political system is now mixed with feudal bureaucratic allegiances towards the administration of the province and Kabul.

Looking across the country one might see fortified castles or *qalas*, either standing alone or surrounded by the clay houses of the landless farmers. Once these forts with look-out towers served purposes rather like medieval castles. One would also see compact villages where the farmers live. These villages had no electricity or kerosene machines until the late 1960s.

Let us enter one of these villages in late winter and see what is going on. As we wander through the narrow streets bordered by houses built around open yards, we are led, being strangers, to the house of the most important man, the *malik*. He is the elected leader of the village who deals with provincial government. Inside we find other visitors already sitting in the guest room. Tea and sweets are served by the *malik's* son and his brother's son. They are all talking about local politics and after our interruption they carry on. Two big landowners who are competing and fighting for power in the valley are discussing which of them is to be invited to a coming village wedding. In the evening an enormous chicken and rice dish is served. Next morning we peep into the inner yard, where women are busy churning butter, by rotating a quirl-stick in sour milk. Later on we wander through the village. Next door is a carpenter, a Tajik, whose main job is to make and maintain all wooden parts for agricultural implements in return for a share in all harvested crops. His wife is just milking their only cow, while it licks the skin of a calf stuffed with straw. This trick makes it easier to milk since its calf has died. Out in the street a group of nomads with asses loaded with fire-wood for sale are coming in from their winter camp close to the nearby mountains. At a water channel on the outskirts of the village is one of the two mosques with a big platform in front, the village school for boys. The teacher is the *mullah*. Close by in an open square is the village's only shop, kept by a Tajik. He sells tea, sugar, needles, kerosene, matches and other necessities. Next to him is the barber. He works outside. For seven kilos of each harvested crop he will cut a man's hair for a year. He is a Pakhtun, but first he is a barber, which actually means belonging to a kind of occupational caste. He has other important jobs as well. He pulls teeth and performs

The ultimate competition is
face to face wrestling. Not
only a sport, it is sometimes
the substitute for a duel –
a means of settling feuds.

(Over page) The hilltop lakes
of Band-i-Amir are among the
wonders of the world. In winter
they are even more remarkable
as the waterfalls freeze.

bleeding operations. He plays music and dances at weddings and he cooks for festivals. His wife is the village midwife, the fount of information on marriageable girls.

At the other end of the village the smith – a Tajik – works with a small boy puffing the fire with his bellows. He has to maintain all iron parts for agricultural implements for a share of the harvested crops, like the carpenter. Both carpenter and smith will repair the mills for extra payment. Out in a fallow field the weaver – again a Tajik – makes his coarse cotton cloth, for which he is paid one fifth of the finished material, plus an amount of corn. A little further away itinerant weavers from Wardak have just arrived after a month's stay in the nearby nomad camp. They are specialists in heavy woolen and goat hair material for tents, transport bags and other heavy goods. As poor semi-nomadic people with few animals and little land elsewhere they are guests for the winter. They stay as *hamsaya*, or subordinate outsiders, getting free accommodation, but being paid nothing for minor services. They are only paid in cash for repairing walls and roofs.

We have only the mills still to see now. There are ordinary horizontal water mills for grinding wheat, rice or maize, and there is the stamp-mill for husking the rice after a special parboiling treatment, which is done in the surrounding *qalas*. If we had visited the village earlier in the winter we would have seen the sugar cane processed and boiled down into brown sugar.

The Pakhtun are named after an ancestor from their father's line of descent. Their name bears either the suffix *khel* meaning 'group' or *zai* meaning 'son of'. Those with the same surname form descent groups which can ideally all be fitted into a common genealogy going back to a saintly warrior of the 7th century whom the Prophet named Abdur Rashid. The members of a descent group, whether nomads or farmers, hold equal rights to land from their common forefather. (Nomads acknowledge a forefather more distant, perhaps as much as 15 generations ago, but farmers may acknowledge a forefather of only four generations back.) The rights to land held by all members of a descent group are for grazing, farming or collecting wild fruits and timber. Formerly the land belonging to the descent group was redistributed every few years so that no farmer always had the worst land. The ideology of equality based on common descent is important in all dealings with Pakhtun society.

It affects the political area of their lives. Leadership is not hereditary but is built up around men with the right personal qualities. A leader must be a sober judge in human affairs, able to speak well in public, wise over tribal matters, straightforward and brave. He will gain followers if he is generous and gives protection. He will find it easier if he is wealthy and can use force. There are usually several competitors for leadership, each with their own band of followers. These rival leaders may well

During winter and spring flood-waters sweep away bridges along the unpaved road from Bamiyan to Band-i-Amir, making the trip dangerous.

Several men attempt a
precarious crossing of the
River Pech in a raft made from
six cow skins and overloaded
with carpets and provisions.

be from the same descent group for heredity is no
guarantee of cohesion as in many African chiefless
societies. Leaders can be constantly kept in check in the
village councils or *jirga*. At these meetings all adult men
can express their opinions and may change their
allegiances according to the behavior and opinions of the
leaders who are vying with each other for followers.

In Pakhtun society there is a strict code of honor –
pakhto – which all are expected to maintain. A Pakhtun
is expected to retaliate against offense or injustice regardless of cost or consequence. He is expected to offer 'guest
friendship'. This means he must receive, feed and protect
by every available means anyone who comes to his house,
even an enemy. The guest is temporarily accepting his
host's authority and superiority. If he continues to accept

97

Where high-walled villages
and narrow streets provide
little space for animals and
people, roofs become the
logical place for them.

Kabul and the Pakhtun Afghanistan

In the interest of hygiene as well as comfort the men of Kabul keep their heads shaved all summer long. It is a busy time for the city's barbers.

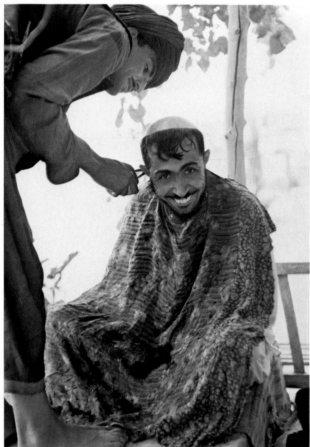

Tashkurghan is a small mountain village where life has not changed for centuries. On market day men bring their flocks to sell and barter.

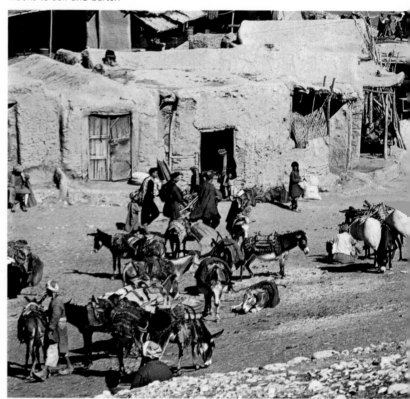

hospitality he is politically dependent on his host. If the host in return accepts hospitality from the guest he is not superior but an ally. In this way political alliances are cemented. Despite his obligation for revenge a Pakhtun must also be ready to forgive. He must always receive a peace messenger and listen to what he has to say.

There is a system of compensation in disputes between men, known as *pakhtunwali*. Compensation is considered in terms of units or *khuns*. One dead man equals one *khun*, a dead woman equals half a *khun*. Loss of a tooth, finger, ear or eye varies between a tenth and half a *khun*. Compensation must be paid in relation to how many *khuns* have been lost. It is often paid in women. For instance a woman might be given in marriage without her family receiving the bride-price due to them. But it is sometimes paid in cash or in kind.

Pakhto, besides being the code of honor Pakhtun must uphold, is also their language. It is *Pakhto* in both senses that unites the Pakhtun. According to a local saying a Pakhtun is one who does *Pakhto* and not merely speaks it.

The men of Tashkurghan spend long hours in tea houses, which women may not enter. The cups and teapots are imported from Russia and recently from Japan.

98

On special occasions Pakhtun
women put on their traditional
finery. The embroidery, coins
and beadwork enhance the
features of the tattooed face.

Chahar Aimaq
Afghanistan

Afghanistan is often called the 'cross-roads of Asia'. Khurasan is the center of that cross. Khurasan which today is a Persian province in the northeast of the country included, before the establishment of the border between Persia, Afghanistan and Russia in the late 19th century, parts of Afghanistan as well. The armies of the great conquerors have throughout history marched through Khurasan. Some left destruction. Others just passed through en route to bigger conquests elsewhere. In the tribes of Khurasan today can be seen the imprint of Alexander the Great, of Genghis Khan, of Tamerlane, of the Mogul Emperors, the Persians and Turks and of the White Huns and Arabs. As a result the ethnic make-up of the inhabitants is probably the greatest admixture of people anywhere. The largest group of tribes in Khurasan is called the Chahar Aimaq.

Of the Chahar Aimaq, or Four Aimaq – although there are usually more than four tribes included under this name – the most important are the Timuri and the Taimanni. Other Aimaq tribes include the Firuz Kuhi, the Jamshidi and the Baghdis Hazara. The many small tribes still maintain something of an individual identity although, to protect themselves from more powerful tribes such as Turkomen in the north or Baluch in the south, the smaller tribes have linked up through alliance and marriage to larger Aimaq groups. By religion the Aimaq tribes are, like most of the population of Afghanistan, of the Sunni faith of Islam. Most people in Persia are Shi'a Muslims.

The rural peoples of Khurasan tend either to be nomadic herdsmen or settled farmers. Most of the population combines both activities. The nomads are sheep and goat herders who use the mountain pastures in spring and summer, and the foothills and valleys in autumn and winter. The way of life of the tribes living in these mountain regions has persisted for centuries despite innumerable political upheavals in the area.

19th century history in Khurasan shows a struggle between Britain, Russia and Persia for control over the area. The role of the local tribes in this struggle has been a complicated and turbulent one. The issue of protecting the British route to India was only important to them when their own pasturelands and security were threatened. During the Anglo-Afghan wars the Aimaq tribes were weakened as powerful autonomous political units. With the final establishment of the Persian-Afghan-Russian border in the late 19th century they found themselves divided between the three countries, although most remained in Afghanistan.

The last population estimate of the Aimaq was made in 1815 when they were thought to number about 400,000. Today they are thought to number about 250,000. Many live all year round in black goat-hair

100

(Above) The country of the Chahar Aimaq is barren and mountainous, and the semi-nomadic tribes have always competed for the thin pasture.

For some Chahar Aimaq nomads, a *yurt* is a spring or summer dwelling. Some, like the Firuz Kuhi, however, use this kind of tent permanently.

(Center) The *yurt* has a circular stressed wooden frame, draped with felt, and bound with decorative, woven goat-hair braids.

Among these tribes, any attempt at government control is bound to be complicated by nomadic movements and the system of clans or *taifehs*.

tents or, in the case of the Firuz Kuhi and some Taimanni and Baghdis Hazara, in *yurts* – light structures with a wooden hooped frame and covered with felt tied by woven goat-hair braids. A large proportion of the Chahar Aimaq however live in permanent domed village houses and only use their tents or *yurts* in the spring and early summer.

Yassin Salehi of the Timuri tribe leads a busy life with his three wives, ten sons and one daughter. As *kadkhoda* (village headman) he has in the past been responsible to the government for his village and he is also an important man in the Salehi clan, or *taifeh*.

Yassin has handed over many of his political duties to his third son Ma'sud so that he can concentrate on the administration of his household. With 120 sheep and goats, two cows and fields of melons, wheat, barley and sugar-beet to organize, his hands are full. His life would be easier if all his sons helped. But his eldest son is married with his own small herd to manage. The next has joined the growing numbers of young men who move to towns to find new work and a new life. The third is busy with village affairs. The fourth is at school in the local town. And the others are too young. Next year things will improve. Then he will have had time to recover from the drought that has decimated his live-stock and crops. And his daughter Fatimeh will have brought him 30,000 tomans (approximately $3,750) of livestock, seed, money and goods in bridewealth by her marriage to Mohsen Taheri, Yassin's sister's son. Also Yassin has made a good arrangement for spring pastures in the mountains 50 miles to the north of his village. When the five families from his *taifeh* that he camps with arrive for their four months' stay in the mountains they are sure to have enough fresh grassland for the herds. He will keep his herd and his brother's herd together during the spring grazing so that their dogs can jointly provide more protection against wolves. His brother's black goat-hair tent can be used by his sons, thus leaving more room in his crowded tent. His wives have to cook inside the tent. The whole family has to eat and sleep there. With such a large family a second tent will be very useful. Perhaps instead of making the traditional carpets, his daughters and youngest wife can weave more goat-hair material for another tent in the autumn, although it will mean a loss in revenue. He could, on the other hand, hire the tractor and harvester of a *khan* from another nearby Timuri *taifeh* who owes him a favor for the use of his two sons during last year's sugar-beet harvest. Then Yassin could save enough time to go and sell his carpets in the city for much more than he would make locally. His traditional subsistence way of life is difficult but known to him so what saddens Yassin most is watching his people slowly lose their tribal identity as the efficient administrative machinery in Persia draws the young towards a new and in a sense a more 'civilized' way of life.

Pakhtun nomads
Afghanistan and Pakistan

Sheep are the nomad's livelihood. Each spring the household moves to the mountains where summer pastures will fatten the flock.

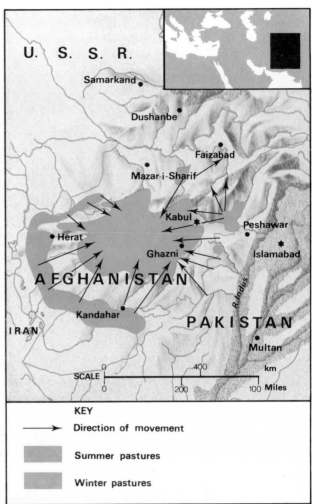

The central mountains of Afghanistan which form the westernmost extensions of the Himalaya and Karakorum ranges are flanked by vast lowland areas on the north, west, south-west and east. These are the arid steppes of Afghan Turkistan and the Iran and Baluchistan borderlands, and to the east the more fertile monsoon-fed valleys of Pakistan's north-west frontier province, known to the Afghans as Pashtunistan. In these lowland areas and in the foothills by which they approach the mountains, the Pashtun nomads have their winter quarters.

The nomads move in response to the demands of their pastoral way of life and to seasonal variations, migrating between low-lying winter quarters and mountain summer pastures for the sake of their animals. The climate is comparatively mild between October and May, though there may be snow in the north for a month or so. In the steppes and foothills March and April rains bring up abundant grass, but from June to September temperatures regularly exceed 100 degrees Fahrenheit, and May sees a mass exodus of the nomads inland, converging on the mountains of the Afghan interior, which have been under

103

Pakhtun nomads Afghanistan and Pakistan

Nomad girls marry young. The groom's family pays 100 sheep and $725. Most of the cash pays for the trousseau — tent, clothes and household goods.

snow for up to six months. In late summer and autumn they move back to the peripheral lowlands.

The nomads spend the greater part of the year camped in their winter quarters. From September until March groups of up to a hundred families settle near some water source, a river, spring or underground channel.

Of the ten to fifteen million people – half each in Afghanistan and Pakistan – who speak dialects of the Pashtu or Pakhtu language and call themselves Pashtun or Pakhtun (otherwise known as Afghans or Pathan), some two to three million lead this nomadic or semi-nomadic life. The majority of the nomads are of the two great Pashtun tribes of Durrani and Ghiljai.

Not all the various Pashtun nomadic groups are pastoralists. They differ greatly in their customs and circumstances: some specialize in long-distance trading, others sell their labor as harvesters. But the nomads of the west, the Durrani tribe and other culturally similar groups, are almost all sheep-breeders. They live in the area that reaches west from Kandahar to Herat. They are distinguished by speaking Kandahari, the 'soft' dialect of Pashtu, by their dress, their customs and by their tents which differ from those of the Ghiljai and other eastern groups.

104

Loaded camels do not travel well under a hot sun so the nomads make camp before noon. The young men dance in the hot afternoons.

Unloaded, the camels kneel
in the sun while the camp
is set up, ignoring the
small dusty children
who romp around them.

Their distinctive tents, *kizhdey,* are made of several strips of black goat-hair cloth which they sew or peg together and throw over three parallel rows of tent-poles. A transverse ridge-pole lies over the long poles of the center row and gives the tent its characteristic humped spine. The cloth is stretched over and held to the ground outside the shorter poles of the two rows. It gives only limited shelter: even when it is woven with an admixture of wool both the rays of the sun and a fine shower of rain during a storm can penetrate it. A man like a camp leader, who expects many guests, may have a separate tent to entertain them in. Today this guest tent is often a western-style canvas structure, bought from traders from Pakistan. Inside it has no hearth and is laid with carpets and cushions. Many families keep half the tent as a sleeping place for their camels. Otherwise they normally pile all the household goods – bedding, felts, storage bags – at the back and cover this wall with carpets or kelims, while in front the housewife has her hearth. Here she keeps her cooking utensils, pots and cauldrons, an iron disc griddle for baking flat bread over the fire, and a number of goat-skins in which water and food are stored.

When the time comes to move they transport their goods and supplies by camel and donkey. Any horses they keep are for riding only. Their livelihood comes from their flocks of sheep. From these they must produce enough meat, wool, skins and various forms of processed milk, not only to supply their own needs but also to sell or exchange for other goods, particularly grain, which they need but do not normally produce themselves. They depend on any profits they may make from their flocks to finance marriage payments, wedding ceremonies, funerals, festivals and other incidental expenses.

The nomad's sheep are fat-tailed sheep of several breeds of which the commonest is the Kandahari. This is well adapted to semi-desert conditions and produces reasonable wool and meat. In Turkistan the Pashtun have adopted the Arabic breed, which is well suited to conditions there and renowned for its meat, and also the Karakul breed, from which come the famous Persian lambskins. They herd the sheep in flocks of about five to six hundred head. These are the property of some five families, the 'herding unit', although some rich men may own one or more whole flocks. Each flock is in the care of two paid herdsmen, who may either be members of the herding unit or complete strangers. As the leader, the shepherd is hired on an annual contract and paid a proportion, usually ten per cent of all produce, in lambs

105

(Over page) From time
immemorial caravans of camels
bearing nomad families or
trade goods have passed this
way across the stony desert.

Pakhtun nomads Afghanistan and Pakistan

Muslim nomads pass one of the Buddhas sculpted in the 4th century from the cliff face in Bamiyan valley in the heart of the Hindu Kush.

Prospective buyers watch as a dealer puts a camel through its paces. Some nomads have trucks now, but for most camels remain as draft animals.

and wool and it is in his interest to tend the animals well. His subordinate, the drover, who follows behind the flock, is employed on a monthly basis for an agreed wage, but does not stand to gain or lose according to the condition of the flock. He is still entitled to his wages even if the whole flock is lost. The shepherds receive in addition their daily keep in food and clothing, which must be enough to protect them from all weathers as they sleep rough.

In March, with the approach of spring, the winter camps break up, and the families of each herding unit go out and camp together near their flock. Fresh, rich grass appears, the lambs are thrown, the ewes have to be milked and the milk processed, turned into yogurt and churned for butter, and the whey reduced into a hard cheese. Around New Year, 21 March, the first shearing is done. The wool from this long rough clip is mostly sold. With the end of April the spring rains cease, the heat sets in and the water supplies may fail; most important, the snow is known to be melting from the high mountain pastures, and soon the nomads begin their trek to the summer pastures.

There are some nomadic groups who build mud-brick houses in their winter quarters, making permanent villages. Many nomads often cultivate some of the land nearby for grain, or get local non-nomadic peasants to do it for them, paying them a fixed share of the crop. In many groups, particularly where the winter settlements are permanent villages with cultivated lands, a large part of the community remains behind during the summer, their brief nomadic life confined to the two months of spring when they go out with the flocks like their nomadic cousins.

The families who go on the spring trek vary from year to year. Often two brothers take it in turns to go. They sell a few lambs, lay in supplies of flour, salt and whatever else is likely to be lacking en route, lighten their baggage, reduce their tents by as much as half the size – and then one night when the moon is full they set off. Close relatives and friends say goodbye to each other for four to five months, and often many tears are shed. But in other groups, whose attachment to the land in their winter quarters is less, no-one at all is left behind during the summer.

To reach their summer quarters the western nomads, whether from Kandahar, Farah, Badghis or Turkistan, have to travel over rough country, ascending river valleys

Marching through clouds of
their own dust, sheep, dogs
and hired shepherds travel a
few days ahead of the rest
of the nomad group.

With the return to winter camp,
the headman's tent is filled
with a constant stream of
visitors — renewing contacts,
trading, catching up on news.

through deep precipitous gorges and across raging
torrents, over 12,000 foot passes and the snows of mighty
ranges. A few groups reach their traditional mountain
pastures in less than ten days, others take a month to
cover the two to three hundred miles' journey. Often,
while the camel trains follow the river courses and valley
bottoms, where possible the shepherds take the flocks
over the shorter but colder route along the mountain
crests where the grazing is easier. Sheep and their
owners may not meet more than once or twice during the
whole trek.

Each daily move begins before dawn and stops before
the sun is very far up, for the loaded camels find the
going hard under the sun, particularly at lower altitudes.
At first light, or earlier if the moon is up, the camp
begins to stir. Older men and small children huddle
round a small fire while the women and young men busy
themselves packing the baggage and loading the camels.
In half an hour or so they are ready and each family
ropes its five or six camels neck to tail. On the first camel,
which is loaded with bedding under the best carpet or
black felt and decked out in fine shell-ornamented
trappings, rides the housewife with her youngest children.
On the next camels ride any other girls. However when
the track gets steep, uphill or downhill, the women all

dismount and walk. The last camel bears the awkward
load of tent poles. The men and boys walk beside the
train or ride on horses or donkeys. The householder may
ride ahead with other men of the camp, perhaps to stop at
a wayside village where they have friends who will offer
an early breakfast of tea and bread.

After about four hours on the road, when they have
covered about ten miles, the nomads choose a suitable
place to make camp, somewhere with grazing for the
camels not too far away. They make the camels kneel,
unload them and pile up the household goods into a
wind-break. If the flocks are not to come into camp, the
nomads take the day easy, with a snack soon after
arrival and perhaps a main meal towards nightfall, after
the wife has baked bread. Otherwise people sleep, sit
around and talk, or entertain visitors from the nearby
villages – often quite close friends or trading partners.

Throughout their summer migration the nomads trade
with the villagers along the route. Village women come to
the camps offering local herbs, eggs, fresh and dried fruit
and, in north Afghanistan, a special dish made of
noodles and yogurt, in exchange for much-needed scraps
of wool. The nomad men give animals or cash advances
to their friends who promise repayment next year or later,
usually in grain or fodder. This credit is expensive, and

110

The nomad's sheep provide most of the meat for settled villagers who pay in grain or fodder to be collected later in the year.

(Bottom) Nomad camels wait in the shade in a bazaar town while their owners buy goods for the year on credit to be paid off in the spring.

neighbors. The housewife remains, and in the small hours starts the slow boiling of the curds, which must not hear a human voice or they will catch fire – which is a real enough danger. By dawn the job is finished. She calls for help to pour the clarified butter from the cauldrons into the storage skins, and the neighbors come round to ask how much she has made, and to congratulate her.

Around the same time, the sheep are shorn again. Men of the camp and often neighboring camps come to help and local villagers may be employed as well. Nearly all the short summer clip of wool is then given over to the women. They tease and card it, then roll and press it into felt, a job again requiring assistance, particularly for the big black felts which form the center pieces of the daughters' trousseaux. They also make smaller gray felts to be used as blankets and rugs. Wherever the neighbors, men or women, come to help the host feeds them a meat stew for lunch.

While they are still at the summer camp the men usually visit the large nomad bazaars at Kasi or Charas. Here traders, mainly Ghiljai Pashtun from east Afghanistan, bring goods from the towns and from Pakistan by camel train and nowadays by truck. They set up white canvas tents as shops. The western nomads, and also local villagers, bring animals for sale, but come mainly to buy grain and other food supplies, cloth, second-hand American jackets and coats, guns and ammunition, dyes, and many other things. The nomads buy on credit which they will pay off the following spring.

By the end of July it is time to start for the homeland, as the winter quarters are called. The camel trains set off straight away – camels in particular should not stay much later or they are said to catch a fatal rheumatism. The flocks may well stay with the shepherds for a month longer so that they can continue benefiting from the cool mountain summer and the succession of alpine grasses. The nomad families arrive back around the end of August, at the time of the Independence Day celebrations. The harvest is in, and the fruit crops – apricots, grapes, melons – are to be enjoyed. It is a time of comparative plenty. Work, however, remains to be done. Fodder must be laid in for the winter. The farmlands must be prepared for the next sowing. In September the festivities season begins: big weddings, large gatherings, accompanied in Turkistan by Buzkashi games.

Daily social life in the camps is intense. The nomads hate to be alone and like nothing better than a heated conversation. Even where a herding unit of perhaps only two tents is camped in summer in an isolated valley or on a hilltop there will probably be a daily stream of visitors to the camp of friends, neighbors, tradesmen. Men regularly invite each other to meals, and so do women. Passing strangers are always bidden to stop for a meal or for the night, and though they may not be asked their own name or business, they are expected to communicate any other information or news they have. Whenever a

with nomads from the east – though less so from the west – the villagers often get deeply into debt and have to forfeit their lands. Although the mountain villagers speak only Persian, a most important aspect of these exchanges, particularly for the normally isolated villagers, is the news, ideas and information that the nomads bring with them.

In the summer quarters sometimes several herding units camp together, though more often each unit camps separately in its own pasture. The nomads have their traditional areas, but may have to pay a due, either to their chief or to a local village landowner. Although they remain there for only about two months it is a busy time for all the family. The sheep thrive on the strong mountain grazing and continue to produce milk until July. The housewife turns the milk to yogurt almost every day. Each morning in the cool before dawn she churns the yogurt to separate the curds and whey. She reduces the whey to a hard cheese and stores the curds until the end of the milking season. Then she sets aside one night in July for making ghee.

That evening the children bring in plants, rubbish, old shoes, anything to symbolize the summer camp, and hang them up around the tent. Then after dinner all the family except the wife leave the tent and go to sleep with

Sitting in the doorway of his tent a nomad can see far across the horizon while with the help of a friend he twists animal hairs into a rope.

A tent is woven from goat hair. Perhaps it is intended for the daughter of the family — all brides must have their own new tent.

wedding is held, anyone within hearing is welcome at the feast.

Each winter camp or settlement is occupied by a group of kinsmen related to each other through the male line, with a common ancestor whose name the group and probably the settlement bears. Many of the residents, however, are of other groups by origin, unrelated, or related only by marriage, to the 'core' members of the camp. These attached residents are known as neighbors, though often their status is more that of clients or even retainers. Every camp has a leader who owes his position to wealth and personality, rather than to age or simple succession from father to son. Apart from this recognized leader, who has the status of official headman responsible for dealings with government authorities, the old men of standing, the heads of the more important families, form a body of elders who are consulted for their opinions in community disputes. They may call a *jirga,* a general assembly which all adult males are eligible to attend. No leader can enforce his will and decisions are reached by persuasion and consensus.

112 All Pashtun have a strict code of behavior and

Each time the nomads make camp, and as soon as her belongings are unloaded, the housewife begins making flat bread for the evening meal.

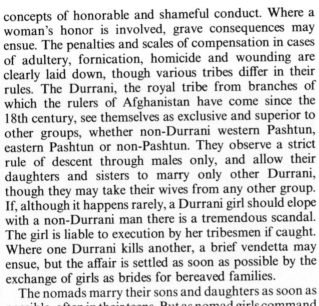

While the younger men take the camels down to water an old man has time to sit in the sun playing a two-stringed fiddle.

concepts of honorable and shameful conduct. Where a woman's honor is involved, grave consequences may ensue. The penalties and scales of compensation in cases of adultery, fornication, homicide and wounding are clearly laid down, though various tribes differ in their rules. The Durrani, the royal tribe from branches of which the rulers of Afghanistan have come since the 18th century, see themselves as exclusive and superior to other groups, whether non-Durrani western Pashtun, eastern Pashtun or non-Pashtun. They observe a strict rule of descent through males only, and allow their daughters and sisters to marry only other Durrani, though they may take their wives from any other group. If, although it happens rarely, a Durrani girl should elope with a non-Durrani man there is a tremendous scandal. The girl is liable to execution by her tribesmen if caught. Where one Durrani kills another, a brief vendetta may ensue, but the affair is settled as soon as possible by the exchange of girls as brides for bereaved families.

The nomads marry their sons and daughters as soon as possible, often in their teens. But as nomad girls command a bride price of up to 100 sheep and 50,000 Afghanis ($725) in cash, and the average drover's monthly wage is only 500 Afghanis a poor man's son may not be able to marry for many years. In a marriage in which already related families are united the price may be reduced substantially. Poorer families may well arrange an exchange of girls in which no bride-price is paid either way. Otherwise in wealthier families, and particularly in the case of eldest sons, heads of families normally choose their children's spouses for them, hoping thereby to further the family interests by arranging advantageous alliances. In some cases both the boy and the girl may be allowed some freedom of choice. Much of the cash part of the payment received by the bride's father is spent on amassing her trousseau, the goods and clothes she takes to her husband which should be enough for them to set up a new household. Every married woman should have a room or tent of her own however small. Second or further wives are the privilege of the wealthy or the resort of those whose first wives have failed to bear sons.

Compared with many other nomadic societies in the Muslim world the Pashtun are devoutly religious. They try hard to observe the formal duties of Islam. Many camps have a resident mullah, one of the family who has been to study in a religious school for some years and returned with the ability to lead prayers, to contract weddings, to conduct funerals and mourning ceremonies, and to teach the nomad children not only how to pray and perform their religious duties, but also how to read and write. Many camp sites, however briefly occupied, include a small area marked off by stones, which acts as the mosque. Here the men gather for the evening prayers at least. Even women, who are not allowed in the mosques, pray quite frequently at home. At Pamazan the nomads fast strictly. At the Id which concludes the fast, and again at the Id of Sacrifice, particularly when they occur in the winter quarters, big gatherings and ceremonies are held, with massive attendance at the mosque, followed by fairs, dancing, games and competitions. But formal religious life is on the whole sober and unemotional. Many Durrani men belong, at least nominally, to one of the dervish brotherhoods. Once or twice a year their spiritual leader or *pir,* comes round to visit, to collect his tithes, and to hold Zikr ceremonies where his followers, particularly the younger men, attain trance states through controlled breathing and body movements. This ecstatic experience is held to be a proper counterpart of the formal mosque religion, and just as important.

The nomad women, who are cheerful, although their life is one long drudge are not veiled. They are hardly secluded in normal camp life, and they are outspoken in their opinions on whatever is the issue of the moment, whether a daily household budgeting detail or a major tribal scandal. But a woman may not normally attend the *jirga* assemblies, except when she has a personal cause to argue, and then the camp women's leader, a respected old woman, will argue for her. The women gather separately from the men on festive occasions. And the nomad women are not normally allowed to participate in either the mosque or the Zikr ceremonies, and are definitely deprived in matters of religious experience. Perhaps as a reflection of this, many of the nomad women, particularly those unable to bear sons, or otherwise in conflict with their husbands, are liable to fits.

The Pashtun have a romantic appeal. They are an attractive people. But the nomads' way of life is nevertheless a harsh one and highly vulnerable to climatic disasters. Moreover, their nomadism is seen by the authorities as an obstacle to attempts to bring them the benefits, such as education and health facilities which the modernizing Afghan State can offer. The nomads play an important role in the Afghan economy, however, for they exploit otherwise unused range lands and contribute pastoral produce much needed by settled society.

113

Hazara
Afghanistan

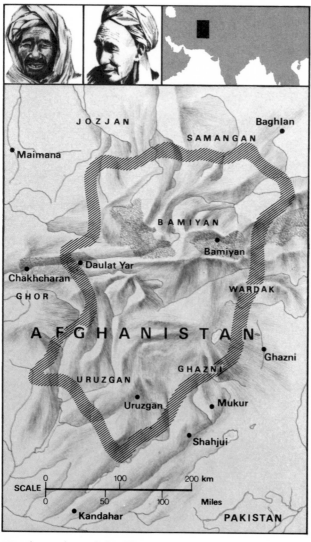

In the region of the Hazara one-roomed houses often have a mud wall, squarely adjusted around a mud dome, as though in imitation of a *yurt*, the felt tent used by central Asian nomads. Groups of these houses, held together by an encircling wall, easily conjure up the camps of Genghis Khan as they were described by 13th century missionaries and Chinese travelers: scaffoldings under domes and banners, walls of silk, wool or brocade, where the royal wives walked under headdresses so tall that they had to move into their tents backwards. The wives ruled the royal camps and sat at the Khan's side at his banquets, each wife in her appointed place. The Mongols are believed to be among the ancestors of the Hazara, but all that remains to display such a past are the tent-shaped houses and the flattish, mongoloid faces of the Hazara people.

The one million Hazara are second in size only to the Tajik, the largest Afghan Persian ethnic group in Afghanistan. They live mainly in the Hazarajat, the

114

115

Less than 100 years ago,
warring Hazara tribes made the
mountains unsafe. Now, in
peace, women return to their
village after work.

Water trickles over the Band-i-Haibat (Dam of Awe), to be harnessed by the Hazara for the grinding wheels of their flour mills.

In winter in Hazarajat, villagers are often isolated for 6 months. In summer, however, village schools are able to open every day.

The face of a young Hazara boy reveals marked Mongoloid features — among his ancestors were troops of the armies of Genghis Khan.

mountainous eastern half of the country. Although they speak a dialect of Persian their language also has an admixture of Turkish and many pure Mongolian words and grammatical features.

The Hazara have their own tradition of their Mongolian origins. According to some written legends they were originally remnants of Genghis Khan's occupation army. Indeed the name Hazara may reflect this as it probably derives from the Persian word *hazar*, meaning one thousand, and referring to a division of the Turko-Mongol armies. But the Hazara are almost certainly of mixed origin, descended from the successive waves of Turko-Mongols who settled in Afghanistan in the 13th, 14th and 15th centuries, mixed with the local tribes and absorbed their culture.

By 1500 the Hazara had settled in their present, mountainous land and thanks to its inaccessibility and their own belligerence, they succeeded in maintaining the independence of their territory until 1892. In that year, Amir Abdur Rahman Khan finally defeated the Hazara, after which they came under Afghan administration. Administrative centers, roads and caravanserais

Hazara people who have left
Hazarajat for towns and
cities are often forced to take
the heaviest work as
water-carriers or porters.

were built and peace established so that caravans and travelers no longer had to by-pass Hazaraja.

In Hazarajat almost every stretch of ground which can be irrigated is cultivated, sown with wheat or barley, pulses or plants for fodder and, towards the south, with maize. Cows, sheep and goats are kept around the villages for their meat and milk; oxen are kept to pull the plows, and, with asses and horses, are used as pack animals. They keep as many animals in fact as they have winter fodder to feed. They are a self-sufficient people who produce all they need apart from luxuries like tea and sugar. They barter their surplus wheat and clarified butter with the Pakhtun (Pashtun – see page 100) nomads; they sell woven materials and felt mats. In return the Pakhtun nomads give them cheap cotton cloth, sugar and tea. The Pakhtun have often allowed them credit, with the result that the Hazara frequently fell into debt and the nomads increasingly took over their lands and became absentee landlords. To avoid hardship many Hazara then moved to the Afghan towns where they took work as porters, water carriers and refuse collectors.

Nevertheless Hazarajat, despite its sparse natural resources, seems a densely populated country. The compact villages ring the irrigated zones. The houses, made mainly of mud and stone, are well adapted to the climate. In the coldest regions a house consists of one windowless room with a porch. The only light is from a smoke-hole in the roof, and even that can be closed. Elsewhere there are two- or three-roomed houses; but there is always a fireplace in the stable, so that, as in the one-roomed houses, the animals are cared for in a severe winter.

In the house of a Hazara family there is only simple furniture. In a corner an open fire-place or a baking oven is built into the floor. There are small recesses in the clay walls where oil lamps and other possessions are kept. One contains the family's wooden chest of clothes and treasures. In others stand woven bags and skin sacks. There are earthenware pots, imported copperware, wooden bowls and other utensils. At night the

family sleeps under quilted cotton blankets on home-made felt mats spread on the floor.

Although in the highest regions of the mountains the Hazara stay in their villages all the year round, in the warmer regions they generally move for three summer months to small mud huts in the fallow fields for their winter houses become unbearably infested with insects.

In regions towards the north they trek up into the mountains to the high pastures for the summer. Here they live in felt-covered round tents (*chapari*), of a kind also dwelt in by the Uzbek. Summer and autumn are the active seasons for the Hazara. In winter, the Hazara explain, they do nothing but eat and sleep, for often they are cut off from the outside world for up to six months. It is therefore essential that in the summer they busy themselves gathering and storing fuel and fodder for the isolated winter months. Throughout Hazarajat, these necessities are stored in stacks.

Hazara women weave, make pottery and felt, and process the dairy foods which are kept for the winter. They employ simple horizontal ground looms for weaving the heavy *barak* cloth which is used in men's clothes and rugs, blankets and the sacks which are slung across the pack animals. The women make felt by spreading the loose carded wool on an old felt mat, sprinkling it with water, rolling it up and tying it together and finally rolling it hundreds of times over the ground.

In the morning the women bring the milk taken from the cows to the boil – the first stage in milk preparation. They then make butter from the soured milk of the day before, churning it in goatskins hung beneath a tripod, finally turning it into ghee, or clarified butter, by boiling it so that the water content is reduced to a minimum. This ghee will keep for anything up to eight months. But the Hazara have many other ways of using the milk. Buttermilk from the churn can be boiled, hung up in a cloth to drain the whey so that the remaining solids can be pressed into round lumps and dried in the sun. The result is *grut*, a favorite winter food, which keeps for years.

Traditionally the Hazara have never been a politically united people. Instead they have always been split into a number of tribal and regional divisions with hereditary, almost feudal, leaders called *khans* or *mirs*. Many of the Hazara people have names with the prefix *day* (Day-Zangi, Day-Hundi for example) the meaning of which is unknown. But an Afghan proverb says that a Hazara without a *day* is like an Afghan without a *-zai*, a word which means son of. This all reflects the importance of tribal affiliations, even in these times since the tribal leaders, or *khans*, have been stripped of their feudal powers. Today, although the *khan* families are still influential, the people of Hazarajat belong to seven different, multi-ethnic provinces. It seems that while tribal identities within the society of the Hazara are crumbling, their common identity in relation to outsiders has become more marked.

117

Nuristani
Afghanistan

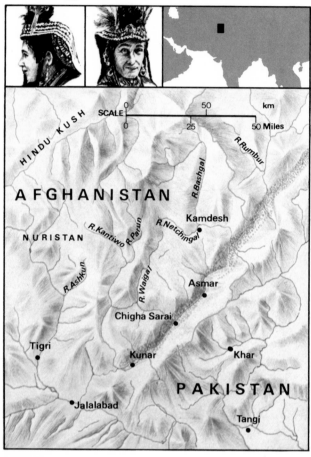

Nuristan, a mountainous region some 5,000 square miles in extent, lies on the southern slopes of the Hindu Kush Range in north-eastern Afghanistan. It is a land of forests with deep ravines separated by high mountains. Perhaps sixty to eighty thousand people live in these isolated valleys. In the lower part of one valley – the Bashgul – there is now a motorable road, but in the rest of Nuristan there are not only no roads, the mountain trails are not even suitable for horses, mules, or donkeys. One must walk. In winter deep snow may isolate one village from another for weeks at a time and the high mountain passes which connect one valley with another are often closed from December to April.

There are four main valley systems in Nuristan; there are also numerous tributary valleys which contain important settlements. In each of the main drainage areas the inhabitants speak a different language. These are Kati, Waigali, Ashkuni and Paruni; they have been classified as Dardic languages and belong to the Indo-Iranian family.

The earliest known European penetration of this 'Kafiristan' (land of infidels) occurred in 1885 with the Lockhart expedition, but it was a medical doctor from the Orkneys – George Scott Robertson – who was the

119

Perhaps more than 60,000
people live in Nuristan in
villages — clusters of timber
houses clinging to almost
inaccessible mountain slopes.

first to explore and map the country. He spent a year
among the Kafirs (1889-90) and published a book called
the *Kafirs of the Hindu Kush* which is still the standard
work on the area. In 1896-98 the Amir of Afghanistan
made war on these independent peoples and forced them
to accept Islam. The name of the country was then
changed to Nuristan – 'land of light'.

The people of Nuristan are proud, and though they are
hospitable and friendly, they are also aggressive and
quick to avenge any injury. They enjoyed centuries of
independence and raised their sons to be warriors, training them to be skilled hunters with spear and bow, and
later with matchlocks and flintlocks. Today a man's most
prized possession may be a British army Enfield rifle.

For eight or nine centuries they held out against the
tide of Islam which had spread eastward across Asia
from Arabia. They raided Muslim settlements and passing caravans in the Kunar valley, the Alingar valley, and
the Kabul valley. These raids against the encroaching
Muslim population became institutionalized, that is, a
successful warrior was rewarded according to the
number of men he had killed. He could achieve rank in
this way and so improve his status at home.

Another way in which a man could become important
in this society was to give a series of public feasts over a
period of years, inviting everyone in his village to
attend – perhaps 1,000 to 2,000 people at a time. Later,
as he aspired to achieve still higher rank, he would invite
other villages as well. In order to understand how such
large scale feasting was possible, let us look at the
economics of village life in Nuristan.

The people live in permanent villages located on steep
mountain slopes at about 2,000 meters above sea level.
These villages may vary in size from two dozen households to more than 300. Each village has round it the
terraced fields, irrigation channels, mountain streams and
pastures which provide the basis for the kind of 'alpine'
economy that is characteristic of Nuristan.

The basic division of labor in the society coincides with
a division in the economic system: a combination of
arable agriculture and transhumant (semi-nomadic)
herding. The women are responsible for the raising of
grain on irrigated terraces. In spring they clean and repair
the irrigation channels, dig the small terraces with spades,
plant the grain (barley, millet, maize and wheat), weed
and water the crops and, at the end of August or early
September, harvest the grain. Most fields in Nuristan are
too small to make plowing practical; though plows are
used in parts of the Bashgul and Parun valleys.

The men, meanwhile, have been herding livestock on
distant pastures. The transhumant movement of herdsmen and livestock from permanent villages to seasonal
pastures begins in spring, when all livestock are taken
from the winter stables on a certain day and moved out
to the early pastures. These herds consist of goats, cattle,
and sheep, in that order. In Waigal valley they say a rich

The Kalash take great care
to stock up with meat, cheeses
and liquid butter, for winter
feasts. Here they skin a beast
before salting and storing it.

(Center) Nuristani 'People
of Light' call the Kalash
kafir. Unlike the Nuristani
the *kafir* are infidels,
unconverted to Islam.

Kalash love an excuse to sing
and dance — as at the great
outdoor spring and autumn
festivals for Jestak,
goddess of home and family.

Nuristani Afghanistan

Nuristani men build houses by jamming stones between a timber framework and then plastering the walls. A house may cost 10 cows or 60 goats.

The isolation of Nuristani hilltop villages like Malil and the shortage of pasture makes inhabitants wary of people from other villages.

122

man has at least 500 head of livestock. Of these, approximately 450 will be goats, twenty or thirty cattle, and the rest sheep. In other areas, according to altitude, relief and the accessibility of pastures, the proportion of cattle may be higher.

When the first pastures have been thoroughly grazed and as the snow line retreats with the onset of warmer weather, the herds move up to the next set of pastures together. These herd movements are carefully controlled by a special group of villagers who are elected for this purpose each spring. They have the authority to levy fines on those who fail to move their animals out of the winter stables on the appointed day. They can also fine a herdsman who allows his livestock to stray onto the wrong pastures or into cultivated fields. These men are also responsible for seeing that the terraced fields are watered in strict rotation according to village rules; anyone who takes water from the channels out of turn is liable to be fined. In the autumn they must see that no one picks grapes or walnuts before the harvest for these fruits has been announced. Fines may vary from one big cheese to a goat, or even a cow. The fines that have been collected belong to those elected members who have been charged with these supervisory responsibilities. Usually they meet in autumn at the end of their tour of duty and, using the fines they have collected, give themselves a feast. This is the only 'pay' they receive.

Meanwhile, the herdsmen have moved from one set of pastures to another, changing every 15 or 20 days, until by midsummer they have reached the highest pastures at 3,000-3,500 meters above sea level. Here they milk the animals and make butter and cheese. The cheeses, weighing 5 to 8 kilograms, will keep for a long time if properly salted. These foods are carried down to the village and stored away for the autumn feasts and long winter months ahead.

As midsummer passes, the herds move on to other pastures, gradually descending to lower altitudes so that by first frost they are back in the neighborhood of the winter stables. By this time the women will have harvested the grain, gathered hay on the mountainsides, and collected a good supply of firewood.

When the harvest is in and the herdsmen are back from the mountains there is a festive air in the village. It is at this season that most marriages take place, as the supplies needed for wedding feasts are at hand. This is also the time of the year when feasts of merit are most likely to be given by men who wish to achieve rank and improve their social and political standing in the community.

In Nuristan the important economic group is the extended family – that is, a family consisting of an old patriarch, his married sons and their wives and children. In agricultural affairs, and on certain occasions in political matters, these extended families compete with each other. The shepherds, for example, compete among themselves to see who can get the most milk, who can make the most

clarified butter, who can produce the greatest number of cheeses. Back in the village, the women compete to see who can harvest the greatest number of baskets of grain. No one in Nuristan is really satisfied to produce just enough to supply his family with food: everyone strives to achieve a surplus. They work hard, not just to achieve a subsistence minimum, but to produce far more than they can actually consume.

From this we might conclude that they intend to market their surplus foods, or to exchange them for other goods. But this is not the case. The sole purpose for amassing surplus foodstuffs in this society is so that they may be given away. In short, they are used to achieve social goals, rather than economic goals.

On the 20th July, 1970 I attended such a feast in the village of Nisheigrom in Waigal valley. The feast was held out of doors on the rooftops and the entire village was present. My informants estimated that the feast required at least 5 cows, 35 big goats, 565 kilograms of wheat, 565 kilograms of millet, 160 liters of clarified butter, and 160 kilograms of cheese. The host, a man named Kuvera, offered this feast to the village to celebrate the raising of the roof beams on the new village mosque. By doing so his status in the community was greatly enhanced.

Before the Afghan invasions of 1895, when Nuristan (or Kafiristan, as it was then called) was completely independent, there were these two ways for a man to become important in his community. He could embark upon a career as a warrior and achieve rank according to the number of enemies (ie Muslims) he killed, or he could stay at home and give feasts of merit. The most important men usually did both, though an influential position in Nuristani society required, and still requires, more than mere rank.

A man of influence is above all else a good public speaker with a reputation for persuasive argument and a clear grasp of the problems relating to a given issue. This brings us to consider what form of 'government' exists in traditional Nuristani society, for there are no chiefs or princes, no judges or jury, no written laws, no police or army. And yet social order is maintained and those who break village laws are punished. How then does the system work?

Everyone in Nuristan is a member of a named descent group by virtue of birth. Descent is traced through the male line; the larger groups which are formed according to this principle are usually termed lineages and clans by anthropologists. Members of a lineage co-operate with one another. If a man needs assistance it is to his kinsmen that he looks for help. If a man is involved in a dispute, the members of his lineage rally round to give support. Both plaintiff and defendant can normally expect such support; indeed, they have a right to it. Membership in a lineage carries with it certain rights, duties, and obligations, and because of this, the 'lineage system' is an organizing principle in social, economic, religious and political affairs.

Disputes are settled by mediators. Having said this, we must qualify it, for it gives the impression that they hear a case and then announce a verdict. In fact, they cannot do this. They are mediators, not judges. Having heard one side of the story they go to the home of the other party involved in the dispute and listen to his version of what happened. They may do this several times, as they hear evidence and question witnesses. Then, in the end, they try to propose a workable solution. When both sides agree and the fines are paid, the case is over.

Today in Nuristan the important man is not necessarily a famous warrior, or outstanding giver of feasts, though these virtues are still much admired, he is rather the man who has repeatedly demonstrated his skill as a mediator. As his reputation grows he will be invited to settle 'big' disputes in neighboring villages and his fame will spread throughout the valley. He has become a man of influence and is respected by all members of the society. In Nuristan one cannot go higher than this.

Striking features of Nuristani culture are building techniques and architectural styles. Cantilever bridges span the rivers; large timber houses perch on steep rocky slopes; complex irrigation systems run for miles along the mountains. The houses are often covered with finely chiseled geometric designs cut into the wood; household utensils such as bowls and tables are carved in detail with elaborate designs. Such patterns are not just decoration: they represent the rank of the owner. The iron and silver work provides evidence of a long tradition that has developed many special features. Potters, weavers, leather-workers, and basket makers also contribute to the material culture of Nuristan.

All these things are produced by a small hereditary group of craftsmen who form a separate class in Nuristani society. In nearly every village there are a few families of these craftsmen who practise and pass on traditional skills. Socially, they occupy a low position in the society. In the hands of these few people – not more than 10 per cent of the population at most – rest all the skills capable of producing and perpetuating the material culture of Nuristan.

Although many features of Kalash culture are similar to those of Nuristan, they are in some respects a rather different people as their language – Kalasha – is an Indian language. Certainly they pursue the same modes of livelihood as the Nuristani and share many other cultural characteristics with them.

In 1895 when the 'Durand Line' was demarcated to separate Afghanistan from India, the Kalash Kafir Valleys of Rumbur, Bomboret and Berir were left on the Chitral side (now part of West Pakistan). This apparently minor detail in the work of the Boundary Commission had profound implications for the Kalash. Had they been

One of the jobs of the village wood-carver is to make grave statues. Though socially inferior, he is vital to the Kalash culture.

Detailed geometric carvings on houses and possessions denote the status of the Kalash inhabitant, reached through wisdom and generous feasts.

Although Kalash women do not wear veils and are more independent than Afghan women, they are kept separate during ceremonies and feasts.

(Bottom) Kalash women work very hard, growing rice and maize and collecting wood. The men herd livestock on distant pastures, or sit at home.

included within the confines of Afghanistan they would have been converted to Islam in the Afghan invasions of 1895-98. As it is, they have been left in these isolated valleys to continue their traditional way of life and their ancient religious observances.

The Kalash Kafir population is small: not more than 3,000 or 4,000 altogether, and as they are slowly accepting Islam it may be that there are now no more than 1,500 who actually practise the old religion.

Many Kalash villages have temples to Jestak – a goddess protecting the family, children and the home. Numerous ceremonies concerning family life are performed there during the year. At the great spring and autumn festivals which are held out of doors by the Jestak temple, the villagers assemble to dance and sing. Several Kalash villages also have open air shrines to the god Mahandeo. These usually have a stone base and a large carved wooden box on top, from which project carved wooden heads of horses. Opposite there are wooden benches with carved vertical planks commemorating great sacrifices of the past.

The shrine of Sajigor in Rumbur Valley is a holy place of major importance. On August 27th 1967 I was present when 40 or 50 shepherds came down from the mountain pastures carrying baskets of cheese. On top of each basket were juniper branches for the sacred fire. The shrine is only a few yards from the river and is set in a grove of trees. From the branches of these trees hang the horns of goats sacrificed at the shrine. The shrine itself is a stone platform some ten feet square and about four feet high which is said to contain the body of a sacrificed goat with an ancient knife obtained in battle against the Bashgul Valley Kafirs. The carved wooden heads of horses project from the structure.

As their baskets were unloaded and the large round cheeses set out round the edge of a cloth that had been spread on the ground, the juniper branches were piled in a heap beside the shrine. By this time nearly a hundred men and youths had gathered in the sacred grove (women are not allowed to enter the area); others were coming up from villages down the valley carrying goat-skin sacks full of round flat cakes of bread.

A fire was made in front of the shrine and when it was burning well, fresh green juniper branches were piled on; at once thick clouds of white smoke rose in the air. A goat was led forward and a virgin boy milked it so that a few drops fell on a cake of bread. The bread was then broken and the pieces thrown through the smoke onto the shrine.

The priest stepped forward, raised his arms and began to chant; a cry that was taken up and repeated by the assembled crowd until the grove echoed with sound. Then the cheeses were cut into thick wedges and everyone present – even Muslim visitors – received one of these on a piece of bread. In a few moments the solemn religious atmosphere of the grove had changed to take on the air of an afternoon picnic.

Hunza
Pakistan

Legend and romance weave a
dream around this valley which
some call Shangri-La, peopled
by the descendants of
Alexander the Great's soldiers.

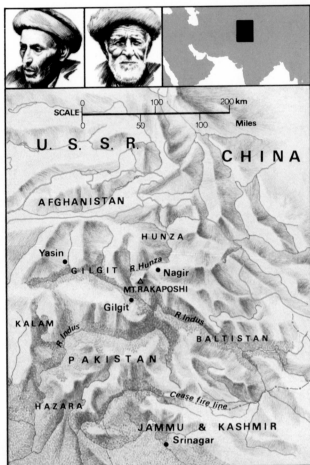

When a Burusho man from Hunza gives directions he will not talk about the cardinal points of the compass. He will speak of going up or down river, or up or down hill. He locates houses by the channel they draw water from. In Hunza land and water dominate life.

The state of Hunza is locked in at the extreme north-west of the Himalayas where the Karakoram mountains join the Hindu Kush and Pamir ranges. They form a nexus which the people of Hunza aptly call the 'Roof of the World', a place where Pakistan meets China, Afghanistan and Russia.

The rugged land is cut by high and narrow rock-strewn valleys ending in white glaciers. There are jagged crags above barren black walls of rock with an occasional background of giant white peaks sharp against the deep blue of the sky. Much of the Hunza is uninhabitable, for it is only where there is a lucky coincidence of soil and water that men can settle.

There are two geographically and culturally distinct peoples living on the strips of land along the mud-cliffed Hunza river gorge – the Wakhi and the Burusho. The Wakhi were nomads in Russian Turkistan and Afghani-

stan, some of whom settled with their flocks alongside the Chapursan river and the Hunza river north of its west-ward loop. Rising above 9,000 feet, their land is too high to grow wheat or really good fruit; only their pastures are better than those of the Burusho further down the river gorge. The Burusho live, at 7,800 feet, in an eight-mile-valley on the right river bank of the Hunza gorge and form the majority of the population. Their language, Burushaski, is unique. Some claim that the Burusho are descended from men of Alexander the Great's army; others say they originally came from the north or lived in Baltistan, in the east.

In late spring the Hunza valley becomes a mass of bush-green terraces, fields studded with leafy willows and poplars, orchards of apples, peaches and pears, mul-berries and swelling red apricot buds. These spring colors fall against a crimson-brown background of rocks rising to snow-laced crags, with the giant white pyramid of Rakaposhi standing opposite. Approaching Hunza after three dusty days on foot along the bleak, tortuous path from Gilgit you can understand why travelers should have called it a Shangri-La.

A myth of Hunza has grown up presenting an image of the Hunzakut as a wise old people who know neither strife nor illness but live on peacefully into ripe old age, undisturbed in a perfect society and a land of plenty. The myth is not without some truth. Almost all who have visited the Hunza have commented on their cheerfulness, courtesy and tolerance, and above all their spirit of co-operation; but this spirit existed in a struggle against both the harsh land and other peoples, in a society that has been radically changing over the last century.

The oral traditions of Hunza tell of the common origin of the royal families of Hunza and its twin state of Nagar across the river gorge. They also mentioned an exchange of princesses between these families. In the eastern Asian kingdoms these exchanges were signs of alliance, and the first mention of Hunza in Chinese annals records such an exchange between Hunza and Tibet in the 7th century AD. The castles of the early settlement in the Hunza valley were built by craftsmen from Baltistan who accompanied a princess on another exchange as part of her dowry. And yet despite these alliances, the states were frequently at war with one another. Houses were clustered around the castles into which the inhabitants would withdraw and light fires as beacons when they were attacked.

The Hunzakut, described in 1891 as the "terror of all the people from Afghanistan to Yarkand", were particularly successful and enterprising brigands. They regarded their raiding as a right conferred on them by the proximity of the trade routes. Their ruler, the Mir, even exchanged gifts with the Chinese resident in Turkistan at Kashgar, while at the same time raiding the main caravan routes in his territory. Hearing from his agents of a rich caravan setting out from Yarkand south towards Leh, the Mir

(Left) A mountain wall rises behind the Mir's palace to cloud-capped peaks which the people of Hunza call the 'roof of the world'.

Surrounded by his ministers, the Mir holds the daily *durbar*. The final authority in a land without police or jail is open to anyone with a grievance.

(Bottom) For centuries the Hunzakut terrorized the trade routes from Afghanistan to Yarkand. No caravan was safe from their savage raids.

129

Children have plenty of time
to play and to practise the
dances their elders perform
at the annual marriage
celebrations after the harvest.

had a goat sacrificed and its head paraded around in front of his men, then dispatched them east over the desolate Shimshal pass to set an ambush. From these caravans in the north-east the Hunzakut plundered jewelry, silks, animals and other goods. And from the south they took slaves – Balti, Nagari and Kashmiri – for sale to the Badaksh merchants in the north.

On occasions Hunza was attacked by Sikhs from Gilgit in the south but, well protected by her difficult passes, remained undefeated. In 1866 the Kashmiri attacked, again helped by the Nagari, but the Nagari sided with the people of Hunza to rout the expedition, capturing sepoys of the British Raj who could be sold in the slave markets of Turkistan.

In 1891 the British, fearing Imperial Russia's expansion south from the Pamirs towards India, dispatched a mission under Colonel Algernon Durand to ensure a military road and lines of communication back up through Hunza to the Pamirs. His armed force, attacking first up the Nagar bank of the river, inflicted the first military defeat on the Hunzakut. The precarious track up from Gilgit was widened to take pack animals; a telegraph line was installed up to Misgar near the Turkistan border, and a new Mir installed to replace the intriguing Safdar Ali who had fled over the roof of the world to Kashgar.

The new Mir, Sir Mohammed Nazim Khan KCIE, ruled peacefully over Hunza from 1892 to 1938. He was the first Mir for over a hundred years to die a natural death while still in office. He governed the distant parts of his realm by telephone, and in his lifetime the population of the valley increased from 6,000 to over 10,000. The multitude of villages grew, where possible, to meet this increase.

But the valley can only support a limited number of people. Hunzakut techniques of husbandry have exploited this land to the full. So much of the land is terraced into fields that there is only one road through Hunza and even that is nowhere more than six feet wide. Elsewhere the people must climb or walk in single file beside water channels or along the edges of the terraces. The terrace walls are carefully revetted up with stones, large at the bottom and small at the top, each locking into the next. They have even made land by building up a steep terrace wall on the mountainside, crushing or removing rocks from the inside and alternately flooding and draining the space between. Within a few years there is enough rock dust and mud to make a narrow strip field a few feet across.

Fields must have water but there is not enough rainwater for irrigation. Hundreds of feet below, the river is

Jan Mohammed earns his living as a teacher but at prayer and feast times he acts as a priest and leads the singing of love songs to the Prophet.

Women move to their husband's village on marriage but each returns home proudly with her new-born child for a visit which may last a year.

(Bottom) Although Muslim, the women of Hunza wear no veil, but an embroidered hat, scarf, and a brightly colored tunic and baggy trousers.

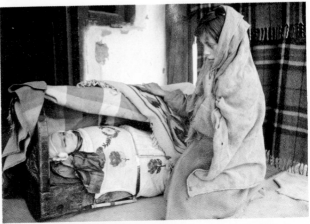

racing away down the gorge, its waters inaccessible. And so a system of narrow aqueducts carry water down from glaciers far above. The aqueducts are channeled out of the rock face or suspended along it in wooden troughs, crossing seemingly sheer mountain faces. These channels are up to six miles long and made and maintained with no better tools than wooden poles, shovels and soft iron picks. Like all other constructions here, aqueducts are made without mortar. When a section disappears in one of the frequent landslides, a man has to be lowered on the end of rope to construct the new ledge, wedging shallow stones into crevices, widening the shelf and padding in loose soil to complete the channel.

Although most villages have their own direct channel to the glacier, the water is never plentiful and has to be regulated. This is easily done and – except at certain times of the year, as during sowing – children operate the sluices. The people store their supply of water in stone-walled reservoirs, which are emptied by removing a wooden plug at times when water from the glaciers does not flow. In the summer children swim in these same pools. Drinking water is stored separately in similar dug-out pits that are roofed over and approached down steps to keep animals away.

13

There is little pasture in Hunza and few livestock. In summer sheep live on fruit and foliage in the villages; cattle are taken up the mountainside above 12,000 feet where they are herded by young boys. The boys also feed them with fodder and make a kind of butter from the meager fat produce. The trees are stripped of their leaves, the fields literally swept for tufts which, with the little hay they have is stored as winter fodder. And with few animals, dung for manure is scarce. It is normal for a small boy to follow a beast around with a small bowl, especially when the animal is in the village or being used to thresh crops, to collect the droppings. The dung is then stored, together with the odd twigs it has picked up, until the winter manuring of the fields. Fresh human dung, is also kept away from the fields and it is possible that this custom (together with the individual supply of glacier water to each village and a separate store of drinking water) has kept the Hunzakut free from the endemic goiter and epidemics that afflict the surrounding hill peoples.

In Hunza, fields are not only rotated, they are also used twice over each year. The barley fields of the late summer are sown with millet; the wheat fields, which ripen a few weeks later, are sown with winter buckwheat. This last crop is grown as an insurance, for buckwheat is hardy and can survive a bad winter. But the people have no real love of scones made from this buckwheat. Along with their own vegetables they also grow potatoes and tomatoes, introduced by the British, and then the summer is the season of abundant fruits – apricots, for one, are a staple also dried and stored for the winter.

In spite of their careful husbandry, food is often scarce in late winter. The animals, lean at the best of times, have to be kept in byres feeding on scant fodder during the winter cold. There is not enough of this to keep all the animals alive, nor enough stored food for the people themselves. Weeks before the new barley is ready most households run out of flour, and many run short of dried apricots and vegetables. At this time of year an animal killed for the winter festival of Tumushelling gives welcome meat to supplement this diet.

A child's portion of food depends on his age. An able-bodied man is entitled to double a woman's ration, and an expectant mother gets a larger share than the other women. It is the job of the chief housewife to store and ration out the foodstuffs over the whole year – a difficult job in which the experience of an old woman is much valued. If too much is given out in the summer months of plenty the family may starve before the next year. A wife's incompetence at this job is grounds for divorce.

Among the people of Hunza a man and wife, his sons and their wives and their children all live and work together. In the winter cold, with temperatures well below zero, they all sleep together in the common living room on raised platforms around the walls, bachelors together, unmarried women together and couples together. During the day they sit around a small central fire from which smoke meanders outwards, filling the whole room and blackening the pillars and walls before finally escaping through the smoke-hole in the roof. There are no windows, and if it is very cold with snow or a powerful wind the skylight is shut leaving the room in darkness. Only the glow of the fire remains and as there is little fuel the fire itself burns slowly when the wife is baking chapatis or boiling vegetables. The women sew, bake and tend their babies. Outside it is gray and bleak, clouds hang low over the rocks, stark trees and desolate fields into which the men venture only occasionally, perhaps to break ice for water. Otherwise they stay inside with the family, mending their tools. Old people recount tales to the young; stories of their bygone brigand days and heroes, and of clan history and everyday events. This is their literature, the store of their wisdom from which the children learn of the life and ways of Hunza.

In the other world of the hot dry summer the people live out on the roof, spinning wool or drying apricots, talking and visiting with their neighbors, cooking and sleeping in the open. The houses are built in small groups within which the families co-operate with each other; harvesting, threshing and taking their grain to the miller together; exchanging gifts of food between each other.

The people live outside in the hot dry summer and the village barber must take care not to become too interested in the gossip around him.

(Top) Bericho bands of pipers, drummers and kettle drummers play all through wedding feasts, taunting the men whose dancing is not vigorous enough.

Every village has a weaver
who makes the men's 9-foot-
long cloaks, called *chogas*.
The edges of the best, festival
chogas are embroidered.

A housewife grinds grain to
make chapatis of millet or
wheat. In hard times she
makes them with buckwheat,
though they are less popular.

There is no hard and fast line between a man's and a
woman's work. A man will happily drive the threshing
team or look after a baby, a woman will readily work
with a shovel, but normally the heavy jobs – plowing and
maintaining the terraces – are done by men. In the
evening men sit and smoke pipes of scarce tobacco picked
from tiny plots in the corner of a field.

It is the children of the family who carry presents
between houses. Perhaps they take early-ripening fruit to
their mother's family in another village where fruit ripens
later. The children help their parents in work only so long
as they are interested. Otherwise they roam around in
groups. Boys play a kind of football called *mindak* in
which they kick a lead and cloth ball up into the air, and
score by the number of times they keep it aloft. Girls
practise embroidery, and all the children – boys and girls
alike – play a game similar to rounders, or in twos, on
each other's backs, play horses. Some retire to play with
pebbles on a scratched-out piece of ground. The elder
children willingly look after all the younger ones. It is
quite impossible to tell whether it is their brother or sister
or some neighbor's infant that they lead by the hand.

There are a few experts within the Burusho community,
like millers and the master carpenter who fixes the doors
on the houses and the weavers who make the men's
nine-foot-long homespun cloaks called *chogas*. There is 133

Hunza Pakistan

High up on the mountainside with the village cattle, the young herdsman must make his own 'boots' to keep out the cold Himalayan wind.

(Bottom) Hunza has no doctor and a man must splint and bandage a broken foot himself or get the skilled village elders to take care of it.

Land is so precious in Hunza that there is only one road, barely 6 feet wide. Elsewhere, people must clamber along the edges of the terraced fields.

Storing and rationing out the food supply for the year is a wife's most important task. Incompetence is grounds for a divorce.

also a group of outsiders called the Bericho who work as blacksmiths and musicians in the villages. These Bericho are a separate community, with their own customs, language and village, and they do not marry among the Burusho. At one time the Burusho regarded them as inferior and would not accept food from them. Bericho blacksmiths tour the Hunza villages each year with their hammers, using a stone forge and bellows supplied by the villagers. They repair the few iron goods, the shears, tripods, sickles and plow tips, owned by the Burusho. In return each Burusho village pays a small annual tax to the Bericho community.

If there is a dispute between two people the first to try to settle it are the heads of the families. If the dispute is then between households they put it in front of the village's open court, known as a *durbar*, for each village is an administrative unit supervised by a headman appointed by the Mir. Plaintiffs can go still higher, to the *durbar* of 'the headmen of the four clans' at the capital Baltit; or even to the *durbar* of the Mir's advisor, the Wazir, with a final appeal to the daily governing *durbar* of the Mir himself. The Mir's decision in the *durbar*, as it is in all matters, is absolute and final. But court action does not pay in Hunza; it is customary for the winner of a case to thank the court with a gift roughly equal to the fine imposed on the loser. The extreme punishment that the Mir's court inflicts is banishment, generally to the oppressive Shimshal valley to tend the Mir's flocks for a number of years. Crime itself is rare; the censure of the community is a sufficient check on behavior.

There is a story of a young married woman who faked a fatal accident, leaving her hat at the side of the river gorge to make people think that she had fallen in and drowned, after which she went to live with another man. The pair were eventually discovered and, coming before the Mir's *durbar*, he judged that she should be divorced and married to her lover. The man's family did not approve, and one month later the woman committed suicide by walking off the cliff edge into the torrent below.

Girls are normally married by 16, boys by the age of 18. It is the parents who arrange the match. They take into account the desirability of marrying where the family has married before, a preference for marrying outside their own clan (which was part of the law until 1930). The desires of the girl and boy are secondary, but if the couple prove totally incompatible they can obtain a divorce. The families negotiate the marriage, exchanging gifts with an extra payment from the groom's family as a token recompense for the expense of bringing up a daughter. Not that a wife is utterly separated from her kin by moving to her husband's family's house. Visits sometimes lasting a year take her back to her family with a new-born child. Land and property are inherited by the sons of the house, but the wife-to-be receives a small dowry amongst which will be rights to certain of her family's fruit trees.

Although the Hunzakut are nominally Muslim their women are neither secluded nor veiled, but treated in an open and equal manner. The Hunzakut, whose previous religion is not known, became Muslims of the Shi'a sect 600 years ago when the royal family married with the royalty of Baltistan. It was only four generations ago that they converted to the freer Ismaili sect, with the Aga Khan as its spiritual head.

A part-time priest, a *khalifa*, supervises the marriage ceremony. He has been appointed by the Mir and qualifies for his position by being sufficiently literate in Parsee or Arabic to lead the Islamic prayers. The ceremony is conducted at the bride's family house in front of both families, and a few weeks later is followed by the great wedding day. This is a reciprocal feast for the men at the man's family house. But only after a further public celebration, which to the Hunzakut is known as the 'Great Wedding Day', can he take his new bride home. All the new marriages in each village are celebrated on this one day, appointed by the Mir, in the middle of December, after the harvest and sowing of the winter barley. People pack the entrance to their village, dressed in their brightest embroidered clothes. Women sport silken scarves, the men with colored shirts and embroidered rims to their *chogas*. The men and boys to be married wear a loose silk robe and a bright feathered turban instead of the normal round cap. The men dance, each bridegroom and his clan brothers dancing in turn in the clearing. Throughout there is the music of the Bericho band of drummers, pipers and kettledrummers who taunt the party if the dancers are not jumping or moving their arms vigorously enough.

Frequently the high-point of this celebration among the Burusho is a game of polo. Not the ordered western game but perhaps more as it used to be, for polo originally came from this part of Asia. It is a wild six-a-side rampage to the accompaniment of music that continues with neither interval nor change of mount until one team has scored nine goals. In Hunza valley every village has its long stretch of narrow field surrounded by a low stone wall, reserved for polo.

The main ground where Burusho polo is played at the capital is 300 yards long, and here the 70-year-old Mir sometimes starts the game. He gallops from one end holding the stick and ball in one hand, and as he approaches the center of the ground he throws the ball into the air and hits it hard – over 100 yards – before it touches the ground. He repeats this feat, known as *tamba*, no less than seven times in succession. It used to be just the losers who danced in the center of the field for the winners. Possibly this was a ritual sign of submission, but nowadays both the teams dance. The Burusho, whose name means arrow, used to hold archery competitions on horseback. But now there are few, if any, who still have this skill. The Burusho are no longer the terror of Yarkand, no longer arrows.

13

Glossary to the peoples of western and central Asia

In this area, stretching west to east from Turkey to the Indus and south to north from the Indian ocean to the Russian steppes, most of the people are basically caucasoid. The exceptions are a few mongoloid enclaves like the Hazara in Afghanistan, and a mongoloid strain is visible among many groups, especially in Soviet Asia.

The caucasoids of this area are similar to the Europeans from Greece to France. Most comparable to them are the highlanders of western Asia. They have light brown skins and black or dark brown hair. Their eyes are usually brown but there is a notable proportion of people with light eyes: gray, blue, green or hazel. Compared to Europeans the west Asian highlanders, especially the Armenians, have a lot of body hair. They have large, sometimes curly, beards, and bushy eyebrows that meet in a tuft in the middle. The hair on their heads is straight or wavy. They have high, narrow noses, straight or, more commonly, curved, and angular faces with jaw and forehead not much narrower than their mid-facial breadth. The lightest skins are seen along the Aegean coast of Turkey and the darkest on the Persian Gulf, particularly in Baluchistan. The color of their eyes gets darker from west to east as well. The percentage of light-colored eyes ranges from 85 per cent among the western Turks to less than 5 per cent among the Baluchi.

As one moves into the steppe lands of Turkmenistan, Uzbekistan and Tajikistan and into northern Afghanistan, the highland west Asian influence is less pronounced. The Tajik are the north-easternmost representatives of the highland west Asians. They have sallow skins and nearly half of them have light-colored eyes. They are less hairy than the highlanders from further south. Some of them have mixed with the mongoloids and have epicanthine eye folds. But the Uzbek have even more mongoloid characteristics: some with upturned noses, weaker beard growths and more with epicanthine eye folds. Fewer have light eyes.

There are a few other racial influences too. The Arabs, who are strictly those people from the Arabian peninsula but who spread from Morocco to India after the 7th century, have intermixed with the peoples of the area. People who bear traces of Arab influence tend to be more lightly built with longer legs, smaller chests and finer hands and feet. In some of the gypsies of the area there are distinct traces of negro blood resulting from years of negro slavery.

The languages of this area are, on the whole, as uniform as the people. Most speak Indo-Aryan languages. The people of the steppes – the Turkomen, Kirghiz, Uzbek, Kazak and Uighur – all speak Turkic languages. In the Caucasus there are Caucasian speakers. The Brahui speak a Dravidian language and in this respect are unique to the area.

Most of the people in this area are Muslim. The Soviet states are officially atheist and there all religion is discouraged as superstition. In Iran they are mostly Shi'a Muslim. Unlike the Sunni Muslims, they believe the Caliph, or Imam, as they call him, should be a divinely appointed descendant of Ali, the Prophet's son-in-law. Sunni Muslims elect their Caliph. There are several different Shi'a sects who dispute the succession of Ali. The concept of divine rulers was part of the ancient Persian religion and is possibly the reason that Shi'a Muslims tend to come from Iran.

Some words in Arctic
languages are similar to
Turkish words. The Turks are
thought to have originated
in the Arctic region.

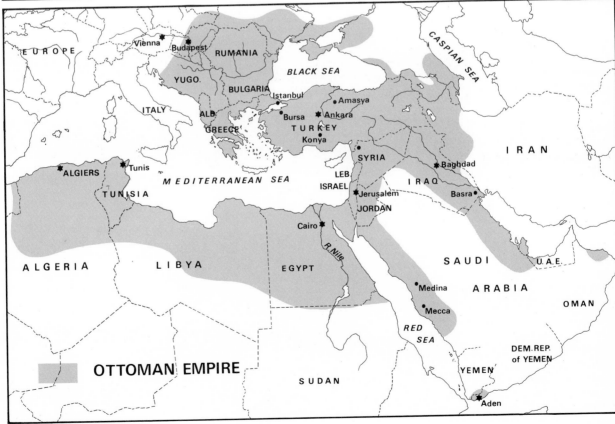

The Ottoman Empire, heir
to the eastern Roman Empire,
lasted from 1281 to 1924 and
made its capital Istanbul,
once called Constantinople.

ADYGE see CHERKESS

ADZHAR *Population*: 10,000. Language group: Caucasian. The Adzhar are a southern lowland tribe of Caucasian (q.v.) people living on the Black Sea coast near the Turkish border. They grow millet, barley, wheat, vegetables and vines. They are Muslim.

AFGHAN see PATHAN

AFRIDI see PATHAN

AISOR see ASSYRIANS

ALIELI see TURKOMEN

AL KATHIR see ARABS

ARABS *Population*: 900,000. Language group: Semitic. Arabs live scattered throughout central Asia. Turkey has some 300,000 but there are only 10,000 to 20,000 in the central Asian Russian Republics. Here they live in ancient communities scattered throughout the eastern oases. About half a million live in Iran. Several Arab tribes, chiefly the Al Kathir and Bani Lam, live in the Zagros mountains of southern Persia. And settled villages of Arab fishermen and fruit growers live along the Persian Gulf coast. There are still some Arab nomads and sheep herders. The Arabs are Sunni Muslim. A few in Afghan Turkistan retain their ethnic identity, but most in Afghanistan have been assimilated by other peoples, except for the Sayyid, a highly inbred self-isolating group who claim descent from the Prophet Mohammed.

ASERI see AZERBAIJANI

ASSYRIANS *Population*: 40,000. Language group: Semitic. The Assyrians live in the Soviet Armenian Republic, near lake Urmia in north-west Iran and in Iraq. Most of them are farmers who grow mainly millet, barley and wheat, but many others are mechanics in the cities. Some are mountaineers with a reputation as fierce, aggressive fighters. Many Assyrians fled to Russian territory at the end of World War I and now live mainly in the cities of the Caucasus, where they are called Aisor. Their religion—the Nestorian branch of Christianity—gives them a great cohesive force.

AVAR *Population*: 250,000. Language group: Caucasian. The Avar are north Caucasian (q.v.) people who live in the highlands of west Dagestan, USSR. In the 7th century they had a vast European Empire. Now they are stock-breeders and vegetable growers. In their homes they make Caucasian felt cloaks, leather and wooden goods, metalware, tapestries and embroidery. They are Sunni Muslim.

AWAN see HINDKI

AYNARLU see KAMSEH

AZERBAIJANI *Population*: 4·1 million. Language group: Turkic. The Azerbaijani or Aseri live in northern Iran and the Azerbaijan Soviet Republic across the border. Some Azerbaijani are farmers whose main crops are wheat and rice. Others work in the oil fields. There are stock-raising families who migrate between summer and winter quarters, but most of the rural population in Russia now live on collective farms. Their traditional craft is rug-weaving. Village life alters little between Russia and Iran. They are all Shi'a Muslim although they are the most westernized of the Turkic-speaking groups.

BAHARLU see KHAMSEH

BAIKA see KHO

BAKHTIARI (pages 58–67)

BALUCHI *Population*: 1·1 million. Language group: Iranian. Most of the Baluchi tribes live in the Baluchistan area of Pakistan. Another half million live in Iran from the Gulf of Oman to Seistan on the Afghan border. In southern Turkmenistan there are 10,000. Everywhere their land is dry and inhospitable. Most of them are pastoral nomads, and have been for generations, but some are settled farmers who grow mainly wheat. Others are soldiers, policemen and rent collectors for the big landlords. The nomadic Baluchi are continually crossing the Pakistan, Afghanistan and Iranian borders and tend to engage in such profitable enterprises as smuggling. The Baluchi are Sunni Muslim.

BANI LAM see ARABS

BASSERI see KAMSEH

BELORUSSIAN see SLAVS

BERBERI see HAZARA MONGOLS

BESUD see HAZARA MONGOLS

BRAHUI *Population:* 600,000. Language group: Dravidian. Most Brahui live in Pakistan. About 250,000 live in various parts of Afghanistan and 100,000 in the Seistan region of Iran. Most Brahui are nomadic farmers and herdsmen. From March to October they settle down to grow cereals, mainly wheat and maize, fruit and vegetables. In November they move south with their fattened cattle and handicrafts, to work as seasonal laborers, returning north again in the spring. Many have settled in the Sind on land opened up for irrigation. They are Sunni Muslim.

CAUCASIANS *Population:* 3·5 million. Language group: Caucasian. The Caucasian peoples live in the narrow mountain valleys from the northern slopes of the Caucasus southward into Georgia and Azerbaijan. They speak many different dialects but their customs and religion—Sunni Muslim—are similar. Many groups have a history of long resistance to Russian rule and are fiercely independent. Most of them are farmers and stock-breeders. In the more inaccessible hills they hunt and occasionally raid their more settled neighbors. They are excellent shots and horsemen and preserve a romantic reputation despite widespread poverty and disease. The giving of bridewealth, bride capture and family blood feuds persist today in some areas. Western dress is now beginning to replace their ages-old long coats, cartridge belts and fleece caps. The rich Caucasian folklore includes the Prometheus legend and, in the north, the epic of the *Narts*, or mythical heroes.

CHAHAR AIMAQ (pages 112-113)

CHERKESS *Population:* 80,000. Language group: Caucasian. The Cherkess or Adyge are Caucasian (q.v.) people who live in the north-west Caucasus near the Black Sea. There are several thousand more in northern Turkey. They are pastoral farmers, horse-breeders and fruit growers. Until recently the Cherkess had slaves. They are officially Sunni Muslim although there have been recent reports of still-existent early cults, associated with thunder, fertility rites and the sacred grove.

CHITRALI see KHO

CHUGI see GYPSIES

DAGH CHUFUTI see TAT

DARZADA see MAKRANI

DERVISH (pages 56-57)

DHUND see HINDKI

DUNGAN *Population:* 40,000. Language group: Sinitic. The Dungan or Tung-an are a small group of Chinese Muslims settled along the Chu river in the Soviet Republics of Kirghizia and Kazakstan. They found refuge here after an unsuccessful revolt against the Manchu dynasty of China in the 1870s. They are now skilled farmers who are said to have exerted a strong cultural influence. They are believed to have initiated rice and tea cultivation in the Fergana valley.

ERSARI see TURKOMEN

FEILI LUR see LUR

FIRUZ KUHI see CHAHAR AIMAQ

GASHGAI see QASHQA'I

GERMANS *Population:* 750,000. Language group: Germanic. These Germans live mostly in Kazakstan in the USSR where they work on collective farms and in the cities. They were once the Volga Germans who were exiled to Soviet Central Asia during World War II when several autonomous republics in southern Russia were liquidated on the orders of Stalin.

GHAKAR see HINDKI

GUJAR see HINDKI

GUKLAN see TURKOMEN

GYPSIES *Population:* 50,000. Gypsies live in most central Asian countries as a small minority. Those in the Soviet Union are known as Luli or Chugi. There are about 8,000 in Tajikistan and Uzbekistan. The Soviet government attempted to settle them on collective farms but most of them remain nomadic. The 30,000 Iranian gypsies who live mainly in the Caspian provinces are nomads, following their traditional crafts and trades, such as basketmaking, carving and smithing.

HAZARA MONGOLS (pages 114-117)

HINDKI *Population:* 250,000. Language group: Indo-Aryan. The Hindki tribes live scattered throughout the central part of Pakistan's northern frontier area. They are Sunni Muslim of Indian origin and include the Awan, Gujar, Karral, Dhund and Ghakar peoples. The Gujar live among the Yusufzai Pathan, serving them as artisans and peasant farmers. The hill Hindki are very poor. Some

139

are tenants, cultivating land for others, and some are nomadic graziers.

HUNZA (pages 126-135)

JAMSHIDI see CHAHAR AIMAQ

JEWS *Population:* 270,000. Language group: Semitic. Jews are a minority in all the central Asian countries. Most of them live in much the same way as their neighbors whether they be Kazak (q.v.), Persian (q.v.) or Turks (q.v.). There are 75,000 Iranian Jews who have been in Persia since ancient times and who all speak Persian today. The Jews preserve their ethnicity, including their religion, by inbreeding and segregation. They usually live in the cities where they are merchants, importers and money-lenders. There are nearly 160,000 Jews in Soviet central Asia and some 20,000 in Georgia. There have been small Jewish communities in Afghanistan for centuries, particularly in Herat, Kabul and in the cities of Afghan Turkistan. In Turkey they are a small minority, living mostly around Istanbul and Izmir.

KABARDIN *Population:* 300,000. Language group: Caucasian. The Kabardin are part of the western group of north Caucasian (q.v.) peoples who live along the Kuban and upper Terek river basins. Several thousand others live in northern Turkey. They grow crops, especially millet, barley and wheat, and vegetables. They breed cattle, and horses for which they are famed. Once there was a Kabardin prince and a feudal aristocracy. Most of them are Sunni Muslim but a few around Mozdok are Christian.

KAFIR see NURISTANI

KARAKALPAK *Population:* 250,000. Language group: Turkic. Most of the Karakalpak live in the USSR near the southern shores of the Aral sea. There are several thousand in Afghanistan. 'Karakalpak' means 'Black caps', referring to the black fleece headgear of the men. They are nearly all farmers, growing wheat, barley,

maize and cotton. On the desert pastures they raise cattle and Karakul sheep. The Karakalpak are Muslim.

KARRAL see HINDKI

KATURE see KHO

KAZAK *Population:* 4 million. Language group: Turkic. The Kazak are widely scattered throughout Kazakhstan in the USSR and Afghanistan, where many have assimilated with the Uzbek (q.v.) people. Only in the city of Herât do they live in a single compact settlement. The Kazak are Turko-Mongols. Traditionally they were divided into 'hordes'. They lived in *yurts*, raised horses and cattle and loved horse-racing and falconry. Now they are mostly settled cultivators, growing wheat, barley and maize. They were vigorous resisters of Sovietization and many were killed or deported to forced labor camps, and their traditional territory has now been mostly colonized by Russians. Numerous others emigrated to China. Kazak religion has some Islamic elements but these are incorporated into an indigenous religion which includes shamans, clans and ancestor cults. The Kazak shaman or *bagsha* is believed to be especially adept at curing nervous diseases, besides combating fevers, rheumatism and paralysis.

KHAMSEH *Population:* 90,000. Language groups: Iranian, Turkic and Semitic. The Khamseh tribes pivot around the town of Shiraz in the southern Iranian province of Fars. They are made up of five main tribes – Arabs (q.v.), Baharlu, Aynarlu, Basseri and Nafar who joined together to resist the Qashqa'i (q.v.). It is a political alliance and the ways of life of these peoples continue to vary. The Arabs, who speak Arabic and Persian dialects, are nomads at heart and those who settle down to farm are generally poor and unsuccessful. The nomadic Arabs hire out their mules and camels for transport. They are good rug-weavers and produce most of the Fars carpets. The Nafar live in a dry and barren region. The Aynarlu and Baharlu are Turkish speakers. The Basseri are the richest tribe. They are nomadic pastoralists who move their sheep and goats in a north-south direction, living in small camps along the way. They have a chain of market contacts on their route to whom they can sell their animals and handicrafts. They are increasingly becoming settled farmers.

KHO *Population:* 100,000. Language group: Indo-Aryan. The Kho, or Chitrali, live in the remote mountain valleys of Pakistan's northern frontier. They are a group of tribes, the most important of whom are the Kature, Khushwaqti, Rezakhel, Khoshne and Baika. They farm, raise cattle, weave cloth and make carpets. In winter thousands of the young men migrate to the plains as manual laborers, to build roads etc. Each household has a fruit orchard attached. Kho society is graded into the *adamzada*, the nobility, headed by the family of the ruler or *mehtar*, the *arbabzada*, the petty officials and tradespeople, and the *fakir-i-miskin*, the 'people of poverty'. Polo is the national sport and most Kho are fond of music, dancing and festivities. They are Sunni Muslim.

KHOSHNE see KHO

KHUSHWAQTI see KHO

KIRGHIZ (pages 74-79)

40

KOHISTANI *Population:* 209,000. Language group: Indo-Aryan. The Kohistani include several different racial groups and languages, the apparent result of centuries of inter-mingling of Chinese, Mongol (q.v.), Iranian (q.v.) and Pathan (q.v.) with the original Aryan invaders. They live in the northern Hazara, Gilgit, Upper Swat and Chitral regions of Pakistan. One tribe, the Swati, who live along the upper Indus, are thought to be the original inhabitants of the Swat valley. They are called Kohistani by the Pathan. The name also means 'people of the mountains'. They cultivate wheat and other grain crops on terraced fields, irrigated and plowed by bullocks. They breed oxen, buffalo, sheep, goats and donkeys. Between summer and winter they move their herds from as high as 14,000 feet down to 2,000 feet. Most families have houses in four or five different settlements and nearly the whole population is concentrated throughout the year in the altitude appropriate to the season. Most Kohistani are Shi'a Muslim.

KOREANS *Population:* 220,000. Language groups: Slavic and Korean. The Koreans or 'Kulaks' of central Asia were sent to Uzbekistan and Kazakstan from Korea, under the Soviet régime of the 1930s, possibly because of their resistance to collectivization. They formerly lived in villages scattered throughout the areas where rice could be grown. Now they are successful pig and poultry breeders and are good at vegetable growing. In Uzbekistan most of them grow cotton, as well as rice. Their collective farms have acquired a certain fame because of their success.

KUHGILUYE see LUR

KULAK see KOREANS

KUMYK *Population:* 135,000. Language group: Turkic. The Kumyk live on the north-west shores of the Caspian sea in the lower regions of Soviet Dagestan. They farm, breed cattle and fish. They are Sunni Muslim.

KURDS (pages 36-43)

LASSI *Population:* 70,000. Language group: Indo-Aryan. The Lassi live in the former Las Bela state of Pakistan. Most of them are poor farmers, but many have to seek employment in Karachi and Sind. They are Muslim.

LAZ *Population:* 60,000. Language group: Caucasian. Most Laz live on the Black Sea coast, east of Trabzon in Turkey. About 1,000 live in Soviet Caucasia between Batum and Trabzon. They cultivate millet, barley and wheat, and fish and trade. They are Sunni Muslim.

LEZGIN *Population:* 100,000. Language group: Caucasian. The Lezgin are north Caucasian (q.v.) people who live along the Samur river in southern Dagestan, USSR. They breed cattle and grow crops, especially millet, barley, wheat and vegetables. In their homes they make tapestries and wrought-iron ware. They are Sunni Muslim.

LORI see MAKRANI

LULI see GYPSIES

LUR *Population:* 2 million. Language group: Iranian. The Lur are a confederation of four main groups: Feili Lur (Lesser Lur), Bakhtiari (q.v., Greater Lur), Kuhgiluye and Mamassani. They live south of the Kurds (q.v.) in the Zagros mountains of Iran. They are a proud people with a reputation among the settled Iranians of being great hunters. The Mamassani are particularly inaccessible and fierce. The Lur are nomadic and semi-nomadic sheep herders. They grow a few crops but often buy their staple foods of wheat and barley from sedentary valley dwellers. They wear simple black clothing. They are Shi'a Muslim.

MAKRANI *Population:* 160,000. Language group: Indo-Aryan. The name 'Makrani' covers the tribes in the Makran area of Pakistan, including Darzada, Nakib, Lori and Med peoples. Many of the tribes are occupational groups: most Darzada, for example, are landless laborers and most Lori are poor artisans. Some of them are by tradition gypsies, tinkers and minstrels who display marked negroid features and have moved into Karachi as stevedores and unskilled laborers. The rural Makrani keep sheep, goats, camels, donkeys and buffalo and are renowned for greyhound breeding. They are also famed for their embroidered leather work. The Med are a coastal fishing group. The wandering Lori are jugglers, palmists and fortune tellers. The favorite sports of the Makrani are wrestling and racing. Most of them are Sunni Muslim and have a firm belief in the powers of holy men (*pirs*) and spirits.

MAMASSANI see LUR

MED see MAKRANI

NAFAR see KHAMSEH

NAKIB see MAKRANI

NOGAI *Population:* 41,000. Language group: Turkic. The Nogai live on the northern foothills of the Russian Caucasus between the lower Kuma and Telek rivers. They are

14

farmers and cattle-breeders. The Nogai are Sunni Muslim.

NURISTANI (pages 118-125)

PAKHTUN see PATHAN

PATHAN (pages 86-99 and 100-111)

PERSIANS (pages 44-55)

PUSHTUN see PATHAN

QAJAR *Population:* 70,000. Language group: Turkic. The Qajar are a small Iranian tribe who live along the Elburz in Mazanderan and Gilan. They produced a dynasty of shahs who ruled Persia from 1796 until 1926. Once they were nomadic but most are now settled wheat and maize growing farmers. They are Muslim.

QARAMA see TURKOMEN

QASHQA'I *Population:* 300,000. Language group: Turkic. The Qashqa'i or Gashgai are the largest single tribe in the Fars area of southern Iran. They have been described as one of the happiest and best organized of the big tribal groups that have survived the measures the late Reza Shah took to control them. Their annual migration from the Isfahan area to the Persian Gulf is the longest in Iran. Their flocks provide them with milk products and with wool to weave or to sell. They also grow cereals, and their orchards and nut tree groves provide them with extra income. The horses they breed are famous. Their black tents, made of goat hair, are woven by the women. Theoretically the tribe's *khan* or chief decides the migration route and the allocation of the grazing land to the herding units. Their costume is distinguished by a felt cap, with flaps which they often turn up. The Qashqa'i have been politically active and the former Shah's effort to disarm them led to the imprisonment and death of their chief. They are Shi'a Muslim.

QIZIL BASH *Population:* 110,000. Language group: Iranian. The Qizil Bash or 'Red Heads' are so called because of the red caps they wear. They live scattered throughout Afghanistan. One group occupies a quarter of Kabul where, unlike the rest of the people, they are Shi'a Muslim. They hold respected positions as clerical officials in government offices. Some of them are traders and craftsmen. Another colony of Qizil Bash live in the high valleys of Foladi, at the western edge of the Hazarajat.

REZAKHEL see KHO

RUSSIANS see SLAVS

SARIQ see TURKOMEN

SAYYID see ARABS

SHAHSAVAN *Population:* 100,000. Language group: Turkic. The Shahsavan live south-west of the Caspian Sea in the Azerbaijan area of Iran. There is a smaller group near Teheran. The Shahsavan or 'followers of the Shah' consist of several tribes set up in this area to protect the Shah's interests. The nomadic Shahsavan have their summer pastures at the foot of the Sabalan mountains and their winter pastures at Dashte-Moghan. The tribal heads or *begs* organize and coordinate the migration, and have lately become intermediaries between tribe and government. Due to the joint Irano-Russian irrigation project on the Aras river many Shahsavan have become settled farmers.

SLAVS *Population:* 14 million. Language group: Slavonic. Russian Slavs live throughout Soviet central Asia in the countryside as well as in the cities. Originally they brought several innovations such as potatoes and pigs to the area. In Kazakstan they outnumber the Kazak (q.v.). The farming Russians are mainly grain growers but many work in the cities. There are about 6.5 million Russians in the Caucasus. The Ukrainians and Belorussians, other Slavic peoples, each number over one million in the central Asian Republics. There is a small Bulgar minority in Turkey.

SWATI see KOHISTANI

TAIMANNI see CHAHAR AIMAQ

TAIMURI see CHAHAR AIMAQ

TAJIK (pages 80-85)

TALYSH *Population:* 150,000. Language group: Iranian. Most Talysh live on the Caspian coast in the Soviet Republic of Azerbaijan, but some 50,000 live in the Caspian district of Iran. They grow crops and vegetables, raise stock and have cottage industries. They all know Aseri as a second language. Most Talysh are Sunni Muslim but there is a Shi'a minority.

TAT *Population:* 90,000. Language group:

Iranian. The Tat live in south-western Azerbaijan, USSR, mainly on the Apsheron peninsula. They grow vegetables and millet, barley and wheat. In their homes they make tapestries and metalware. Nearly all of them can speak Aseri (q.v.) as a second language. They are Shi'a Muslim, except for 8,000 Tat-speaking Jews known as Dagh Chufuti or 'Mountain Jews'.

TATARS *Population:* 1 million. Language group: Turkic. The Kazan Tatars have lived in central Asia since the 18th century. Many more joined them in 1945 when the Soviet government exiled thousands of Crimean Tatars. By tradition the Tatars are teachers, missionaries and merchants. Their eminent position is due to the strategic position of Kazan and to their historical relations with the Kazak (q.v.) and Uzbek (q.v.). Most Tatars live in the cities. They are Muslim but are more russianized than any other Muslim people.

TEKKE see TURKOMEN

TROGLODYTES (pages 32-35)

TUNG-AN see DUNGAN

TURKS (pages 24-31)

TURKOMEN *Population:* 1·5 million. Language group: Turkic. Most of the Turkomen or Turkmen, live in Turkomeniya in southern Russia, but they also extend into northern Iran and north-west Afghanistan. There are several Turkomen tribes each centered on an oasis. The two great Turkomen tribes of Iran, the Guklan and the Yamut, were once raiders. A few of the Yamut are still nomadic but most Turkomen are now settled farmers. Near the Caspian sea they are fishermen, sailors and traders. Those in Afghanistan supplement their stock-breeding by cultivating crops, but they still live in dome-shaped tents. Others have become impoverished village-dwelling servants. Much of their cultivation depends on the Uzbek (q.v.) constructed irrigation facilities. Almost

all Turkomen have large herds of sheep, goats, horses and camels. They wear high fleeced caps and long fur-lined coats. In summer they wear a brightly colored light gown called a *khala'at.* Turkomen women are renowned for the Bukhara rugs which they weave. Most Turkomen are Muslim.

UIGHUR *Population:* 180,000. Language group: Turkic. The Uighur live in several small groups near Alma-Ata in the Kazak Soviet Republic. A further four million live in the Chinese province of Sinkiang. The Uighur are closely akin to the Uzbek (q.v.) in looks, language and customs, although in their farming techniques and food habits particularly they have been influenced by the Chinese. Most of them are now collective farmers. They are devout Sunni Muslim. Uighur shamans or *bakshi* practise their curing techniques in a state of trance. Uighur make pilgrimages to the holy man's tomb *(mazar)* for help with spiritual and practical problems.

UKRAINIANS see SLAVS

UZBEK (pages 68-73)

YAMUT see TURKMEN

YURUK *Population:* 5,000. Language group: Turkic. The Yuruk live in the remoter parts of northern and central Turkey. They preserve in a relatively pure form the language, economy, customs and probably the physical type of the old Turks who migrated from central Asia. The Yuruk are semi-nomadic shepherds and it is difficult to estimate their exact numbers.

All population figures are approximate.